SINGING BONES

INDIGENOUS MUSIC OF AUSTRALIA
MYFANY TURPIN, SERIES EDITOR

The many forms of Australia's Indigenous music have ancient roots, huge diversity and global reach. The Indigenous Music of Australia series aims to stimulate discussion and development of the field of Australian Indigenous music (including Aboriginal and Torres Strait Islander music) in both subject matter and approach.

Archival Returns: Central Australia and Beyond
Edited by Linda Barwick, Jennifer Green, and Petronella Vaarzon-Morel

For the Sake of a Song: Wangga Songmen and Their Repertories
Allan Marett, Linda Barwick, and Lysbeth Ford

Reflections and Voices: Exploring the Music of Yothu Yindi with Mandawuy Yunupingu
Aaron Corn

Singing Bones: Ancestral Creativity and Collaboration
Samuel Curkpatrick

Songs from the Stations: Wajarra as Sung by Ronnie Wavehill Wirrpnga, Topsy Dodd Ngarnjal and Dandy Danbayarri at Kalkaringi
Myfany Turpin and Felicity Meakins

Wurrurrumi Kun-Borrk: Songs from Western Arnhem Land
Kevin Djimar

SINGING BONES

ANCESTRAL CREATIVITY AND COLLABORATION

SAMUEL CURKPATRICK

SYDNEY UNIVERSITY PRESS

First published by Sydney University Press 2020

Sydney University Press
Fisher Library F03
University of Sydney NSW 2006
AUSTRALIA
sup.info@sydney.edu.au
sydneyuniversitypress.com.au

 A catalogue record for this book is available from the National Library of Australia.

ISBN 9781743326770 paperback
ISBN 9781743326787 epub
ISBN 9781743326923 mobi
ISBN 9781743327111 pdf

Artwork: *Devil Devil* (2012) by Wally Wilfred; used with permission
Cover design by Miguel Yamin

The musical examples referred to in the text can be found at
https://sydneyuniversitypress.com.au/singing-bones

CONTENTS

LIST OF FIGURES

COLLABORATION

This project would not have been possible without the friendship of Daniel Wilfred, Benjamin Wilfred, David Wilfred, Wally Wilfred, Andy Peters, Roy Natilma, and their families. In turn, these connections would not have come about or been sustained without the enthusiasm of Aaron Corn, Paul Grabowsky, Peter Knight, and the Australian Art Orchestra. I am grateful for the support of Frances Morphy, the Ngukurr Language Centre, the Ngukurr Art Centre, the National Centre for Indigenous Studies at the Australian National University, the Australian Institute of Aboriginal and Torres Strait Islander Studies, and the Sir Zelman Cowan School of Music at Monash University.

PREFACE

Benjamin Miyala Wilfred

The first time I found Sam [the author], he came to Ngukurr with the Australian Art Orchestra. He wanted to make recordings for everything. I thought we could use these recordings to tell everyone why our ceremony is important. But also, if anything happens, that recording is going to be there for my kids. We will use it in the school, the language centre, the aged care centre, the library.

That orchestra mob came and asked me to do *Crossing Roper Bar*, and I said yes because I wanted to do something new—keeping culture strong and keeping healthy by singing and dancing. And so we can make new history.

This word is from me, Benjamin: Keep strong. I'm passing it over to you mob and my kids, John, Rodney, Talia, and Maxine.

And I want you mob to hold this Wägilak *buŋgul* [ceremony] strong. When I get crook, you mob keep rolling it—the string. Be strong.

I write this down now, for you mob: my history, Wägilak history from 2005. John, this is for you. Eight years I have been touring, right up to London. I have been singing and talking too.

It's right this book. I got permission from my elders, from Sambo Barabara for this *Crossing Roper Bar*.

And I hope you mob like this book for my history; for the Young Wägilak Group.

Ngukurr, October 2014

Daniel Warrathuma Wilfred

Well, that ceremony for me, it's keeping me. Sometimes we want to stop, but we can't stop, because our ceremony tells us, "Keep going. Maybe your kids might learn the song."

It's going from here to *Crossing Roper Bar*. Blackfella side is proper one—strong culture. I use the ceremony song. But whitefella side, we enjoy ourselves and we are sharing with whitefellas. And they are sharing with us, and we are sharing our ceremony.

And I do this *Crossing Roper Bar*. I never stop. My kids are following my tracks; what I do, in different places. And they can know what I'm doing, on the ceremony side.

That culture, it's *manikay*, Wägilak *manikay*. So I'm playing those songs, different bits and pieces, all the words—I'm playing *manikay* now with *Crossing Roper Bar*.

We sit down and talk, telling stories for our song. This song, it's ceremony; this blackfella way is strong for us. We grow up with this *buŋgul* [ceremony]; we learnt from the elders, passed on to young generations. I am trying to teach my kids. I hope Isaiah picks it up, and Tryson. Breanna is a dancer too.

The *manikay*, we sing that with our language: it stays in language. It didn't come from a book or anywhere. It came from the mouth, and sticks—we call *biḻma* [clapsticks]. We sing in Wägilak, not in Kriol or English. With *manikay* we never stop. This song never stops: it's still there, it never changes—my song! Today I'm the youngest singer and I'm still working with my songs.

Sometimes we do new songs, but it still comes up with our language. New songs, it never stops. Sometimes I mix it up: *yiḏaki* (didjeridu) and *biḻma* (clapsticks) with jazz, and guitar. But my instrument is the *yiḏaki* and *biḻma*. Mix it up with the whitefella music.

And I still love to do my *Crossing Roper Bar* and I keep teaching the Balanda mob (non-Aboriginal people). Teach them my language too—always tell them.

And this book, you're going to learn about my songs and language.

Ngukurr, October 2014

GLOSSARY

Balanda. Non-Aboriginal person, from the word "Hollander".

bäpurru. Literally "father's group", a group identity expressing shared connections to ancestrally bestowed homelands and ceremonial repertoires.

bilma. Clapsticks.

buŋgul. Dance, accompanying song in public performance; ceremony.

Dhuwa. One of two moieties in Yolŋu society and culture. See also Yirritja.

Djuwalpada. Ancestral *mokuy* who established the Wägilak homeland and public ceremony.

madayin. Ancestral law, performed through dance, song, design, story, language, country, and kinship.

manikay. Ceremonial song performed in public contexts, such as funerals, circumcisions, or for entertainment. See also *buŋgul.*

miny'tji. Sacred designs; painting; colour.

mokuy. A type of *waŋarr* that bestows public law and ceremony; a malignant ghost associated with death. See also Djuwalpada.

ŋärra'. Restricted or secret ceremonies and knowledge.

Ŋärra'. A gathering of leaders and families for law and ceremony of the highest importance; sometimes referred to as "parliament"; a ceremony that brings together *bäpurru* related through *riŋgitj.*

ŋalabuluŋu rom. Following law; correct living; life that reflects ancestral pattern and precedence, which involves the continuation of ceremonial performance.

ŋaraka. Bones; integral structural forms of *manikay.*

ŋaraka-wäŋa. Bone-country; the hereditary estate bestowed upon a *bäpurru* by their founding *mokuy.*

riŋgitj. Alliance; ceremonial, political and familial connections between *bäpurru* of the same moiety; a ceremonial site belonging to one *bäpurru* but located in the territory of another. See also Ŋärra.

Ritharrŋu. A language group in South East Arnhem Land, closely related to Wägilak. Although Ritharrŋu people have different homelands and ceremonial repertoires to Wägilak people, these are closely intertwined; Ritharrŋu are considered "the same" as Wägilak, and this is a mutually dependent relationship like marriage.

Wägilak. A language group and collection of families in South East Arnhem Land with distinct lineage, ceremonial repertoires, and homelands.

waŋarr. Creative beings that shaped the land, people, and culture.

yäku. Names; sacred lexicon; song texts.

yuṯa. New, as in *yuṯa manikay.*

yiḏaki. Didjeridu. Known in Kriol as *bambu.*

Yirritja. One of two moieties in Yolŋu society and culture. See also Dhuwa.

yolŋu. The generic word for a *person* in various Yolŋu languages.

Yolŋu. A broader identification of similar but distinct languages and cultural practices; people whose traditional homelands centre around the north east of Arnhem Land. See also *Wägilak.*

Yolŋu-matha. The "tongues" or languages of the Yolŋu.

Orthography and Pronunciation

ä. Long "a" as in *far*; written as "aa" in older texts.

ḏ, ṯ, ḷ, ṟ. Underlined consonants are retroflexed, with the tongue curled back and touching the roof of the mouth.

dh, nh, th. Lamino-dental consonants pronounced with the tip of the tongue between the teeth.

glottal stop ('). As in the word Djaŋ'kawu.

Ŋ or ŋ. The letter eng, shown capital and lowercase; pronounced "ng" as in *song*.

rr. Trilled "r".

Abbreviations

AAO	Australian Art Orchestra
CMI	Creative Music Intensive, of the Australian Art Orchestra
CRB	*Crossing Roper Bar*
YWG	Young Wägilak Group

INTRODUCTION

Of my earliest encounters with Wägilak *manikay* (song), one memory stands out strongly. I had just heard a performance of *Crossing Roper Bar* (*CRB*) in Darwin, a wild admixture of free-jazz improvisation and ceremonial *manikay*, bringing together musicians from Melbourne and Ngukurr, a community located on the southern border of Arnhem Land. While this hectic, densely woven entanglement of musical voices seemed impenetrable on first hearing, more perplexing was the description given by songman Daniel Wilfred: "What we are doing is the same as our grandfather did. It's not new, it's the same." This seemingly novel approach to musical performance in Australia was at once appropriated into the *manikay* tradition by an assertion of ancestral continuity and expression.

While inquiry into the shape and direction of a project like *CRB* might typically follow questions of power and agency, Daniel's understanding of tradition and creativity inverts the usual gaze of critical theory: here, it is the *manikay* tradition that enfolds contemporary performance within established narratives and institutions. This book is an attempt to better understand the hermeneutic behind such a statement, and the ideas of tradition that shape Wägilak creativity. Despite the comments of one distinguished anthropology professor who dismissed a research focus on *CRB* out-of-hand as "bourgeois rubbish", this is an exploration of *CRB* as a legitimate and authentic expression of *manikay*. At least for practising musicians and those seeking a better understanding of Indigenous Australian performance traditions, this seems a more productive and engaging approach than a critique of inherent political agendas. While such a critique might be valuable for self-reflection, the point is to explore the ways *manikay* opens new relationships and new futures through

1

creative processes, rather than constraining relationality through postcolonial ethical framings.

This book seeks to show how meaningful engagement with the orthodox *ŋaraka* (bones) of *manikay* is always involved and collaborative, as individuals grapple with tradition through the unfolding conversations of improvisation, the layering of new stories onto established narratives, and the generation of movement and textual density that contributes to an aesthetic of *bir'yun* (brilliance). Through *CRB*, *manikay* is sustained as it is carried into new contexts and affirmed as a valuable tradition for contemporary Australia, as it draws individuals into new relationships across cultural difference.

Wägilak *Manikay* and *Crossing Roper Bar*—"Keeping Culture Strong"

The twentieth century unravelled the ancient cultural fabric of much of Australia's north. Connections of belonging to past, place, and purpose were stretched and frayed, with countless communities fragmented and individuals isolated from the traditions that once sustained them. Many families and language groups, strained by unprecedented cultural and political disruptions brought about by colonisation, lost their songs and language, and with these the means of perceiving everyday life interwoven with ancestral reality.

Within these communities today, there remains a deep and legitimate concern over ongoing cultural loss. Individuals and organisations are working to stem the tide of attrition and revitalise cultural practices. A degree of urgency is often expressed in calls to action, something clearly demonstrated in the National Recording Project for Indigenous Performance in Australia's "Garma Statement":

> Performance traditions are the foundation of social and personal wellbeing, and with the ever-increasing loss of these traditions, the toll grows every year. The preservation of performance traditions is therefore one of the highest priorities for Indigenous people … These ancient musical traditions were once everywhere in Australia, and now survive as living traditions only in several regions. Many of these are now in danger of being lost forever … Indigenous performances are one of our most rich and beautiful forms of artistic expression, and yet they remain unheard and invisible within the national cultural heritage.[1]

Despite immense cultural loss across Australia, the Wägilak *manikay* repertoire is one of dozens of *manikay* repertoires in Arnhem Land that are still performed today. Wägilak *manikay* tell of the foundation of the Wägilak homeland at Ŋilipidji, and tie into larger narrative sequences linking together related estates,

---

1   "Garma Statement on Indigenous Music and Dance", The National Recording Project for Indigenous Performance in Australia, http://www.aboriginalartists.com.au/NRP_statement.htm.

different *bäpurru* (father's group), and sacred sites across the region in a complex of intercultural relations.[2] *Manikay* shapes individuals and communities as they follow the tracks of ancestral precedence. Not only do songs and narratives carry a wealth of experience and knowledge, passed down through successive generations, they also enrich experiences of human relationships and connection to place. Traditionally, *manikay* has been integral to education, social arrangement, land ownership, religious ceremony, and law.

In recent years, Wägilak have extended their ceremonial practices to incorporate the sounds and voices of some of Australia's leading jazz musicians and proponents of contemporary improvisation, gathered under the auspices of the Australian Art Orchestra (AAO). Known as *Crossing Roper Bar*, this dynamic project enriches *manikay* with new sonic colours, twists, and turns, and is performed for new audiences across the country. *CRB* performs the *manikay* for a smoking (purification) ceremony with grooving bass, drums, and free-jazz improvisation. This has come about through the desire to "keep culture strong," as a relevant, interconnected ancestral voice in the present.

Many Indigenous Australians, ethnomusicologists, and linguists are involved in projects seeking to revitalise and sustain cultural traditions. Such projects require more than documentation, which creates only a representation of the past. The desire to engage with Indigenous song traditions has led to genuine partnerships between researchers and Indigenous performers, friendships between colleagues who are brought closer together through their activities. *CRB* is one such partnership. This book seeks to show just how the vibrancy of *manikay* is sustained through *CRB*, arguing that creativity and collaboration are vital to our collective efforts to ensure Indigenous Australian performance traditions are not lost.

CRB might seem like a radical departure from the ways of the ancestors, and the irrepressible drive toward individual freedom of voice—characteristic of improvised traditions that originated in America—might seem a world away from the orthodox, guarded musical forms of *manikay*. Yet the distinct and even disparate voices of *CRB* are held together as a performed conversation, a meeting of different families and repertoires on the *bambula* (ceremonial ground) of the present. Coming chapters will show how *manikay* and jazz traditions enable this coincidence of expression.

A visible, audible process of engagement unfolds on stage, between individuals who are seeking new ways of playing together, of extending their traditions through creativity and collaboration. Daniel explains to participants taking part in the AAO's Creative Music Intensive, "You share your songs with me, I'm sharing my songs with you. I always listen to what you play, with your

---

2   See Chapter One for discussion about the nomenclature *clan*.

instruments, and I feel a new song coming up."[3] For whitefella musicians looking beyond histories of appropriation and indifference, this partnership frames a respectful and innovative approach to musical collaboration.

Here, we discover a process of active collaboration, abounding with imagination, in which *manikay* is sustained with vibrancy and colour. For Daniel and David Wilfred, the AAO and *CRB* offer a platform to "keep culture strong", to sustain their ancestral traditions as a living conversation. Because musical contributions from the AAO are largely improvised, new ideas and sounds continually emerge, multimedia elements are incorporated, and *yuṯa manikay* (new songs) are composed. Significantly, the narratives and sounds of *manikay* are learnt through this living, generative process.

Amid the complex interactions of cultures and traditions that make up contemporary Australian society, Wägilak continue to weave their present experiences and relationships into the *raki* (string) of ancestral identity through song. Continually integrated, expanded, and transposed into new contexts and relationships, *manikay* remains ever "the same but different, just like my grandfather used to do".[4]

Blown Together

In Wägilak *manikay*, the wind blows together different groups for ceremony, which is always a meeting of diverse individuals, families, languages, and histories. So too, the various issues and philosophical influences that pervade this book are blown together by *manikay*. Some of these are introduced below. What emerges is a unique conversation, a performance that gathers multiple voices and histories.

After introducing these themes below, the book proceeds through the following chapters. Chapters One through Five build a rich picture of *manikay* in Wägilak ceremonial expression, law, thought, and history. Chapter One introduces Wägilak storytelling, the homeland at Ṉilipidji, and the basic narrative of Wägilak *manikay* (song). Chapter Two outlines the recent social history of the Wägilak and their role in performing ceremony. This chapter shows the mix of cultural influences and technologies that shape contemporary performance. Chapter Three explores some philosophic and ontological dimensions of *manikay*. In performing ceremony, Wägilak follow the footprints of elders, sustaining engagement with the ancestral text. Chapter Four unpacks some of the poetic layers of Wägilak *manikay*. Short sections build a multi-layered exposition of key narratives and images. Chapter Five offers an overview

---

3   Daniel Wilfred, conversation with the author, 15 September 2017.
4   Benjamin Wilfred, conversation with the author, 12 August 2013.

of the structural forms of *manikay*, especially its rhythmical modes which carry narrative and dance. The ongoing composition of new songs is also introduced.

Chapters Six through Eight then turn to *Crossing Roper Bar* (*CRB*). Chapter Six outlines the early patterns of engagement that shaped *CRB*. Wresting ideas of *groove* from notions of *primitivism*, musical examples from *CRB* show that groove can generate formal complexity and pull individuals together into new relationships. Chapter Seven explores the rich, heterophonic textures of *manikay* in improvisation, multimedia, and performance contexts. Examples relate to the Yolŋu aesthetic of *bir'yun* (shimmering brilliance). Chapter Eight focuses on the unique musical voices and traditions that the Australian Art Orchestra brings to *CRB*. Various projects of the AAO are introduced, showing their conversational approach to collaboration in different settings. This chapter argues that jazz can be typified as a tradition that emphasises free, vocative expression.

Raki

The subject *raki* (string) in Wägilak *manikay* suggests that present life is woven into the past, which extends like a string through the generations. To perform ceremony is to weave the present into this ancestral string. *Raki* is about continuing in the patterns established by ancestral progenitors. Just as the ceremonial string is carried over the heads of family who process in a line, *manikay* connects the generations. Through ceremony, the past continually speaks into human lives and substantiates existence. Expressions of tradition prompt us to respond, recognise, and consider our own unique place and purpose within this history.

> When Wägilak people perform *manikay*, they continue to extend the *raki*, taking on the responsibility to "keep culture strong". Through performance, the *raki* grows in length; new fibrous strands are twisted together.[5] Present life extends from ancestral origins as new generations are woven in through performance. Benjamin Wilfred holds this hope for his children: "My little boy, he's going to be a didj man, like me. And he's a dancer. Even Daniel's sons, they all dance, and they respect the culture. So we are giving them culture, when they are young. And I know that my kids [will] just keep rolling it, and they want more knowledge from me."[6]

---

5 *Raki* (string) is a theme with similar but different meanings in the *manikay* of other *bäpurru*. Cf. Corn and Gumbula's description of Baripuy *manikay* and the subject of *wunybuḻ* (possum-fur string). Aaron Corn and Neparrŋa Gumbula, "'Buḏutthun Ratja Wiyinymirri': Formal Flexibility in the Yolŋu Manikay Tradition and the Challenge of Recording a Compete Repertoire", *Australian Aboriginal Studies*, no. 2 (2007): 122.

6 Benjamin Wilfred, interview with Daniel Browning, "Crossing Boundaries", *Awaye* (Radio National, Melbourne, Australian Broadcasting Corporation), 2 November 2013.

Performances of *CRB* occur within various *manikay* and jazz histories, different strings that extend back into separate pasts but also forward into an increasingly interwoven future. Through their musical voices, individuals come to understand their unique place within the greater movements of history beyond the present situation.

In this book, multiple strands of voices merge, like singers improvising independent lines in *manikay*. The juxtaposition of diverse ideas, intellectual traditions, and cultural metaphors generates conversation. This never settles into definitive representation but contributes to understanding as a continually emerging process. While this book carries its own unique voice, it nevertheless weaves yet another fibre into the ongoing string of *manikay*.

Encounter

Does Indigenous culture represent a fascinating but unreachable *other*? Many university-level music students desire greater engagement with Indigenous Australian cultures but are afraid of breaching unknown ethical protocols ascribed to these cultures as other. This rigid notion of difference stymies human relationships, invoking separation. Ironically, even as Indigenous Australian cultures are held in high esteem, distance can be exacerbated by good intentions.

Many Australians rightly celebrate the abundance of Aboriginal and Torres Strait Islander cultures. Most visibly, our art galleries hold Indigenous Australian painters in high esteem. There are wonderful artists in this country who truly deserve this renown. Yet even as Indigenous Australian eyes have conveyed the land and its people in art for tens of thousands of years, contemporary Indigenous Australian art is not hung beside iconic Australian landscape paintings from the last 250 years. The potential for discursive interplay is diminished.

Similarly, non-Indigenous musicians and composers celebrate Indigenous Australian music through placements that separate. Didjeridu virtuosi sit in front of symphony orchestras, outside of a score's internal dialogue. The pedestal may hold up a person or culture with pride, but it also alienates. In many ways, we have become stuck in our cultural separations rather than reconciled to the wonderful possibilities of intermingling difference. Fixated on an unapproachable other—whose difference is exacerbated by the moral injunctions of cultural relativism—vibrant discourse with *yet another* individual, culture, or history subsides.

Daniel Wilfred's words—"What we are doing is the same as our grandfather did. It's not new"—present a striking challenge to this situation. In *CRB*, musicians and songmen encounter the *manikay* tradition as they interact with one another and create something new. The unfolding of these relationships is not necessarily neat, simple, definitive, or easily anticipated.

INTRODUCTION

In any form of encounter there is always something about another that we are not justified in maintaining, perhaps a significance or complexity unseen. This is a reality of subjectivity, necessary if we are to be intersubjective. The false self-assurance of a disinterested gaze denies this reality. Therefore, a seriousness of purpose is needed in any such encounter, recognising that the past, a tradition, an interlocutor, or a cultural system, holds certain meanings not presently revealed to our limited understanding; interpretations are provisional and not immutable. Taking stock of decades of academic writing about Indigenous Australian peoples, cultures, and histories, Torres Strait Islander academic Martin Nakata suggests, "The indigenous position must be *complicated* rather than simplified" by applying neat theoretical framings.[7]

For Yolŋu, history is encountered not as a foreign land but as the substantial and tangible ground of present life: ancestral life is carried into new contexts as it engages action and response. Similarly, different cultural perspectives are valued. Prominent Yolŋu advocacy for a "two-ways" or bi-cultural approach to society and polity mirrors an historic openness to cultural adjustment while retaining "relative autonomy".[8] If we are to seek an approach to reconciliation that resonates with this Yolŋu understanding, then difference is not only to be celebrated but engaged as meaningful.

In *CRB*, the AAO allow the Wägilak singers to hold their habitual conceptions of music to account, not conceptually but through the dynamic interactions of performance. This unfolds as a conversation, in which each musical utterance is provisional, responding by offering a perspective on the topic at hand but also moving the conversation forward. By approaching the *manikay* tradition as a voice with something to say, the objective gaze that characterises appropriation is avoided.

This book assumes that it is not inherently unethical to consider or speak about people and cultural situations from another perspective. Where we open ourselves to the voice of another person or tradition, our own ideas are changed and enriched. Such engagement is productive, especially if playful, in allowing the grooving momentum of conversation to carry us along. While essentialising something about an *other* always remains a danger in any understanding, ongoing conversation with *another* continually surprises us as relationships shift and grow in ways not yet imagined. Together in relationship, we move beyond situated anticipations and forge *yet another* possibility.

---

7   Martin Nakata, *Disciplining the Savages, Savaging the Disciplines* (Canberra: Aboriginal Studies Press, 2007), 12.

8   Morphy and Morphy develop the term *relative autonomy* "in apposition to the idea of the intercultural". Frances Morphy and Howard Morphy, "Anthropological Theory and Government Policy in Australia's Northern Territory: The Hegemony of the 'Mainstream'", *American Anthropologist* 115, no. 2 (2013): 176. See Mandawuy Yunupingu's Boyer lectures for more on a "two-ways" approach to society and culture. *Voices from the Land* (Sydney: ABC Books, 1994).

Hermeneutics

Hermeneutics concerns interpretation and the way we come to understand. Human understanding is confronted with much diversity of expression and so hermeneutics is a pertinent focus when coming face to face with largely unknown cultures—where one does not inhabit many of the unconscious assumptions, inferences, and subjectivities of another cultural world. As in reading a text, music is performed and heard through interpretations.

To perform or listen is to interpret; to interpret brings subjectivities into being, influencing what one plays, sings, or hears. An individual's hermeneutic of tradition directly shapes musical performance and understanding. This book is concerned with two planes of interpretation: between individuals and their indigenous traditions, and intercultural interactions.

A pervasive influence on the ideas of tradition in this book has been the work of philosopher Hans-Georg Gadamer, whose hermeneutics variously resonate with *CRB* and *manikay*. Gadamer's magnum opus *Truth and Method* observes that understanding and interpretation are indissolubly bound together.[9] Shifting away from classical hermeneutic method, which was concerned with developing appropriate and justified methods for interpreting texts, Gadamer questions the legacy of Enlightenment objectivity. Enlightenment approaches to hermeneutics emphasised objectivity through reasoned or empirical argument and method, in overcoming "the negative implications of a recourse to the authority of tradition".[10] Such methodology assumed a need for the interpreter to transcend his or her situation and, through the application of correct procedure, arrive at the truth behind the historically constituted text.

Gadamer subverts these assumptions. He argues instead that, in accepting the reality of subjectivity in understanding, the interpreter supposes that further engagement is necessary to expand, elaborate, refute, or question those very anticipations that enable understanding to take place. To engage with any tradition is to perceive it from ever new, expanding horizons. Situated understanding is *possibility*, the very orientation of engagement and a position from which we begin to think, question, and discuss. Prejudices are revealed and transformed only as we open ourselves to different voices, situations, and traditions, not "in preliminary methodological self-purgations".[11]

This book assumes a similar approach: it is in performed musical conversation, in hearing and responding to the voice of another, that we become critically conscious of our present horizons. Understanding begins in speaking

---

9   Hans-Georg Gadmer, *Truth and Method*, trans. Joel Weinsheimer and Donald G. Marshall, 2nd revised edition (London: Continuum, 2006).

10 Georgia Warnke, *Gadamer: Hermeneutics, Tradition, and Reason* (Oxford: Polity Press, 1987), 75.

11 David Linge, editor's introduction, in Hans-Georg Gadamer, *Philosophical Hermeneutics*, trans. David Linge (Berkeley: University of California Press, 2008), xxi.

of one situation from another, where such speaking is open ended, rather than closing down in definitive representation.

Ŋaraka (bones)

To talk of hermeneutics is to speak of texts. Yet the term *text*, with all its complex associations and uses in philosophy, seems irrelevant to *manikay* as an oral tradition. *Text* is used in this book to refer to the stable forms and narratives that provide impetus for performance, and is not limited to graphic representation. A similar concept for Wägilak is the *ŋaraka* (bones) that underpin all performance of *manikay*. These *ŋaraka* can be read in the land, ecology, and people. Benjamin Wilfred often asserts, "All the songs come out of the land, the animals, the ground." In this sense, we might rightly understand *manikay* to be underpinned by a tangible text. To overlook this is unintentionally to invoke *terra nullius*.

Manikay opens a conversation with certain social, religious, and existential concerns—the text of human existence—articulating a response to these perennial features of life through song, dance, and narrative. Performance articulates various connections to land, patterns of social relationship, ancestral constitution, and teleological orientation—*ŋaraka* (bones) that are the essential identities carried in *manikay*. The performance of *manikay* sustains constitutions of *bäpurru* (father's group), *gurruṯu* (kinship) relations, *wäŋa* (homeland), *matha* (tongue), and ways of knowing and perceiving the world. As a complex whole, *manikay* represents an interconnected web of texts.

Performance is generated and impelled by pervasive structures of *manikay*, yet those structures can never fully represent a performance. Perhaps the difficulty comes in thinking of structure as prior to performance. The same could be said of country. We know the land as we interact with it—hunting, burning off, gathering for ceremony—and in doing so, we are sustained by the land. The ancestral *ŋaraka* are not static but present in all forms of life. Only through our relationships and performance do the the bones of *manikay* sing.

Performing Tradition

Understanding could be expressed as a conceptual process: someone who wants to understand *manikay* must question what lies behind what is performed. Yet to go back *behind* what is said—to discover the *ŋaraka* (bones) that give rise to ceremonial expressions—is also to ask questions *beyond* what is said. Tradition is eventful: in the unique context of the present, a new horizon is opened by the event of tradition.[12]

---

12 Cf. Gadamer, *Truth and Method*, 370.

An intimate relationship between the past and present is not necessarily reflected in the performance and musicology of the modern music conservatory. This is exacerbated by a polarisation between practical performance (*praxis*) and musicological writing and ideas (*dicta*).[13] Pervasively, musical traditions are understood as distinct clusters of stylistic attributes, conceptually over-and-apart from us, requiring emulation and imitation, *praxis* informed by *dicta*.

Hegel's ideas about history, an important influence on Gadamer, challenge this view of tradition. Hegel speaks of historical situation with poetic language, imagining cultural forms of the past as fruits ripened on a tree, living and constituted within the historical climate that shaped their growth, "the spring and summer of the moral life in which they bloomed and ripened".[14] With this imagery established, his critique of historicism is penetrating. The historicist relationship to the past, he claims, is an "external activity" that merely "wipes spots of rain or dust from this fruit". Hegel continues:

> Instead of the internal elements of the surrounding, productive, and lifegiving reality of the moral world, it [historicism] substitutes the elaborate structure of the dead elements of its external existence, of language, of its historical features and so forth. And this not in order to live within that reality but merely to represent it within oneself.[15]

Historicism is a view of the past that can only deal in representations of that past. On the contrary, Wägilak *manikay* is concerned with the past living through the present. The historicist quest dulls the possibility of the past living through new articulations, integrations and adaptions. Historicism is an "external activity" and, for Gadamer, can conjure only a "derivative, cultural existence … A hermeneutics that regarded understanding as reconstructing the original would be no more than handing on a dead meaning."[16]

In a similar denial of historicism, Daniel Wilfred asserts that *CRB* is "the same" as any performance of *manikay* from the past: "What we do today is no different to what our grandfathers did."[17] By performing in *CRB*, the Young Wägilak Group—the name adopted by those Wägilak who collaborate with the AAO—are drawn into an engagement with the *manikay* tradition as present and active in the world around them. The *manikay* tradition speaks through new performances and performers, shaping understandings of kin, society, polity, ecology, and language. This resonates with Gadamer's view of tradition as something known proximately, not as distant from us but effective within

---

13 Carolyn Abbate, "Music—Drastic or Gnostic?" *Critical Inquiry* 30, no. 3 (2004): 507. The terms praxis and dicta reflect this articles title, "Drastic or Gnostic?"

14 G. W. F. Hegel, quoted in Gadamer, *Truth and Method*, 160.

15 Hegel, quoted in Gadamer, *Truth and Method*, 160.

16 Gadamer, *Truth and Method*, 159–60.

17 Daniel Wilfred, in discussion with the author, 2012.

present understanding.[18] "A reconstructed understanding of tradition will not work ... what is said in tradition needs to make sense from the now."[19]

For Yolŋu, pervasive ideas of tradition as an historical other, treated as an artefact apart from us, "do not fit or make any sense to us; in fact they are repulsive".[20] This "fantasy of the origin rendered historical" is a "desperate refusal of the real human condition, which is that of multiplicity at all the level of existence"[21] To view Wägilak tradition as a repository of cultural information to be sustained as artefact would betray a similar fantasy. As a living, thinking relation to the past, tradition transcends Hegel's "external" representation; it breathes anew when creative engagement rips it from its museum-like display.

Approaching *manikay* as a conversation, we recognise that tradition is not ossified heritage: it is vocative. Ubiquitous and infused within all, tradition is known and sustained in an active conversation between the past and the present, and between individuals and cultures.

Phenomenology

In an amorphous and experienced form like music, a quantitative approach to understanding is limited. Music is first and foremost an event, known as it is heard and through the ways it shapes our engagement with the world.

The Wägilak narrative finds expression in many different forms, including song, dance, design, language, and story. Figurative images and themes are layered together, interlocking and carrying nuanced significations and meanings. This complex ceremonial constellation mirrors the phenomenological excess of the natural world. Admiring the endless variety of life in the world around us, we recognise the impossibility of creating any comprehensive record of cultural forms like *manikay*, which is as much a response to the world around it as a set of definitive forms.

The natural abundance of the world extends to include human perception. Jean-Yves Lacoste expands: "Because the work of art possesses a physical reality (sonorous material, cloth, paint, etc.), this material may be perceived in an autonomous way ... we are thus led straightaway to recognize an irreducible plurality."[22] The creation of any definitive or contained record of cultural tradition is a phenomenological impossibility; reification stymies natural excess. Performed iteration is also provisional, capable of offering only one

---

18 Gadamer, *Truth and Method*, 299.

19 Hans-Georg Gadamer, *Truth and Method* (London: Continuum, 2006), 367.

20 Djiniyini Gondarra, "Assent Law of The First People: Views from a Traditional Owner," *National Indigenous Times*, 3 March 2011, 24.

21 Ricoeur, *On Translation*, 33.

22 Jean-Yves Lacoste, "The Phenomenality of Anticipation", in *Phenomenology and Eschatology: Not Yet in the Now*, ed. Neal DeRoo and John Panteleimon Manoussakis (Aldershot, Hampshire: Ashgate, 2009), 16.

perspective in time. Cultural traditions live beyond their peculiar and particular iterations.

The Yolŋu hermeneutic resonates with these observations. Howard Morphy explains that in Yolŋu thought, "the metaphysical core is never merely said because it is itself complex and intertwined with social practice. It cannot be condensed in a single sentence; rather it is performed, painted and danced"[23].

In seeking to capture the ways music is engaged in Indigenous Australian culture, some ethnomusicologists have attempted to complement an objective, documentary gaze—the careful notation of form and function characteristic of early Australian ethnomusicology from the 1960s and '70s—with rich phenomenological description. Writings on *manikay* by Aaron Corn are representative of this approach (Magowan's *Melodies of Mourning* is another example),[24] and attempt to convey something of the way *manikay* shapes human perceptions of people and place. The following passage is a rich example, in which the details of the description convey something of the Yolŋu experience of song as a living, interwoven narrative:

> There is a song in my mind that takes me to a place of great beauty and antiquity. As its melody undulates through my synapses, I can sense this place anew. I can feel the fine white sand squelching between my toes, so soft and light it is like walking on a cloud. The sands whistle with the wind as it ripples across the bay … In the brilliance of the sun silhouetted against an expansive white cloud, a lone gull cries out to her chicks nested on yonder island … The song takes me to that beach as though I were standing there right now with the soft sands between my toes and all the other details I described. Yet now we face a dilemma. At this moment of realisation, I can offer no evidence whatsoever that any such thing is going on in my head—no proof of a song, or the place I say it describes.[25]

At times, a similar style of description is used in this book. One benefit of this is that, in working in between languages—English, Kriol, and Wägilak—a certain opacity of description avoids oversimplification. *Manikay* narratives are themselves densely layered and this writing style preserves something of that richness.

Many expressions and phrases in this book have been used as they were communicated to me, even where a clear meaning may not be evident. Hopefully, this approach leads toward a shared language concerning *manikay*, even if this is a modest and very minimal beginning. Further, my own voice is often blended

---

23 Howard Morphy, "'Joyous Maggots': The Symbolism of Yolngu Mortuary Rituals", in *An Appreciation of Difference: W.E.H. Stanner and Aboriginal Australia*, ed. Melinda Hinkson and Jeremy Beckett (Canberra: Aboriginal Studies Press, 2008), 137.

24 Fiona Magowan, *Melodies of Mourning: Music and Emotion in Northern Australia* (Oxford: James Currey Press, 2007), 15.

25 Aaron Corn, "Nations of Song", 146–47.

with the expressions of Wägilak singers. This lack of delineation can, at times, lead to a loss of critical distance. However, what is gained is a proximity and coincidence of expression that is hopefully enabling of further interaction.

Creative expressions like music demand creative understanding. Here, Paul Ricoeur's words seem pertinent: "Only a poet can translate a poet."[26] The opacity and open-endedness of narrative descriptions can lead to more careful listening and further engagement. Likewise, Ricoeur's words reflect the creative impetus of *CRB* as it engages with *manikay* as a poetic tradition.

Wata

Daniel Wilfred sits beside me. "Can you feel that wind blowing? We sing, and the wind just comes up out of nowhere."

The wind is starting to pick up. Free and fluid, we cannot grasp it. In our separation, each of us can feel it blowing around us, blowing between us.

There is an ancestral wind that stirs today. Can you feel it? It eddies through these words, stirring from another time, another place—far out to sea, the deep ancestral waters also stir.

The wind is blowing. It is a wind that blows people together, blowing different voices together in a sweet cacophony, an animated, rippling song. Situations intermingle. The wind is blowing somewhere new.

---

26 Paul Ricoeur, *On Translation*, trans. Eileen Brennan (London: Routledge, 2006), 38.

1

IMPELLED: SONGS FROM THE GROUND

In the blank air a song is heard. Breaking absence, out of nothing—presence. In the hollow air, the grain of a free-flowing voice, wending and weaving, enchants. Each note passes before its rippling wake, an echo that reveals a voice. The song is carried in its dispersal, heard as it is thrown into the world.

The expectant air brims with anticipation. Hopeful ears strain to hear a living voice. The *bilma* (clapsticks) strike, impelling voices on. And as they listen, creative minds are impelled to sing. Quivering thighs carry feet over the dancing, reverberant ground.

An ancestral voice, which was and is, and called our world into being. Far out to sea toward the sunrise, a song broke the stillness, rippling across the land. The dark land was woken by the *waŋarr* (creative ancestral beings) whose feet danced to an ancestral groove, etching their movements into the land.

That song of old can be sensed today. Through *manikay*, ears become attuned and eyes directed. Every night the singers take up their place in the dust, the ancestral song again finds its voice.

Manikay (song) carries ancestral foundations and presence. Through song, the past animates the present world, moving *yolŋu* (people) to dance. In song, community is established. By song, the past enfolds the present. Today, the unique voices of individuals belonging to the Wägilak resound over the ground and water, and through the country.

To sing, Wägilak sit on dust and rock. But they also sit on the ground of tradition, which gives shape to the present. Whether in the capital cities of the south or the remote outstations of the north, Wägilak sing from the ground of their *ŋaraka-wäŋa* (bone-country). This is their homeland, out of which family and law extend. This Wägilak country is called Ŋilipidji: "My country,

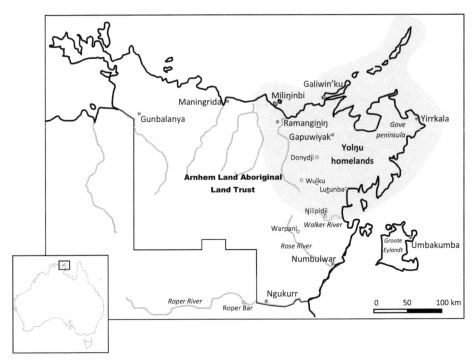

Fig. 1.1. Map of Arnhem Land showing the location of Ŋilipidji on the southern border of the Yolŋu homelands.

it's beautiful country, called Ŋilipidji. And another name, called Lärra, the Stone Spear—that's Wägilak country."[1] Though Wägilak people call the names of Ŋilipidji in song, it is Ŋilipidji that impels their performance.

> *Manikay* is coming out of that ground; comes from that ground at Ŋilipidji. *Manikay* is for country, for leading new generation. *Manikay* is for using in funeral, *wata* [wind], smoking [purification ceremony]. Learn about your country [in song]. *Manikay* means spirit for the country, and songs; where he walked, Djuwalpada [ancestor of Ŋilipidji]. *Manikay* means for the land and for the ground, tree, no matter what animal. Everything. *Manikay* means for the countryside and for land—land and sea—no matter where you go.[2]

Ŋilipidji lies in the far northern reaches of the Australian continent, about two days' drive from the nearest capital city, Darwin (figs. 1.1, 1.2). It is a hot, inland place some thirty-five kilometres west of the coast at Blue Mud

---

1   Benjamin Wilfred, in discussion with the author, "Digital Audio Technologies and Aural Organicism in the Australian Art Orchestra's 'Crossing Roper Bar,'" *Information Technology and Indigenous Communities* conference of the Australian Institute of Aboriginal and Torres Strait Islander Studies (Australian National University, Canberra, ACT, July 13, 2010). In Wägilak, *lärr* denotes the chips that break off a stone spearhead.

2   Benjamin Wilfred, in a conference discussion with the author, "Digital Audio Technologies", 13 July 2010.

Fig. 1.2. The outstation at Ḏilipidji today.

Bay in the Gulf of Carpentaria. During the wet season each year, Ŋilipidji is encircled by floodwaters. These drain away in the dry season, leaving behind dusty riverbanks and deep, dark waterholes. The low-lying hills to the south are covered by scattered stone outcrops, and the landscape is covered sparsely in hardy eucalyptus and ironbark trees. Ŋilipidji is famous for its historic production of greasy, pink-streaked ŋambi (stone spear heads) and knives at numerous open-ground quarries. A valuable commodity, ŋambi were lethal in hunting and combat, and traded across great distances.

Until the fragmented movements of exodus from life on ancestral estates in the mid-1900s, Yolŋu had lived on their traditional homelands for countless generations. Today, Wägilak reside in towns like Ngukurr, hundreds of kilometres away. While the opportunity to get "back to country" is often thwarted by limited access to reliable transport, the possibility never fails to light up excited eyes. When a trip does eventuate every year or so, no one can help but sing all the way home. The *gumurr* (chest) of *manikay*—the main *body* of a song during which sacred names of Ŋilipidji are intoned (see Chapter Five)—pulls swelling hearts back into the embrace of country.

Fig. 1.3. Wunungirrna, the Walker River at Dilipidji.

We arrive at Ṉilipidji after two days' travel via Numbulwar, where, along the way, more family were gathered into the convoy. The old corrugated-iron huts need sweeping, the grass burning to get rid of snakes. Not far from where we are camping is a spring, bubbling through thick foliage and running into still pools. These pools are soft underfoot with thick black silt, making it hard to see any little, shy "snappy ones"—freshwater crocodiles. The spring is an ever-flowing source of life, created when the ancestral Djaŋ'kawu Sisters plunged their sacred digging stick into the ground. A few hundred metres away, this water joins Wunungirrna, the Walker River (fig. 1.3).

We go fishing in one of the freshwater pools that overflow in the wet season. It is full of ŋatban' (rifle fish) and huge madhpuna (black bream). Stomachs rumble. We are not strangers: the land recognises the presence of the wäŋa-waṯaŋu (country owners), smelling our scent and giving up an abundance of natural resources for our sustenance and pleasure. Plenty to catch.

An old rope swing extends across the deepest part of the stream, a playful remnant of the abandoned outstation. Not much infrastructure remains here: a few rotting blankets, some fishing reels and spears, colourfully painted but extremely dusty huts, a defunct solar panel, and one large water tank.

What remains at Ṉilipidji is much more permanent and tangible than a few dilapidated buildings. When we entered Wägilak country, just west of the main track to Gove, we stopped to smoke some many'tjarr (leaves) for the spirit of a recently deceased relative, announcing our presence to the land.

After eating some freshly stewed ŋanaparru (buffalo), we roll out sleeping mats and mosquito nets on a huge tarpaulin—the underside is still covered in buffalo blood—and the sun sets. Benjamin Miyala Wilfred, Andy Lukaman Peters and David Yipininy Wilfred prepare to sing the manikay that narrates the foundation of this homeland.

David Wilfred, a Ritharrŋu man related directly to the Wägilak by marriage, is djuŋgayi (manager) for the singers. The djuŋgayi plays yiḏaki (didjeridu) for his ŋänḏipulu (mother's group; opposite moiety), ensuring that the performance follows the correct narrative sequence. Benjamin Wilfred and Andy Peters are reciprocally obliged to play yiḏaki for Ritharrŋu songs (see Chapter Two, "Wägilak Connections").[3] David addresses the ancestral beings in the Ritharrŋu/ Wägilak language, naming everyone who is present and reflecting pensively on the state of contemporary ceremonial practice: "There is no elder in the Wägilak clan for the buŋgul [ceremony]." Benjamin continues:

---

3   David Wilfred is from the Yirritja moiety; Benjamin Wilfred, Daniel Wilfred, and Andy Peters are from the Dhuwa moiety. Wägilak (Dhuwa) typically marry Ritharrŋu (Yirritja), and descent is agnatic, i.e. through the father's line. In ceremony, both Dhuwa and Yirritja are needed: one group owns and sings the songs, while the other group oversees the ceremony and plays yiḏaki.

Fig. 1.4. Wally Wilfred, *Devil Devil of Dilipitji*, 2011. About 135 x 100 cm. Reproduced with permission.

We are going to start [singing] from Butjulubayi [north of Ṉilipidji]. *Yiḏaki* player is David, and his land, where he came from, is Bunḏuḻum. Where I'm standing now is my home, Ṉilipidji. Tomorrow we are leaving, walking to Warparni.[4] My song is Wägilak. We will start with [the songs] "Yolŋu Man" ["Djuwalpaḏa"], "Gara" [Spear], "Malka" [String bag], "Wadawada" [Wire spear].

Long-time ago our grandfather's father, grandfather's mother, they used to walk everywhere, travel around with the Yolŋu song, "Djuwalpaḏa". This song we are going to start from is where we are now, Ṉilipidji. Ṉilipidji, Lärra [stone spear country]. This is my home, me, Miyala.

All my grandfathers and my in-laws, they are all gone now. All our grandfathers—fathers' fathers—all passed away. We are the only people that know the culture and the secret singing. Only us mob now. Andy [Peters] is the only elder in the Wägilak clan. This is me talking, Miyala. I'm doing this recording for all my children to listen and learn, and move along with our culture … I'm the only person that knows the traditional songs. All the rest are gone. This is for you mob; you mob got to listen properly, learn and carry on. Only then can I stop.[5]

The *biḻma* (clapsticks) break the dark, humid air, dense with insect noise (audio example 1a). The regular and percussive strikes mimic Djuwalpaḏa's footsteps as he begins to walk.

Audio example 1a. "Djuwalpaḏa," *walking* mode. Benjamin Wilfred, Andy Peters, and David Wilfred (*yiḏaki*). Dilipidji, South East Arnhem Land, August 25, 2010.

Djuwalpaḏa, the Wägilak *Mokuy*

Djuwalpaḏa Ṉirriyiŋirriyi dhawal-wal ḏuy'yun
Ḻikandhu-ŋupan Djuwalpaḏa

Djuwalpaḏa, Ṉirriyiŋirriyi, walking across the country
Djuwalpaḏa, with elbows pointing

("Djuwalpaḏa" song text)[6]

---

4   Warpani, an important waterhole in Ṉandi (Miṉiŋiri patrigroup) country, some 40km southwest of Ṉilipidji.

5   Benjamin Wilfred speaking at Ṉilipidji, Arnhem Land, 25 August 2010.

6   Unless otherwise noted, all translations and transcriptions in this chapter were recorded with Daniel and Benjamin Wilfred between 2010 and 2012. Translations attempt to capture the explanations as they were provided.

Setting out from Butjulubayi, that wild man Djuwalpada searched far and wide across the land (fig. 1.4). Dangerous animals threatened him, surrounded him. "Waahh!"—his voice broke through fear. Brandishing his *gudjarra'*, a razor-sharp stone-head spear, he advanced. Warily Djuwalpada walked, lifting his thighs high, knowing each foot placement before it landed. Through the bush he went, searching for a home.

The walking *mokuy* (ghost) Djuwalpada carried many things. From his shoulders hung *malka* (string bags), woven from carefully spun *raki* (string). Around his neck was the *galpan* (dillybag), the bush bag—I can't tell you what's inside that one.

> Galpan galpan wayidjila
> Birrinyinbirrinyin maninyala

> Dillybag dillybag dillybag
> carried by the ghost Birrinyinbirrinyin

> ("Galpan" Dillybag song text)

The hunting *mokuy* (ghost) Djuwalpada, he has his *galpu* (spear-thrower) too, to send his *gara* (spear) straight and fast. The searching *mokuy*, he tracks his food. He also follows the bees, looking for the law. The *mokuy* journeys to his *naraka-wäna* (bone-country).

"He got the spear, he got woomera, he got dillybag. He walks with that and he will always get bush food and fish and put it in his dillybag. That's where he puts the honey. And he's always walking: Yolŋu, Wild Blackfella, Djuwalpada we call him. He's travelled around the country. Place to place. Djuwalpada. We sing about him."[7]

Djuwalpada walked right up to the Gove peninsula, to Dululrripbi. He left one *gara* (spear) up there, in the ground. Where a spear has been left, something will "come out and grow from that place"—*galtha* (a course of action) has been set in motion.[8] At another place he left a *galpan* (dillybag) and at another some *bilma* (clapsticks), places where people are blown together for ceremony. As he walked, Djuwalpada looked at the world, naming the plants and animals he saw (audio example 1b).

Audio example 1b. "Djuwalpada," *walking* mode. Benjamin Wilfred, Roy Natilma (higher voice), and David Wilfred (*yidaki*). Recording made during sessions for the *CRB* album, Melbourne, 13 April 2009.

But still Djuwalpada had no home. With elbows pointed, he looked high in the treetops of the *gadayka* (stringybark tree), searching for some *guku* (honey).

---

7   Benjamin Wilfred, quoted in Grabowsky et al., "Forum on *CRB*."
8   Raymattja Marika-Mununggiritj and Michael Christie, "Yolngu Metaphors for Learning", *International Journal of the Sociology of Language* 113, no. 1 (1995): 60.

He needed that honey first. "Where is the *jugabeg blai* [native honey bee]? There, near the *dhaŋgarra* [stringybark flowers]." High in the tree, he spotted a hive.

Djuwalpada tried to climb up but the blades on his elbows were too sharp. The tree was cut down, splintering. It cracked open. Oh, those bees were angry! They attacked, swarming around. Djuwalpada fought them off and took the *guku* (honey). And the honey was good. "Hey, gu gu gu gu gu gu, gey gey!" Singing and dancing with joy, Djuwalpada put the honey in his *galpan* (dillybag) (audio example 1c). "Dillybag, it's a bush bag. Where he put his beef, honey, sugarbag from the tree, he put in his bag."[9]

Audio example 1c. "Djuwalpada," *dancing* mode. Benjamin Wilfred, Roy Natilma, and David Wilfred (*yidaki*). Vocal interjections by Wesley Wilfred. Recording made during sessions for the *CRB* album, Melbourne, 13 April 2009.

As he continued walking, Djuwalpada felt the breeze on the back of his neck, tickling. Slowly it started to pick up, getting stronger and stronger. He was frightened. Listen now: can you hear a song carried on the wind? The song of a bird, crying, the *birrkpirrk* (lapped-wing plover).

Djuwalpada called out, "Birrkpirrk-Birrkpirrk, where am I going to stay? I'm staying now at this place but I don't want to stay here because otherwise a big wind will come."[10] The *birrkpirrk* was also frightened by the big wind that was coming and flew away.

His spear would show him where to go. Djuwalpada looked north, shaking his spear. No, his home was not there. He looked south—not there either. Then, still pointing his elbow, he looked west. There was his home. His spear flies, entering the ground in the low-lying hills of Ŋilipidji (audio example 1d).

Audio example 1d. "Gara" (Spear) *throwing* mode, with Benjamin Wilfred, Roy Natilma, and David Wilfred (*yidaki*). Vocal interjections by Wesley Wilfred. Recording made during sessions for the *CRB* album, Melbourne, 13 April 2009.

> Marrayunmara gara guthanbiny nhalaŋu
> Marrayunmara gara guthanbiny nhalaŋu
> Yarrarra, yarrarra, yarrarra [wahhh!]
> Gulyunmirr galpu, madayin-marrayi
>
> Aiming, he shakes his spear. Which way now?
> Aiming, he shakes his spear. Which way now?
> Ready to throw
> Thrown from the spear-thrower, making the sacred law
>
> ("Gara" spear song text)

---

9   Daniel Wilfred, comment during a dance workshop, Melbourne, 29 May 2014.
10 Benjamin Wilfred, interview with the author, Ngukurr, 19 July 2011.

Wägilak law *is*, now and here.

"'This is my land, where I'm going to live. I'm going to live here and I'm going to stay here.' And he starts dancing now, in that place."[11]

This is their place, *ŋaraka-wäŋa* (bone country). Like the straight flight of the spear, their path is set.

"He [Djuwalpada] was a long time ago and he's still here today. What those elders handed over is still going to be there for the young people."[12] "That's where his elbows are pointing, where he walks, looking for the place and for the land, when he finds the land he stops. He walks along, giving each tribe a song. How he came back, right through to my land, to a place called Ŋilipidji. He's pointing with his elbow, tracking fish, bush honey, making a string, skinning the bark, walking, when he find the land, Ŋilipidji, and there he stays."[13]

Lärra. Stone spear county.

"'Ah yeah. This is my land. Alright then, I'll stop here.' This is where Ŋilipidji is. That's how the Young Wägilak's *buŋgul* [ceremony] goes. From the beginning to the end."[14]

"That's where he went, pointing with his elbow. And that's how he found the place, and now he's still there. That's Ŋilipidji."[15]

Narrative Ground

Through song, Wägilak announce the arrival and presence of Djuwalpada's spear at Ŋilipidji, which is still "in the ground" today. "By painting the designs in ceremonies, by singing the songs and performing the dances, Yolngu are re-creating ancestral events."[16] The country at Ŋilipidji remains a tangible inscription of ancestral action. The site where Djuwalpada's spear went into the ground at Ŋilipidji is a sacred place, located in low lying hills south of the outstation. Ŋilipidji is the Wägilak constitution, the breathing chest of an identity, a corporeal body that entails ethical responsibility: to relate, live and act as Wägilak.

This is by no means an exclusive or singular identity: there are many affiliations overlapping and intersecting with the travels of Djuwalpada and the ground at Ŋilipidji, connecting different sites, ancestral characters, ecological features and animals. Wägilak identity is created and sustained as it performed in ceremony; this is extensional, as performance generates a complex web of

---

11 Daniel Wilfred, comment during a dance workshop, Melbourne, 29 May 2014.
12 Daniel Wilfred, interview with the author, Ngukurr, 19 July 2011.
13 Daniel Wilfred, comment during a dance workshop, Melbourne, 29 May 2014.
14 Justin Nunggarrgalug, in a conference discussion with the author, "Digital Audio Technologies", 13 July 2010.
15 Daniel Wilfred, comment during a dance workshop, Melbourne, 29 May 2014.
16 Howard Morphy, *Ancestral Connections: Art and an Aboriginal System of Knowledge* (Chicago: University of Chicago Press, 1991), 102

connections. Just as personal identities and responsibilities are only discovered in relation to others, so too the collective identity of the Wägilak is formed through song. This collective identity is not circumscribed by definite boundaries, as the problematic term *clan* might suggest.[17]

For example, Wägilak man Andy Peters' country is Wulku, which was also founded by Djuwalpada with the same spear.[18] Wulku and Ṉilipidji are connected in *manikay* narratives that join together these two places (see Chapter Four). Common ancestry is significant, as Peters belongs to a different yet closely related *bäpurru* (lit. father's group, but a sense of *connection* rather than *group* is probably more appropriate) within the greater Wägilak identity and language. Yet perhaps just as important is the present-day embodiment of these connections expressed in *manikay*, through ceremonial responsibilities and family connections. References to the Wägilak *clan* are sometimes used in this book, as the term is commonly used by Wägilak from Ngukurr. Yet it is always conditioned by the assertion, "We are the same." The term *clan* figures interdependence and connection (see Chapter Two).[19] Similarly, *manikay* are less *sets* or *cycles* of songs than narrative constellations, with potential to branch off in multiple directions.

The Wägilak narrative of foundation begins with the journey of Djuwalpada, an ancestral *mokuy* (ghost) also known as Yolŋu Man, Birriyinbirriyin, Ṉirriyiṉirriyi, or Ṉänuk. Brimming with associations, this is the story recounted all public performances of *manikay* by Wägilak. The basic structures and figurative action of this narrative are always present in performance. Deeper layers of meaning, intricate connections with other narratives, philosophic concepts, and phenomenological observations emerge from this basic story. These layered stories and connections come to be understood over time, the meanings of song enriched and further revealed within lived situations.

The above retelling of Djuwalpada's journey is merely one narrative thread that draws on an extended network of metonymic allusions and expressions

---

17 We can learn more about Yolŋu identity from the metaphors of song than from anthropological nomenclature like *clan*, which carries with it a variety of assumptions, such as bounded spatial rights or exclusivity of membership based on lineage. Keen, who seems primarily concerned with the rigidity of terms like *clan*—a term that carries a long and complex anthropological heritage— follows a similar argument: "Far from being constituted by enclosure within boundaries or related in a taxonomic hierarchy of group and sub-group, Yolngu identities, like their concepts of place, extend outwards from foci. Connections among identities are not those of closed sets but are those of open and extendable 'strings' of connectedness." Ian Keen, "A Bundle of Sticks: The Debate Over Yolŋu Clans", *Journal of the Royal Anthropological Institute* 6, no. 3 (2000), 419–36.

18 Andy Peters, interview with the author, Ngukurr, 12 July 2011.

19 *Bäpurru* is used here as a more specific identification than the broader name Wägilak, relating to immediate descent and ceremonial responsibilities. Usefully, James notes that *bäpurru* are "distinctive, multivalent, dynamic entities … focussed around common connections of shared ancestral essence [*märr*]." Bentley James, "The Language of 'Spiritual Power': From Mana to Märr on the Crocodile Islands," In *Strings of Connectedness: Essays in Honour of Ian Keen*, edited by Peter G. Toner (Canberra: ANU Press, 2015), 257.

concerning relationship, society, history, and ecology. Multiple strands from different narratives weave in and out of this story, crossing over and spinning off—a dynamic play that is part of a greater canvas. While the account of Djuwalpada at Ṉilipidji remains primary, there is an abundance of intersections and potential detours into other narrative sequences. A single, performed story is latent with connections requiring the performance by other families to be more fully revealed. In this sense, *manikay* across a region like South East Arnhem Land can be understood as an interconnected, interwoven amalgam of narrative threads.

Because understanding always emerges amid deepening layers of association, a comprehensive account of Wägilak narrative or identity is impossible. Performance contexts are always changing too: new performances like *CRB* can show different aspects of the Wägilak narrative expressed in song and dance. While there can be great variety in performance, for Wägilak there remains one legitimate encapsulation of this ancestral narrative that encompasses every possible iteration: the Wägilak *ŋaraka-wäŋa* (bone-country), the ground of Ṉilipidji itself. The ground of Ṉilipidji underwrites all performed expressions, including ceremony, people, society, language, culture, and history. In the Wägilak world, "All the songs come from the land."[20] For Wägilak, it is the land that underwrites social connections and groupings.

The geography and topology of Ṉilipidji itself presents a tangible and stable record of ancestral action and creation. Comparatively, the permanence of any digital song archive, or even materials such as paper and ink, are transient, capable of recording only iterations of song. The aural archives of human memory and speech are always one generation away from extinction, but the land itself is permanent, in that it sustains human existence and activity; it is a living archive through which people walk, sing, hunt, grow families, and die.

The images and events of Djuwalpada's travels through this land form a core narrative carried in all performances of *manikay* and complimentary repertories of *buŋgul* (dance), *miny'tji* (design), and *yäku* (sacred lexicon). In *manikay*, both the musical forms (Chapter Five) and song texts dramatise different subjects and events from the narrative of Djuwalpada. For example, the songs "Gara" (Spear), "Gaḻpu" (Spear-thrower), and "Raki" (String). Paintings of Djuwalpada by Wägilak elder Sambo Barabara and Wally Wilfred (see figs. 1.4, 4.1) depict many of these subjects. In appropriate sequence, the songs that make up common Wägilak performances of *manikay* are listed below (table 1.1).

Different sets of *manikay* form narrative sequences for mortuary, purification, circumcision, initiation, and exchange ceremonies; these songs are always performed in the correct order. As well as forming distinct ceremonial programs, these groupings reflect the responsibilities to perform *manikay*

---

20 Daniel Wilfred, comment during a dance workshop, Melbourne, 29 May 2014.

by different Wägilak *bäpurru* (father's groups) for the country at Wulku and Ṉilipidji. It is interesting to note that Andy Peters asserts his responsibility for singing sequences of songs for both Wulku and Ṉilipidji. Note that in sequence five, Roy Natilma has identified as Djambarrpuyŋu—where he typically identifies as Wägilak—demonstrating how *manikay* create affiliation through responsibilities to perform, as well as new meeting places in-between distinct families and homelands.

The different sequence of songs can be referred to by their overall theme, such as the *wata* (wind) songs, which relates to their use in ceremony and overall narrative. Coming chapters explore how these sequences fit together and encode important relational, cultural, and historical connections of the Wägilak.

In performance, the sacred names of places and objects from Djuwalpada's journey are sung. Dancers also mimic the actions of Djuwalpada as he makes string by rolling plant fibres—"He's making a line to go fishing"—or stalks prey with a spear.[21] Paintings on bare chests, canvas, or coffins, depict the various *miny'tji* (designs) of these subjects. From the Yolŋu homelands of North East Arnhem Land, dozens of *manikay* repertoires make use of hundreds of subjects—ancestral characters, animals, actions, and objects, as in the above table of song subjects (1.1)—which form the basic tangible, mnemonic building blocks of ceremony. These subjects are present in natural and social environments, and point toward the actual traces of creative ancestral action that can be perceived in existence, such as ecological processes and kinship relations. Subsequently, songs become a resource for teaching young children about life as Yolŋu—knowing your country, looking for honey or weaving—relating present-day activity to "what the ancestors used to do".

Each individual *manikay* subject, such as "Djuwalpada," has its own series of *bilma* (clapstick) modes, which are essential to the dance choreography of each song. These modes translate narrative action—such as Djuwalpada stalking, dancing, and walking—into rhythmic form (see Chapter Five). Each performance of *manikay* moves through an appropriate sequence of modes selected for the context; not all modes are necessarily used in any given performance. These sequences are generally fixed, however *buŋgul* (song and dance) performed for entertainment at festivals might draw upon any subject listed in any order. For example, songs may alternate between Wägilak *manikay* items and the subjects of different but closely related *bäpurru* (father's groups) such as Marraŋu, Murruŋun, Nuŋgubuyu, and Nunydjirrpi.

Manikay narratives generally represent connections between different groups with images of natural events. Table 1.1 provides us with an example of this. Extending over the country of different *bäpurru*, the *wukuṉ* (clouds) form out at sea in Blue Mud Bay (sequence one), before they are blown over the land

---

21 Daniel Wilfred, comment during a dance workshop, Melbourne, 29 May 2014.

by the *wata* (wind). The wind gathers all the clouds together in a great storm (sequence four), eventually falling as rain (sequence five) and running through the freshwater streams and rivers (see Chapter Three).[22]

Benjamin and Daniel Wilfred's *manikay* are casually referred to as "those *wata* (wind) songs," and Peters' *manikay* as "those cloud songs". The groups responsible for the performance of these songs might be referred to as "that *wukuṉ* (cloud) mob". In *CRB*, the *wata* (wind) songs are sung (sequence four). These songs structure the events of wind-related ceremonies, such as the smoking purification ceremony.

Today, *manikay* is most frequently heard during week-long mortuary rituals, performed outside the house of the deceased or town morgue for a few hours before sundown. Wägilak mortuary rituals often begin with the subject "Dhaṇarra" (White flower)—recalling the start of a person's life in ancestral law (sequence three)—and after a few days climax with a smoking ceremony and the song "Wata" (Wind) (sequence four). When the wind blows, "all good and bad feelings are finished", blown away.[23]

Manikay is highly structured. Yet, as coming chapters will show, creativity within the structures of *manikay* is considered essential to the realisatino of important narrative aspects. Benjamin Wilfred points out that these integral features are not lost in the *CRB* collaboration, which in all its vibrancy and invention extends from the ground at Ṉilipidji:

> Collaboration [*CRB*] coming out from my walk [through country]; collaboration coming out from the ground and from the land; collaboration coming out from my heart, and looking forward, and from the painting, and from the Grandpa's story, and from the *mokuy* [ghost] called Wild Blackfella [Djuwalpada]. Every story and song coming out from … the country, and from the land, and from the ground.[24]

> [In *CRB*] we follow those tracks: just walk and walk. We always sing about Wild Blackfella [Djuwalpada], where he walked. We follow that track, where the elders in the olden days went, we follow them.[25]

In sustaining traditions of song, Wägilak affirm their responsibilities to the land through connections that have been handed down the generations. Ethnomusicologist Aaron Corn elaborates: "In a pragmatic sense", ceremonial expression such as *manikay* "function as title deeds and represent the

---

22 For example, the Djambarrpuyŋu *rain* songs use *biḻma* modes and rhythmic sequences very similar to the Wägilak patterns.
23 Benjamin Wilfred, "Digital Audio Technologies".
24 Benjamin Wilfred, "Digital Audio Technologies".
25 Benjamin Wilfred, interview with Daniel Browning, "Crossing Boundaries".

ancestrally-bestowed proprietary interests of each *mala* [group]."[26] Corn also writes poetically of the difference between this sort of knowledge carried in song and pervasive Western assumptions: "One person's ephemeron is another's foundations. One person's art is another's law. Paintings on bodies versus books bound in leather. Song versus scripture. Our minds, embodied in words and deed, versus theirs."[27]

Song also expresses the responsibilities that accompany legal custodianship of land and cultural forms. *Mokuy* (ancestral ghosts), such as Djuwalpada, are distinct for every *bäpurru* and give *garma* (public) aspects of law that specify country ownership, rights to hunting and resource harvesting, rules for political arrangements, dispute resolution, kinship laws, and other social structures.[28] When Yolŋu live on the land performing traditional activities such as hunting and land management practices (such as burning-off), they are sustained by the land. *Manikay* expresses not only custodianship of the land but the custodianship of the people by the land. While *manikay* celebrates the natural world and human situation within it, it also emerges as wholly dependent on this ancestral ground: this ongoing relationship with Ŋilipidji impels creative responses which reverberate down the generations, pulsating through voices and feet, minds and actions, and animating unique lives. Everything comes out of the ground at Ŋilipidji.

26 Aaron Corn, "Sound Exchanges: An Ethnomusicologists Approach to Interdisciplinary Teaching and Learning in Collaboration with a Remote Indigenous Australian Community," *The World of Music* 51, no. 3 (2009): 34.

27 Aaron Corn, "Land, Song, Constitution: Exploring Expressions of Ancestral Agency, Intercultural Diplomacy and Family Legacy in the Music of Yothu Yindi with Mandawuy Yunupingu", *Popular Music* 29, no. 1 (2010): 12.

28 Corn details some of the knowledge and laws carried in *manikay*: "How to harvest the honey made by nesting bees in tree trunks. How to hunt macropods ... How to locate buried yam roots ... this is the type of knowledge for human existence that ancestral *mokuy* (ghosts) of both patri-moieties codify in [ceremonial] liturgies." While *manikay* is not so much a "how-to" manual of detailed instruction, it informs discussion and emphasises the importance of specific processes, such as the blossoming of flowers at a certain time of year. Aaron Corn, "Dreamtime Wisdom, Modern-time Vision: Tradition and Innovation in the Popular Band Movement of Arnhem Land, Australia" (PhD diss., University of Melbourne, 2002), 103.

2

CONNECTED IN SONG

There are many Aboriginal peoples with their own unique places. We as Yolŋu are separate from them, because we are connected to them. And we keep making new connections and new separations.

—Mandawuy Yunupingu,
"Vision for the North: Bringing Our Pasts into Our Futures," 2003[1]

Families and homelands with distinct *manikay* repertoires are connected, even as they are separate; the term Yolŋu expresses these connections and separations, as a collection of different groups related through language, cultural practices, histories, and politics.[2] Yolŋu are also separated from one another by distinct skin names, dialects, homelands, alliances, and repertoires of song and dance. Such distinct identities might seem partisan and can lead to tensions between groups, but these differences also result in concern for the good of the whole: identities and inheritances bestowed through lineage only have meaning within the context of a greater ceremonial, legal, and narrative constellation. In their differences Yolŋu entwine together, forming connections in all aspects of life.

Yolŋu celebrate their situation as individuals, families and languages of distinction. The huge variety of *manikay* repertoires across Arnhem Land

---

1   Mandawuy Yunupingu, "Vision for the North: Bringing Our Pasts into Our Futures" (keynote address, Charles Darwin University, 21 May 2013).

2   Even if a large, cohesive social identity known as Yolŋu did not exist prior to European contact, the term here follows its common, contemporary usage, referring to the related Yolŋu *matha* (tongues). Simmilarities in the use and meanings of *manikay* abound among Yolŋu, as do connections within *manikay* narratives and song forms.

attests to this celebration of situation: dozens of distinct melodic and harmonic structures, song languages, *bilma* (clapstick) mode sequences, and *yidaki* (didjeridu) patterns belonging to many different families and homelands. These complex and unique repertoires of poetry and song celebrate specific places, narratives, genealogies, and events. Wägilak identify as Yolŋu yet, as this chapter shows, they have as much to do with families and ceremonial repertoires that are not considered Yolŋu. Importantly, the performance of these repertoires relies upon cooperation between groups that are at once different, contiguous and also spliced together. Distinct narratives of identity and belonging are interwoven, embedded in musical forms and in responsibilities to fulfil different roles in performance.

Yolŋu have always been inter-connected. They have formed connections through trade, ceremony, and relationship, with other Aboriginal peoples from the rainforests, the desert, the Gulf, and the Kimberley. For centuries, Macassans from Sulawesi visited the Yolŋu coast, bringing with them new demands for trade that were filled by Yolŋu.[3] The Macassans brought new goods and materials that in turn stoked the fires of commerce and production.

Not all contact with outsiders was productive. As pastoralists began to expand into parts of Arnhem Land in the late nineteenth and early twentieth century, violent skirmishes and retributive killings decimated some groups and pushed others out of their traditional homelands. This was particularly brutal in the south and west of Arnhem Land and for those caught on this frontier, the violence abated only after the arrival of Christian missions in the early twentieth century.[4]

Throughout the twentieth century, new connections continued to materialise in the Yolŋu world in mixed array—sometimes confusing or destructive, sometimes joyful and lifegiving. These influences continue to shape and characterise Arnhem Land communities today. There were Japanese poachers, and then Japanese bombs; new diseases boring into the body; miners boring into the earth; a federal government three-thousand kilometres away reshaping systems of governance; aspirations of sovereignty and autonomy; a federal judicial system illiterate in Yolŋu law; new communities and outstations birthed through the homeland movement; new languages, like Kriol and English, becoming established and widely spoken; money, alcohol, country music, electricity, television, and the electric guitar; four-wheel drives, roads, tourists, national parks, anthropologists, art collectors, and galleries; coke, smokes, and mobile phones.

Through all these changes, Yolŋu continued to open out their cultural practices, sharing information, making new connections in their songs and art, and attempting

---

3   Trudgen, *Why Warriors Lie Down and Die: Djambatj Mala* (Darwin: Aboriginal Resource and Development Services Inc., 2000), 15.

4   Ibid., 12–42.

to educate outsiders in the value of their culture and experiences (see Chapter Three). In an environment of unprecedented goodwill and concern from mainstream Australia, Yolŋu today continue their *outreach* through cultural expressions.

Yolŋu sing to assert their unique identity in history, an ancestral identity that persists amid ever expanding connections and relationships in the contemporary world. The persistence of *manikay* affirms the life of Yolŋu as at once separate yet connected, both inherited and creative. Beginning to explore such ideas, this chapter elaborates a recent history of the Wägilak and their connections, through a time of unprecedented cultural change.

Going to Town

Compared with the south-east of the country, early colonial contact in Australia's Arnhem Land region was relatively minimal. Aside from Matthew Flinders' voyage to map the coast of Arnhem Land in 1802, the first Europeans to enter the region were a team of explorers led by the Prussian naturalist Friedrich Wilhelm Leichhardt. In 1845, this party crossed the Roper River at Leichhardt's Crossing, later Roper Bar, which is some eighty kilometres upstream from the Gulf of Carpentaria.[5]

The vast region Leichhardt and his party had entered was home to thousands of Aboriginal people from dozens of language groups, each with their own clearly delineated homelands and tracts of country. These people also lived by the rule of established laws concerning family proprietorship, rights in resource management, and hunting. In this tropical monsoon country, much more fertile than the desert to the south, Leichhardt recorded his first impressions of the naturally bountiful land in a journal entry on 19 October 1845:

> I found myself on the banks of a large fresh water river from 500–800 yards broad, with not very high banks, densely covered with salt water Hibiscus (Paritium) ... The water was slightly muddy ... and the tide rose a full three feet ... Natives, crows, and kites were always the indications of a good country. Charley, Brown, and John, who had been left at the lagoon to shoot waterfowl, returned with twenty ducks for luncheon, and went out again to procure more for dinner and breakfast.[6]

The Roper River and its adjacent waterholes are still an abundant source of food for those who live in the region today—a favourite subject of Ngukurr artists,

---

5 Friedrich Leichhardt, "Journal Entries from 1 October 1844 to 2 December 1855", in *Australian Explorers: A Selection from Their Writings with an Introduction*, ed. Kathleen Fitzpatrick (London: Oxford University Press, 1958), 210; Mickey Dewar, *The Black War in Arnhem Land: Missionaries and the Yolŋu 1908–40* (Darwin: North Australia Research Unit, Australian National University, 1982), 7.

6 Leichhardt, "Journal Entries", 246.

Fig. 2.1. Jill Daniels, *Landscape*, 2013. About 100 x 40 cm. Reproduced with permission.

such as Ritharrŋu woman Jill Daniels (fig. 2.1). One and a half centuries after Leichhardt, the Roper Bar is still the only river crossing. The town of Ngukurr, home to the Young Wägilak Group, is only accessible by road for two thirds of the year, until floodwaters cut off road access. Roper Bar was also the inspiration for the name of the collaboration *Crossing Roper Bar*—a crossing into new relational and cultural territory.

In the decades following Leichhardt's expedition, there were increasingly frequent outsider incursions into Arnhem Land. Soon after the construction of the Overland Telegraph in the 1870s, a small number of European and Chinese gold miners settled at Leichhardt's Crossing in 1884. Notoriously, cattle farmers and pastoralists were the next to move in, annexing vast portions of Aboriginal land during the following decades, pushing the frontier of colonial settlement further east.[7]

The African Cold Storage Supply Company, which established a cattle station at the Elsey and Hodgson Downs in 1903, stands out in its brutal treatment of the local populations. Many pastoralists from companies like this were extremely violent toward Aboriginal people, sending out punitive parties after any apparent misunderstanding or perceived injustice, such as the slaughter and

---

7   Dewar, *The Black War*, 7–8.

consumption of a bullock that was grazing on Yolŋu land—something entirely acceptable in Yolŋu law. Through numerous conflicts and massacres, some groups were exterminated and others permanently displaced. Any notion of the sanctity of human life was violated by human depravity on a lawless frontier.[8]

Into this context, Christian missionaries sought to provide refuge to Aboriginal people in the region. The development of missions in Arnhem Land began in 1908 with the Church Missionary Society's (Church of England) Roper River Mission. Soon to follow, the Methodist Missionary Society began establishing mission settlements across north Arnhem Land. In the south-east of Arnhem Land, the Church Missionary Society also established missions at the Rose River (Numbulwar) and on Groote Eylandt (see fig. 1.1).

A stated goal of these missionaries was to establish productive settlements of regimented work and timetabled religious instruction in English. Inherited ideas of civilisation and assimilation underpinned this focus on Western forms of domestication, work, and education. Such priorities overshadowed the development of the missionaries' literacy in Aboriginal languages, law, and culture: genuine relational, cultural, and intellectual engagement was effectively stymied.[9] Aboriginal people began to settle on these missions in the early decades of the twentieth century, many living in newly established camps on the periphery of the mission grounds. This gradual movement away from life on hereditary estates was encouraged by the reliable supply of flour and tobacco, in addition to protection from frontier violence.[10] Outside the missions, other Aboriginal people were starting to work as stockmen or station hands in the expanding cattle industry.

Wurrtjumun Dinah Garadji, a Yugul lady whose country was framed on either side by the Rose and Roper rivers, recorded some stories of her grandfather, Dungulurrama, who lived along the banks and billabongs of the Roper River. Garadji's parents were children when the Roper Mission was established on Yugul land in 1908, and her mother's father's people, the "Blanuganuga", lived in the hills on the upper Walker River, quite possibly in the the same area as Wägilak country in the Parsons and Mitchell Ranges.

> My uncle was a stockman and my father was a mission man. He brought in the Ŋandi and Ritharngu people [and by extension, Wägilak]. He used to go out by himself … He used to tell them to come into the

---

8   Frances Morphy, "Whose Governance for Whose Good? The Laynhapuy Homelands Association and the Neo-Assimilationist Turn in Indigenous Policy", in *Contested Governance: Culture, Power, and Institutions in Indigenous Australia*, Centre for Aboriginal Economic Policy research monograph 29, ed. Janet Hunt et al. (Canberra: Australian National University E-Press, 2008), 118; Trudgen, *Why Warriors*, 16–42.

9   John Harris, *We Wish We'd Done More: Ninety Years of CMS and Aboriginal Issues in North Australia* (Adelaide: Openbook Publishers, 1998), 22–34.

10 Dewar, *The Black War*, 23.

mission, to the school. My uncle didn't like the missionaries. He was a stockman at St Vidgeons.[11]

During the early decades of mission settlement, messengers like Garadji's uncle would visit groups like the Wägilak, who were still living "out bush" and on their country. They would say, "Come to Roper River. There are school teachers there who love us as we are. They are very good people who won't hurt others, they won't hurt anyone. They want to teach children about the white man's ways and tell stories about the big spirits up in the sky."[12]

In 1968, increasing federal and state government involvement in Arnhem Land saw the Church Missionary Society cede control of the Roper Mission, and by the mid-1970s the township of Ngukurr was formed. It was around this time that many of today's older-generation Wägilak came to live in Ngukurr, after a life of constant travel between various bush camps, remote outstation settlements, and cattle stations. Such extensive travel on foot between different locations and during different seasons was known as "foot-falcon", after the Ford Falcon. This had been the usual way of life in Australia for millennia, necessary for maintaining family relationships, trade, and political alliances, and sustaining different agricultural and animal husbandry practices over vast tracks of country. Speaking with elders in Ngukurr today, it is evident that the Wägilak were among the last to trickle into town settlements from this dynamic life on the land.

Sambo (Djambu) Barabara (c. 1945–2005) and Andy Lukaman Peters (c. 1957–) are two significant Wägilak elders and ceremonial leaders from Ngukurr. They grew up in the bush, living in bark huts and frequently travelling large distances on foot to hunt. Barabara explains: "I was born in the bush, no doctors, no whitefellas. Mother carried me in a paperbark coolamon [carrying vessel] … Goanna dreaming country, Stone Spear country, Nilipidgi. Stayed there and grew up."[13] After marrying Amy Jirwurlurr Johnson—a significant Roper River artist whose mother was Ṇalakan and father Rembarrṇa—in the 1970s, Barabara spent time at Costello Outstation before settling in Ngukurr in the 1980s. Art curator Cath Bowdler records that, through his paining and ceremonial leadership, Barabara brought "specific and valuable cultural knowledge to the Roper region … a different set of experiences and ritual knowledge to most of the Ngukurr artists who predominantly came from country south of the Roper

---

11 Wurrtjumun Dinah Garadji, *The Unknown Struggles of my People: Stories by Wurrtjumun Dinah Garadji* (Goulbourn Island, NT: Warruwi Literacy Centre, 1996), 8.

12 Ibid., 26.

13 Sambo Barabara, quoted in Cath Bowdler, *Colour Country: Art from Roper River* (Wagga Wagga, NSW: Wagga Wagga Art Gallery, 2009), 57.

River."[14] The main reason Barabara and other Wägilak people settled in Ngukurr rather than towns like Numbulwar or settlements like Donydji—much closer to their traditional homelands—was due to these new relationships and families with non-Yolŋu groups. Nevertheless, connections with Wägilak from places like Donydji, Gapuwiyak, and Beswick are still strong. Singers and dancers will travel between Ngukurr and these other towns to take part in important ceremonies and funerals a few times each year.

During their childhood, Daniel and Benjamin Wilfred also spent much time staying at and visiting Ŋilipidji. The construction of permanent buildings at Ŋilipidji in the 1980s occurred soon after the growth of the Yolŋu homeland movement in Arnhem Land, which had spawned in Yirrkala in the early 1970s, largely "precipitated by the social trauma that followed the building of the mining town and the introduction of alcohol to the area [Gove Peninsula]."[15] Wägilak had skirted around many of these social problems. The Ritharrŋu/Wägilak outstation at Donydji had been built in 1968 and many of those who moved there had never settled in larger towns like Yirrkala, as did other Yolŋu during the preceding decades.[16] Such outstations were to become "bastions of Yolngu identity, where people have the power to filter the influences of the outside world."[17] For the Wägilak, this degree of autonomy was significance in their maintenance of ceremonial traditions, something they were able to do with more success than other non-Yolŋu groups living in Ngukurr (see below).

Wägilak families have made frequent visits to Ŋilipidji over the past few decades, travelling from smaller communities dotted through south-east Arnhem Land such as Donydji and Numbulwar. In 1983, Wägilak elder Diltjima expressed his desire to establish a settlement at Ŋilipidji, "to keep an eye on the country";[18] the basic infrastructure, like corrugated-iron huts and a water tank, that was erected also made visits much easier. Although most Wägilak today desire to spend at least a part of every year at Ŋilipidji, one of the main difficulties remains access to a reliable vehicle for transport. It is also difficult to get away from family responsibilities, ceremonial responsibilities, and paid employment in Ngukurr. A visit of a few days every year or two is more likely.

Presently, the Ngukurr community—of whom more than ninety percent are Indigenous Australians—is an amalgam of seven different language groups

---

14 Bowdler, *Colour Country*, 70. Amy Johnson's hereditary estate was at Marrkalawa, a crossing of the Walker River used by those travelling south from Ŋilipidji (Ibid., 57).

15 Frances Morphy, "Whose Governance", 120.

16 Kim McKenzie, director, *The Spear in the Stone*, film and study guide (Canberra: Australian Institute of Aboriginal Studies, 1983), 5.

17 Frances Morphy, "Whose Governance", 121.

18 McKenzie, *The Spear in the Stone* study guide, 8. There was no outstation at Ŋilipidji at the time of McKenzie's research and filming there in 1983. At the end of the film, Wägilak elder Diltjima expresses his desire to establish a settlement at Ŋilipidji.

forming a population of just over 1000.[19] These languages come from regions surrounding the town within a radius of approximately 200 kilometres and include people from the Mara, Ṇandi, Alawa, Nuṇgubuyu, Ritharrŋu/Wägilak, Waṇdarrang, and Ṇalakan language groups. Although many people still speak multiple languages, a new lingua-franca known as Kriol developed throughout the twentieth century. Kriol is spoken in several different dialects across a vast area of northern Australia.

Ngukurr is booming with young people: the town's median age is twenty-two, compared with a national average of thirty-seven.[20] With the vibrant energy of youth that characterises this colourful community, Ngukurr is a bubbling mixture of cultures and languages. The community is animated by productive tensions of similarity and difference, connection and separation, and the intermingling of tradition in the present. These tensions are shaping contemporary cultural practices such as art, film and music that are dynamic and fluid—fertile ground for collaborations like *CRB*.

Wägilak Connections

Wägilak are connected. This is true in a profound sense but also in everyday life, where mobile phones spread news rapidly through networks of family and friends. As a people, they traverse numerous linguistic, cultural, and relational borders, while retaining distinct identities. It is important to grasp something of this as an historical reality before we look at the role of Wägilak *manikay* in Ngukurr today, which extends traditional schemes of social and political connection between families, *bäpurru*, and ceremonial repertoires.

Pulled by ties of language, kinship, and ceremonial obligation, many Wägilak had settled in and around Ngukurr and Numbulwar in the 1970s. Others had gone north to Donydji.[21] Benjamin Wilfred grew up and went to school in Ngukurr. Despite growing up in town, Benjamin frequently made many long trips "out bush" with his father, Old Cookie. Travelling on foot over hundreds of kilometres, they would cross the country of many different *bäpurru* and language groups. On one such trip in the 1980s, the young Benjamin Wilfred was helping to construct the road to Ṇilipidji and build the corrugated iron huts that are still there today. The joy of those days still lights up his eyes and his feet twitch to get "back to country".

---

19 Australian Bureau of Statistics, "Basic Community Profile: Ngukurr (SSC70143)", *2011 Census of Population and Housing*, http://bit.ly/2wxghDd.

20 Ibid.

21 Wägilak people also reside in Numbulwar and Gapuwiyak (Lake Evella) in significant numbers, and to a lesser extent in Beswick, Barunga, Katherine, and Darwin. Fewer Wägilak reside in the smaller towns along the North Coast of Arnhem Land and at Yirrkala.

BENJAMIN WILFRED: Yeah, he [Old Cookie] walked from Ŋilipidji to Donydji, then Numbulwar. They walked before: a long way. You have to pass the Walker River and then off to Numbulwar. Yeah. They walked with mum. When I was small I walked with my dad and mum, from Ŋilipidji to Walker River, but if the water was still flooded at Marrkalawa [Walker River crossing] we had to stop there. And from that time I started to learn my knowledge from my father.

SAMUEL CURKPATRICK: When you walked from Ŋilipidji to Numbulwar, you must have passed through a lot of different language groups?

BW: Wägilak, Ritharrŋu, Madarrpa, further down, and then we go Nuŋgubuyu.

SC: Did Old Cookie speak Nuŋgubuyu as well?

BW: Yeah, little bit. He understood. And then we stayed there [at Numbulwar]. And then we had to come back here [to Ngukurr].[22]

The Wägilak and Ritharrŋu are stone country people, separated from the coast by other family, homelands, and languages. This is reflected in the lack of saltwater and coastal themes in their *manikay*. While the estate of Ŋilipidji is owned by Wägilak, it is "managed" by Ritharrŋu people. They are the *djungayi* (managers) responsible for ensuring ceremonial protocols are followed, and oversee land management and succession rights. *Djungayi* (managers) are also required to coordinate and supervise any performance of *manikay*. The *yiḏaki* (didjeridu) player for Wägilak *manikay* is always a *djungayi* from the opposite moiety, that is, Ritharrŋu. The opposite moiety also provides dancers for any *buŋgul* (dance; ceremony).

This special paring between the Wägilak and Ritharrŋu is reinforced by a shared language and frequent marriages between them. Wägilak belong to the Dhuwa moiety, Ritharrŋu to the Yirritja moiety, which form the two mutually dependent halves. Marriage is exogamous, meaning that an individual marries outside of their own moiety and into the other: for example, Daniel Wilfred's Wägilak father married a Ritharrŋu woman from Donydji, north of Ŋilipidji. Wägilak–Ritharrŋu marriages are a typical pairing, although Wägilak marriage to other Yirritja moiety groups is not uncommon: Benjamin Wilfred's mother was from the Ritharrŋu–Biḏiŋal group, closely related to the Maḏarrpa whose homelands lie to the east of Ŋilipidji.

---

22 Benjamin Wilfred, interview with the author, Ngukurr, 13 June 2011.

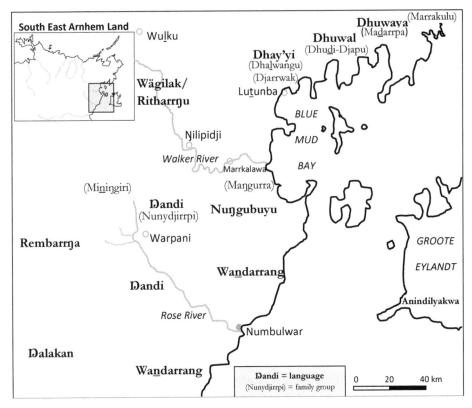

Fig. 2.2. Map of languages and select groups in South East Arnhem Land.

Because legal and ceremonial rights obtained through descent are agnatic and follow the father's line, the children of a Wägilak man will be also identify as Wägilak. Therefore, an individual's mother is always of the opposite moiety. Most commonly, a Wägilak child will have a Ritharrŋu mother. This scheme or principle is known as *yothu-yindi* (child-mother; also the name of a celebrated Yolŋu rock band) and underpins everything in the Yolŋu world. *Yothu-yindi* is about cooperation and productive relationships amid difference: good society comes out of this relationship of difference, especially through reciprocal responsibilities of caring for country and family. Through *yothu-yindi*, Wägilak and Ritharrŋu rely on each other to perform ceremony, requiring organisation by the *djungayi* (manager) as well as needing dancers and a *yidaki* (didjeridu) player from the opposite moiety.

The Wägilak and Ritharrŋu belong to the greater cultural and linguistic bloc known as Yolŋu, whose homelands are concentrated in the north-east of Arnhem Land. Yolŋu culture consists of an intricately woven body of related narratives, ceremonial practices, and family and political relationships. *Yolŋu-matha* (Yolŋu tongues; languages) are also different from surrounding Aboriginal languages, typically suffixing languages.

Yolŋu-matha (Yolŋu tongues) are usually designated on the basis of the different words used for the demonstrative *this*, forming the following divisions: Dhuwal/a, Dhaŋu/Djaŋu, Dhay'yi, Djinaŋ, Djinba, Nhaŋu, and Yakuy. Yakuy is more commonly known as Wägilak or Ritharrŋu, even though the word *yakuy* is used for *this*.[23] The Wägilak/Ritharrŋu (or Yakuy) language comes from an area furthest to the south of the *Yolŋu-matha* grouping, bordering on the substantially different non-Yolŋu prefixing languages Rembarrŋa, Ŋandi, and Nuŋgubuyu (fig. 2.2).

Dozens of different *bäpurru* speak these Yolŋu-matha (Yolŋu tongues), named above. These are not rigidly bounded groups but names the different families who cluster around a homeland like Ŋilipidji and its related ceremonial repertoires; within *bäpurru*, there are overlapping identities and multiple affiliations (see Chapter One).[24] Smaller in number than many of the other Yolŋu languages, there are only one hundred or so Wägilak/Ritharrŋu speakers in Arnhem Land today—there are many more Wägilak/Ritharrŋu individuals who do not speak the language. In 2005, Wägilak was categorised as "extremely endangered" by the most recent National Indigenous Language Survey Report, a classification that takes into consideration changes in the number of speakers and language use by young people.[25]

In 1935, anthropologist Donald Thomson was the first non-Aboriginal person to visit the Wägilak homeland of Ŋilipidji. He wrote of the wide-ranging nomadic lifestyle of the Ritharrŋu (no doubt referring to Ritharrŋu and Wägilak), presenting a picture of a durable and persistent language. It seems that it was this language that allowed Wägilak to live and to relate with other people, clans, and cultures, in distant places. It is worth quoting Thomson at length:

> I have mentioned that both were Ritharrŋu men—members of a group that occupies a very large stretch of country in the interior, behind Blue Mud Bay. This language differs somewhat in vocabulary, but not in structure, from that of the Dhay'yi-speaking people of Blue Mud Bay, but they can understand one another and can converse in Ritharrŋu. These people are the most strongly nomadic of all the Arnhem Landers. Their territory lies in the region of the upper Walker River and extends northwards, inland from Blue Mud Bay, but I found

---

23 Jeffrey Heath, who wrote the first comprehensive grammar of the Ritharrŋu language in 1980, generally uses the term *Ritharrngu* to refer to both Ritharrŋu and Wägilak. Heath designates the following *matha* (tongues) as belonging to the Yakuy language: Madarrpa, Bunanatjini, Buwarrpuwarr, Miniŋiri, Ritharrŋu, Bidiŋal, and Wägilak. Jeffrey Heath, *Basic Materials in Ritharngu: Grammar, Texts, and Dictionary* (Canberra: Pacific Linguistics, Australian National University, 1980), 2.

24 See Keen's extensive discussion in "A Bundle of Sticks".

25 Australian Institute of Aboriginal and Torres Strait Islander Studies with the Federation of Aboriginal and Torres Strait Islander Languages, *National Indigenous Languages Survey Report* (Canberra: Department of Communications, Information Technology and the Arts, 2005), 222.

members of this group quite at home, and still making themselves understood in their own language, in localities as far separated as the Roper River and the Crocodile Islands [Milingimbi]. Their language, therefore, is understood over a wider area than any other in the whole of this country.[26]

A Dynamic Edge

Even though their language and ceremonial expressions are closely related to other Yolŋu groups, the Wägilak and Ritharrŋu clans have many connections with non-Yolŋu clans bordering their estates to the south and west. These connections entail responsibilities for overseeing ceremonial performances and land management practices. Perhaps the most important non-Yolŋu connection for the Wägilak existed with Ŋandi speakers of the upper Rose River. This area was linked to Wägilak lands by an important trade route, running south from Ŋilipidji for about 60 kilometres. Connections between Wägilak and their non-Yolŋu neighbours like the Ŋandi seem to be just as important as those with other Yolŋu groups, suggesting the porous nature of collective identities or labels such as Yolŋu in Arnhem Land.

At Warpani there is a large, permanent body of water. Today, it is difficult to access. When Benjamin Wilfred and Andy Peters walked the route between Ŋilipidji and Warpani with the Yugul Mangi Rangers in 2010, it had been many years since anyone had been there. Artist Simon Normand, who collaborates with Ngukurr artists, records some of the history of this area and people: "Avoided by the first explorers and subsequent police patrols, the first white person to visit here [Warpani] was Ruth Heathcock, the Roper River nurse, guided by local Ngandi people on horseback in 1956."[27]

Wägilak travelled seasonally to Warpani to attend ceremonies and gatherings, and many Wägilak births took place there. The close relationship between Wägilak and Ŋandi, important to the YWG today, is reinforced in *manikay* performance and kinship responsibilities. Benjamin Wilfred's *märipulu* (mother's mother group) is the Ŋandi-speaking Nunydjirrpi clan, another Dhuwa moiety group whose clan estates are situated north of the upper Rose River. Ŋandi is no longer spoken today and is only used in a few *manikay* items that survive in Wägilak memory. It is Benjamin Wilfred's responsibility to continue to "look after" these songs of his *märipulu*—to keep on singing and teaching them to the younger generations.

Ominously, linguist Jeffrey Heath wrote in 1978 about the declining Ŋandi language: "There are probably about six persons who speak Ngandi well now.

---

26 *Donald Thomson in Arnhem Land*, 2010, 58.
27 Simon Normand, *Stone Country to Saltwater: Recent Artwork and Stories from Ngukurr, Arnhem Land* (Melbourne: Simon Normand, 2004), 62.

My principal informant, Sandy (Maḏulpu) is probably in his forties, and so far as I know, persons younger than him do not speak the language well ... Since the Ngandi speakers are scattered at several settlements (Ngukurr, Numbulwar, Roper Valley, etc.), there is no likelihood that the language will survive much longer."[28] The same could have been said of Ŋandi song and dance repertoires.

For Yolŋu, the closest same-moiety relationship other than direct agnatic descent is known as *märi-gutharra*: *märi* is one's mother's mother (or one's mother's mother's brother); *gutharra* is one's daughter's children (or sister's daughter's children). This reciprocal pairing is the relationship Wägilak of Ŋilipidji share with the Nunydjirrpi clan. For Yolŋu, if the continuation of direct agnatic succession within a clan fails, the responsibility to "look after" the land, ceremony, and sacred objects of your *märi*, is enacted.[29] *Gutharra* must also look after the every need of their dying *märi*.[30] In return, there is legitimacy in the claim of a male *gutharra* to the bestowal of his *märi*'s daughter's daughter in marriage.

Some decades ago, custodianship of Nunydjirrpi clan songs was passed on to Wägilak elder Sambo Barabara by Ŋandi elders fearing that their repertoires would be forgotten, and there are archive recordings made by Jeffrey Heath of Barabara singing these songs in 1975.[31] Presumed to be the last remaining Ŋandi language in active use, these songs are today incorporated seamlessly into Wägilak performances for ceremony and entertainment. Most frequently, the Wägilak version of "Wäkwak" (Black crow) is simply replaced by the Nunydjirrpi version, which uses the same rhythmic mode but different melodic constructions (audio example 2a).

Audio example 2a. "Wäkwak" (Crow) *feeding* mode. Nunydjirrpi version sung by the YWG at a funeral in Ngukurr, August 19, 2010.

As in the song "Wäkwak" (Black Crow), similarities in narrative content and rhythmic form are shared by clans with close, same-moiety relationships. This allows the seamless integration of another clan's *manikay* within one clan's typical *manikay* repertoire, without any disruption to the essential narrative or rhythmic momentum. Correlations of musical form allow for greater competence if responsibilities to "look after" a repertoire ever need to be exercised. Parallel forms and narratives in the *manikay* of different clans are

---

28 Jeffrey Heath, *Ngandi Grammar, Texts, and Dictionary* (Canberra: Australian Institute of Aboriginal Studies, 1978), 3.

29 See Howard Morphy and Frances Morphy, "Tasting the Waters: Discriminating Identities in the Waters of Blue Mud Bay", *Journal of Material Culture* 11, no. 1 (2006): 81; Nancy Williams, *The Yolngu and Their Land: A System of Land Tenure and the Fight for Its Recognition* (Stanford: Stanford University Press, 1986), 52.

30 Trudgen, *Why Warriors*, 154.

31 Jeffrey Heath, "Texts Recorded in the Numbulwar Area", tapes 4803–4 (HEATH_J04), Ngukurr, 1975, Australian Institute of Aboriginal and Torres Strait Islander Studies Audio Visual Archives.

often identified with the phrase "It's the same but different." A similar concept of *riŋgitj* (parliamentary) alliance between two groups, also conveyed in *manikay*, will be explored in coming chapters.

Wägilak also "look after" the *manikay* of other clans, singing for ceremonies in Ngukurr if no appropriate singers can be brought in from nearby communities like Numbulwar. Benjamin and Daniel Wilfred may also sing the Ritharrŋu songs of their mother's clan in funerals and at other public ceremonies. Historically, this would have been highly unorthodox; today it seems a necessity. As well as teaching young people at Ngukurr the Dhuwa moiety Wägilak and Nunydjirrpi song repertoires, Benjamin Wilfred also teachers the songs of the Yirritja moiety inland Maḏarrpa, Ritharrŋu, and Bidiŋal clans.

Until the mid-1990s, all these clans—and others such as the Nuŋgubuyu— regularly travelled across south-east Arnhem Land to meet for funerals and other ceremonies. Barabara led many of these gatherings and Daniel Wilfred remembers sitting next to him, learning to sing.[32] In these multilingual, multicultural contexts, Daniel was introduced to Nunydjirrpi and Nuŋgubuyu song repertoires, which were performed alongside Wägilak *manikay* and "mixed together":

> When my dad passed away, Sambo [Barabara] came to pick me up from Numbulwar and started teaching me more manikay … He knew all the songs, from my father who taught him …. And I always listened and went every night. And we made a fire, we got a didj, clapping sticks, and I started to sing along with him—started singing all the songs. He taught me Wägilak songs; he taught me my Grandpa's songs, Nunydjirrpi; he sung those Nuŋgubuyu words, mixed together with Nunydjirrpi singing. I still have those words—sing along [with them today]. And now, when I'm here now, telling my kids now: "You need to learn about these songs."[33]

On a dynamic edge between Yolŋu and non-Yolŋu cultures and languages, and surrounded by a plethora of different homelands and clans, Wägilak have always engaged in intercultural situations. Through ceremony, they have maintained these relationships productively and creatively, while retaining a distinct identity as a people with their own language, ceremonial narratives, and homeland. In this interconnected history, we glimpse precedent for the colourful engagement with improvising musicians in *CRB*. Collaboration with those who are different has always been a way of life—we are all "the same but

---

32 Benjamin calls Barabara *märi'mu* (father's father); Daniel calls him *wäwa* (brother). David Wilfred, who is *djungayi* (ceremonial manager) for the Young Wägilak Group, married Barabara's daughter in Ngukurr.

33 Daniel Wilfred, interview with the author, Ngukurr, 17 June 2011.

different." Wägilak continue in a longstanding tradition of sustaining ancestral narratives and law while creatively embracing cultural and social diversity.[34]

Today, Ngukurr is the home of the self-styled Young Wägilak Group from Ŋilipidji. New relationships, experiences, and responsibilities have tied them to this unique Australian community, a product of continual cultural and social change. Although Ŋilipidji will always be a place of foundational identity and belonging, it is Ngukurr that Benjamin Wilfred misses when he is on tour with the AAO: "When I go out to other places, I always think of Ngukurr. Because we all grew up here, even my brothers and sisters. And I miss my home."[35]

Holding Strong: The Young Wägilak Group

> At Ngukurr, those young people, they lost their language and culture—everything. The Young Wägilak Group is helping them now. They're just lost; only the Wägilak are helping them.—Benjamin Wilfred[36]

With slight exaggeration but certainly with truthful feeling, Benjamin Wilfred expresses a common sentiment held by many Wägilak in Ngukurr. This sense that they are the only ceremonial musicians left is perhaps exacerbated by the distance of Wägilak in Ngukurr from their Yolŋu relatives in communities to the north, who are regularly engaged in ceremonial performance. It also exacerbates a sense of importance and authority within the community. Benjamin asserts an active stance against widespread malaise over the loss of ceremonial performance and law. While Ngukurr has certainly suffered extensive cultural loss when compared to pre-settlement times, it remains culturally vibrant in its own unique way.

Cultural images that might be thought characteristic of Ngukurr include cowboy boots, country music, fluorescent art, and the Kriol language. This contrasts with distinctly Yolŋu communities, which might be typified by ochre-coloured bark paintings, films and radio in traditional languages, and prominent legal representations made to the Australian Parliament by elders. Of the Yolŋu residents in Ngukurr, Wägilak and Ritharrŋu make up the majority. Relatively fortunate in his ceremonial education, Benjamin Wilfred feels keenly the weight of responsibility to sustain these practices in the face of cultural change.

---

34 For a discussion of cultural change and tradition that goes beyond the polarisation between preservation of *cultural autonomy* and its oft-presumed antithesis *intercultural production*, see Morphy and Morphy, "Soon We Will Be Spending All Our Time at Funerals: Yolngu Mortuary Rituals in an Epoch of Constant Change," In *Returns to the Field: Multitemporal Research and Contemporary Anthropology*, ed. Signe Howell and Aud Talle (Bloomington: Indiana University Press, 2012), 51.

35 Benjamin Wilfred, interview with author, Ngukurr, 19 July 2011.

36 Benjamin Wilfred, "Digital Audio Technologies".

It is important to note that other clans in Ngukurr do hold ceremonial repertoires of song and dance, although these are rarely performed. Notably, large regional ceremonies like the Yabaduruwa—which can take a few months to complete—still occur every few years. The Gunapipi ceremony occurs very infrequently at locations such as Numbulwar and Bulman, to which some Ngukurr residents travel to participate.

Performances for public events such as funerals, circumcisions, smoking/purification, building dedications, or festival openings, are generally performed by the YWG—their busy performance schedule attesting to their high demand. Contexts in which the YWG performs are diverse and are not limited to traditions from Yolŋu culture: Wägilak perform their ancestral songs for all language groups in Ngukurr and the surrounding region, including the Mara, Ŋandi, Nuŋgubuyu, Anindilyakwa (Groote Eylandt), Marraŋu, Maŋgurra, and Murruŋun people (see fig. 2.2).[37]

Wägilak elder Andy Peters perpetuates the polarisation that Wägilak in Ngukurr feel as the few remaining *legitimate* practitioners of ceremonial performance: "I don't know about Ngukurr mob—they haven't got the authority from their old people. Like my group, they got authority from me and I got authority from my grandpa and from my dad."[38] Settling relatively late in Ngukurr in the 1970s and 1980s, Wägilak had maintained continual connection with many of the important elements of ceremony passed down the generations, which they believe other clans lost during mission times. This includes a complex web of associations and relationships that constitute ceremony as: connection to elders, family, and history; connection to land and hereditary estates; the continued practise of the Wägilak language and *madayin* law; and a close relationship with the environment through traditional management practices (see Chapters Three and Four). For many in Ngukurr, what the Wägilak sing is not necessarily understood—linguistically or as narrative, religion, or philosophy. Daniel Wilfred explains: "They came here and got married here, and now they stay here, find kids ... They don't know what we sing, they don't know the words."[39] The same might be said of collaborations like *CRB*, which has only performed in Ngukurr twice, in 2005 and 2010. While various recordings of the project have appeared in the Ngukurr Art Centre and Roper Bar Store, *CRB* and other collaborations are events that typically occur outside of Ngukurr, unlike the local bands and music projects which will appear frequently in local festivals.

---

37 The Marraŋu are a Dhuwal-speaking group and the Murruŋun is a Djinaŋ-speaking group. Both come from an area north west of the Wägilak and will not be found on the language map (fig. 2.2).
38 Andy Peters, interview with the author, Ngukurr, 12 July 2011.
39 Daniel Wilfred, interview with the author, Ngukurr, 13 June 2011.

In Ngukurr, the majority the clans that the YWG perform for are non-Yolŋu clans, and so most performances of *manikay* already occur in a local intercultural setting. This has been the case for at least three decades, as Jeffrey Heath records in 1980s:

> The Ritharngu [and Wägilak] are doing remarkably well in preserving their camp songs (buŋgul) and ritual life. Some of my own informants not only carry out their normal rituals, but are in great demand and frequently travel as far south as Elliot, around 500km by road, to perform rituals at the invitation of other Aboriginal groups.[40]

The YWG's imperative to "keep culture strong" acknowledges that today's generation of Wägilak should learn from and respect the embedded knowledge and law carried through ceremonial traditions—even if profound truths are not necessarily or immediately apparent: the Yolŋu hermeneutic always orients toward deeper significances not yet revealed to present understanding. Further, responsibilities to maintain the Wägilak *manikay* narratives extend beyond the wellbeing of a discrete *bäpurru*, as the songs are also integral elements within a greater ceremonial constellation (see Chapter Three).

After the death of Barabara in 2005, the YWG was formed in response to the declining interaction between the younger generations and the dwindling number of living elders educated in traditional ceremonial performance. Benjamin Wilfred explains:

> I lost my elder sister and elder brother, but I still got more brothers. That's why I keep telling them: "Come to me, join me so we can do one job. Be strong together." That's what I always tell my elder brothers. I'm the youngest, and I'm the only one to get the knowledge from Grandpa. I'm teaching some of my brothers, elder brothers, from my heart and spirit from Grandpa, and the painting and the land. Thank you. That's Young Wägilak Group.[41]

It was this group that had, under the quiet guidance and consent of Barabara, begun collaborating with the AAO earlier that year. The YWG's desire to "keep culture strong" is a crucial motivation driving participation in *CRB*. This is serious business, yet it does not preclude innovation: creativity is essential to the renewal of *manikay* as a tradition. Importantly, the musical innovation that occurs in *CRB* is considered authentic to that tradition. Like the use of *manikay* in the rock music of the band Yothu Yindi, "Their songs promote what for them

---

40 Heath, *Basic Materials*, 3.
41 Benjamin Wilfred, "Digital Audio Technologies".

are lawful expressions of hereditary identities, knowledge and values."[42] New collaborations are given purpose and strength as they are connected to the old.

> "We're the Young Wägilak Group now, with my story, with my grandpa's story, and the spirit of Grandpa following me: giving me power, strong power. That's why I'm talking strong. And I love my tour [*CRB*], what I do ... I'm lucky I'm holding this Wägilak culture strong. I'm lucky, that's what my grandpa told me: 'I'm going to give you the *buŋgul*, Wägilak. You have to keep it now.' 'Yeah,' I said, 'no worries.' I have followed my grandpa and I want to be like him. And I did it. I did. I'm standing here and talking for country and I'm walking with the spirit, with Wild Blackfella called Djuwalpada. Even when I tour with the orchestra, that Wild Blackfella [follows], no matter where I go, this Wild Blackfella: country to country ... I have to go for it. And I'm here: a strong man."[43]

Benjamin asserts that "No matter where you go" or in what context you perform, the responsibility to continue ceremonial narratives remains.[44] Ceremony shows you who you are and where you should go, revealing your coordinates within historical life: "*Manikay* is for the new generation. It's going to lead you." As the preceding historical account of Wägilak connections showed, ceremonial performances have always been involved in diverse, intercultural contexts. Like their elders, the YWG seeks opportunities to express their ceremonial narratives and develop skills in their artistic practice through new forums and contexts of presentation.

New Contexts

Aside from *CRB* and other collaborations with the Australian Art Orchestra, the project *Muyngarnbi* is another notable extension of Wägilak *manikay* into new forms and contexts of performance.

Muyngarnbi is a collaboration founded by actor and musician Tom E. Lewis with Wägilak elder Roy Ashley, whom Daniel Wilfred and Sambo Barabara call *maralkur* (poison cousin; mother's mother's brother's son); Dalabon and Rembarrŋa singers are also involved.[45] *Muyngarnbi* aims to record the voices and songs of ageing elders, in most cases for the first time. Lewis also wants to generate greater interest and awareness in the song traditions indigenous to this country, in a way that is accessible to larger audiences: "Everywhere you look, there is music. The wind blows, water runs, in the grass you can hear it.

---

42 Aaron, "Dreamtime Wisdom", 17.

43 Benjamin Wilfred, interview with Jane Ulman, "Cultural Crossings".

44 Benjamin Wilfred, interview with Jane Ulman, "Cultural Crossings".

45 Lewis has a successful career in the Australian film industry and has played leading roles in numerous feature films. Micky Hall Dugurrun from Donydji is another Wägilak elder who features on the *Muyngarnbi* recording.

Sometimes we forget, but if you stop and you listen. Maybe that's the frightening thing, is to stop and listen—because you can hear things."[46]

Since 2002, Lewis has performed with singers from south and west Arnhem Land at Djilpin Arts' annual Walking with Spirits festival at Beswick, supported by a number of musicians from Melbourne. Adopting Roy Ashley's "bush name" Muyngarnbi as the title of their commercial CD, they perform the songs of Ashley's *bäpurru* (father's group). These songs are closely related to the songs in *CRB*. Since 2012, Daniel Wilfred and Andy Peters from Ngukurr have also been involved in this project, which included a tour to Melbourne in 2014. Daniel Wilfred also performs a version of Wäkwäk (Black Crow) at the Australian Art Orchestra's Creative Music Intensive in a similar manner to Ashley's recording on *Muyngarnbi* (see Epilogue).

One clear difference between the *Muyngarnbi* album and the music of *CRB* is that one of Lewis' clearly stated aims is to replace the *yiḏaki* (didjeridu) and *biḻma* (clapsticks) of *manikay* with guitar and electric bass accompaniment. Each track juxtaposes ceremonial song and a standard popular-music accompaniment style, such as country music, Hawaiian slide guitar and blues rock. As a result, each song is given a completely different feel, over which the voice of the unperturbed *manikay* singer features.

Lewis describes the project as a "new platform for the old people". "Going to use *munanga* [non-Aboriginal] instruments like our instruments to carry the song, no *bambu* [didjeridu] or clapsticks … This song is really flamboyant. What about a bossa nova or something?"[47] The music highlights the vocal quality of each elder. As a juxtaposition of styles and traditions that have little historical or stylistic correlation, it takes on a bi-tonal, bi-conceptual feel: the melodic/harmonic constructions of the ceremonial songs continue somewhat independently of the diatonic accompaniments, which never dominate the voices. The transience of styles avoids settling into any definitive identity.

Unlike *Muyngarnbi*, *CRB* does not consciously jettison any musical or instrumental elements from the *manikay* tradition. Yet there remains a clear and common sentiment underpinning both projects, to preserve traditional culture as it is brought into new contexts and forms of expression. Comparatively, *CRB* can seem dense and for those not enamoured by collective free improvisation, which can seem to overwhelm the *manikay*. While this is balanced by a greater flexibility in listening and responding, as well as space provided for the *manikay* singers to shape the overall direction of the performance, *CRB* has less popular appeal.

Yet irrespective of the musical content of these collaborations, *manikay* is *happening*: recordings are being made, festivals are being played, and new

---

46 Lewis, Tom, and Michael Hohnen, *Muyngarnbi: Songs from Walking With Spirits*, audiovisual content on CD

47 Ibid.

audiences are developing an appreciation of ceremonial music and tradition. Resonating with the aims of the YWG, the relevance of *manikay* is being discovered in new situations, relationships, and intercultural settings. As this book shows, it is such creativity that allows traditions to be sustained and remain dynamic—to "hold ceremony strong".

New Technologies

Ngukurr is a mix of different cultures, histories, technologies, and influences. *Maniaky* singers draw on these influences and identities to assert a place for *manikay* within contemporary society, even as they emphasise the difference between *manikay* repertoires and contemporary culture, differences which are as important as connections.

Outside of ceremonial performances of *manikay* in Ngukurr, general musical activity consists of: popular bands, a history beginning with the hugely popular and fondly remembered Yugul Band, a blues band which formed in 1969; hip-hop discos on the basketball court, run by the sport and recreation arm of the Roper Gulf Shire; a women's choir at the Anglican Church and children's action songs with pre-recorded Christian-themed music at the outdoor church stage.

Ethnomusicologist Aaron Corn has written on popular music in Arnhem Land, demonstrating the many creative ways traditional ceremonial narratives and musical forms are perpetuated in conjunction with new technologies and media. In North East Arnhem Land, songs that "specifically incorporate and promote ancestrally given themes, concepts, and identities accounted for more than half of this repertoire" in a study of more than 300 original songs.[48] Comparatively, such numerous and obvious synergies between popular music forms and ceremonial practices are less evident in Ngukurr, although these do exist.

In annual battle-of-the-bands competitions, it is the visiting groups from communities outside Ngukurr, such as Numbulwar, that make the most overt connections to ceremonial traditions in their dance, costume, and inclusion of instruments such as the *yidaki* (didjeridu) and *bilma* (clapsticks). Popular Ngukurr bands over the past few decades like the Yugul Band (for whom Benjamin Wilfred played bass guitar), T-Lynx, Broken English, and the Lonely Boys, have tended to incorporate a sentimental longing for country into their lyrics, rather than seeking a blend of musical forms.

Current local bands, including the Big River Band, the Lonely Eyes Band, and the Lonely Boys, play standard rock and reggae grooves with lyrics concerning love, life experiences, and road and alcohol safety. Sometimes a short *manikay* item used as an introduction—often at the insistence of Benjamin

---

48 Corn, "Dreamtime Wisdom", 75; see also Aaron Corn, "Ngukurr Crying: Male Youth in a Remote Indigenous Community", *South East Arnhem Land Collaborative Research Project* 2 (Woollongong, NSW: University of Woollongong, 2001); Corn, "Land, Song, Constitution."

Wilfred—before the drummer's "1, 2, 3, 4" leads into the latest hit song. It seems the main aim of The Lonely Boys' 2012 song "Baby Come Back!" was to excite screaming youth. Even though this song was introduced with a short *manikay* item, there never was any further musical dialogue with the *manikay* tradition once the electric guitars and drums had started. In this and similar contexts, Benjamin Wilfred is motivated to assert his authority as a ceremonial leader in all local musical contexts, as well as promoting "respect" for the *manikay* tradition. In a way, the local bands provide a platform for such posturing and the implicit claim that *manikay* is "proper culture" is advanced.

While there is little blending of contemporary rock and *manikay* traditions in Ngukurr, ancestral idioms are echoed in the sentimental longing for country, characteristic of many popular songs. In 2010, I helped the Lonely Eyes Band to record some songs. Justin Nunggarrgalug, the young leader of this band, had grown up in Numbulwar and was well educated in Nuŋgubuyu ceremony. Of the six songs recorded, the lyrics of five were recollections and descriptions of his family's country and kin; the sixth was a song about Berrimah Prison in Darwin. Nunggarrgalug sung about his *gagu*'s (mother's mother's) country at Marrkalawa, around the crossing at the Walker River: "My grandmother passed away; the place was lonely. Ohh-ahh, Marrkalawa; *gagu* country."[49] Other songs were about Bickerton Island.

New technologies that have come with mainstream popular music have been embraced by ceremonial singers in Ngukurr.[50] In the 1980s, Barabara created cassette tapes of himself singing *manikay* and sent these to young relatives who were living in different communities. Andy Peters was singing *manikay* alongside Barabara in Ngukurr at that time: "Me and Barabara, we were singing into that cassette, and then sent them to Daniel [Wilfred]. And then Daniel got ideas from that cassette. Then I wanted all the young people to come and help me sing."[51]

Daniel Wilfred recalls receiving the tapes with excitement and working hard to develop his singing skills in the hope that he would one day sing alongside his elder relatives: "My big brother used to stay in Ngukurr—Sambo [Barabara]. When I grew up, maybe ten [years old], he had to record a cassette for me, send it down to Numbulwar. I learnt about it [*manikay*] from the cassette too."[52] As well as bringing new forms of music into Ngukurr, the cassette was a means for elders to retain connection with the dispersed Wägilak population—constantly

---

49 Justin Nunggarrgalug, in discussion with the author, Ngukurr, 2 September 2010.

50 Corn explores the Broadcasting in Remote Aboriginal Communities Scheme (BRACS) of the 1980s, as well as the advent of television, home videos, and video-games in the 1990s. Corn, "Dreamtime Wisdom," 3.

51 Andy Peters, interview with the author, Ngukurr, 12 July 2011.

52 Daniel Wilfred, interview with the author, Ngukurr, 13 June 2011.

shifting between towns, outstations, and the bush—and to instruct the younger generation in ceremonial *manikay*. Daniel Wilfred continues:

> Sambo was doing recording at Ngukurr, and he sent that cassette for me in Numbulwar: "And this is for you, to learn more." And my mum picked it up, to take it back to Ŋilipidji. We moved from Ŋilipidji and stayed at Walker River, and my mum brought it: "This is your big brother, who did that recording for you." "Well mum, can I listen?" And my mum bought a small tape recorder and gave it to me. I listened. I didn't stop listening, you know! And I told my mum, "When you go to Numbulwar, get me a headphone tape [portable cassette player]." And my mum got that headphone tape and brought it to me. When we went fishing, driving with the car, I was still listening … That's how I learnt about [*manikay*].[53]

Daniel Wilfred learnt to sing *manikay* on his visits to Ŋilipidji when he was growing up:

> Ŋilipidji, that's my land. I used to walk around with my mum and dad, getting bush tucker. And my dad took me around to get [find; make] didjeridu, *yidaki*. And we went to get *bilma*—call that "clapping sticks". And I start singing myself … just live there, eating bush tucker, learning manikay.[54]

In a sense, the AAO are another type of technology that Barabara and the YWG have embraced to serve their goals of exercising and disseminating traditional ceremonial practice. Whatever sounds the AAO musicians play with, around, or through the *manikay*, the collaboration allows the inherent musical complexities of *manikay* to persist, giving the project legitimacy and purpose as an expression of *manikay* (see Chapters Three and Four). This is achieved by musical *conversation*, rather than seeking a synthetic blend of musical forms.

While the *manikay* tradition has drawn upon technology and contemporary music to sustain connections to tradition and country, Wägilak performers draw a sense of strength and purpose from their polarisation with more popular, mainstream cultural practices: their *manikay* is ancestral, connected through the generations and supposedly carrying authority. Amid the variegated situations of history, relationships, languages, cultures, and technologies stewing together to form contemporary life in Ngukurr, Wägilak continually assert their connection to ancestral ground. Everything comes out of the land at Ŋilipidji.

---

53 Daniel Wilfred, interview with the author, Ngukurr, 17 June 2011.
54 Daniel Wilfred, interview with the author, Ngukurr, 13 July 2011.

3

ABUNDANT ARTICULATION:
THE LIVING TEXT OF MANIKAY

Trees laden with grey-green leaves are reflected in the glassy waterhole. The surface is a mirror, a covering of moving colour that obscures deep, clear water welling up from the ground. When the wind blows, the surface dances and the leaves are animated; the light plays too. Held up by deep, lifegiving water, it seems that our world dances on the surface of the past.

In stories and song, the Yolŋu tell of a pre-eminent time when creative beings shaped the world and its people. Widely referred to as the dreamtime, this was not just a creative period delineated as past in time or thought. *There and then*, and *here and now*, the dreamtime is continually effective history. Summed up by anthropologist W.E.H. Stanner's neologism "everywhen", its pertinence lies in direct experience as something presently encountered.[1] The dreamtime animates life now, substantiating history, society, ecology, corporeal bodies, and knowledge. It is a movement of past into future, like a deep replenishing spring.

Yolŋu (people) recognise present life as animated through stories and songs passed down the generations. Ceremony recreates the journeys of the great *waŋarr* (creative ancestral beings) who spread out across the land, forming ecology and society—a "true story, no bullshit … It is a true story from my father."[2] *Waŋarr* shaped the natural substance of the world, and the people

---

1   W.E.H. Stanner, *The Dreaming and Other Essays* (Melbourne: Black Inc., 2009), 58. The *dreamtime* was originally a translation of the Aranda word *alcheringa*, made by Spencer and Gillen in 1896— "a sacred, heroic time long ago when man and nature came to be as they are" (Ibid., 57).

2   Paddy Dhathaŋu comments on a painting of the Wägilak Sisters story. These *waŋarr* (ancestral beings) who travelled through Wägilak country are not to be confused with the narrative of Djuwalpada in Wägilak *manikay*. Quoted in Wally Caruana and Nigel Lendon, eds., *The Painters of the Wagilag Sisters Story 1937–1997* (Canberra, ACT: National Gallery of Australia, 1997), 56.

who live on its supporting ground and within its ecological movements. The *waŋarr* gave patterns for human life: for kinship, relationship, politics, and ceremony. Yolŋu follow these patterns of ancestral precedent: through their voices straining in song, the blood coursing in their veins as they dance, and their thoughts played out in improvisation, individuals are connected through the generations to the original creative action.

Under the mundane surface of human relationships, the surface of the land and its features, and behind ecology, there is a living ancestral presence. Ceremonial knowledge reveals this reality that gives shape and sustenance to all life. Knowledge carried in traditions of song illuminates existence as a text that can be seen, heard, smelt—read. Ceremony opens eyes and ears to a profound past that pervades the present, revealing patterns of life set into motion by original creative action. Through performance, knowledge of these patterns is handed down by elders, as laws for living that give shape to present life, to follow in the "foot tracks" of the ancestors.

Similar thought can be seen expressed differently across Australia's top end and central deserts. Warlpiri elder Steven Wanta Jampijinpa Patrick from the Tanami Desert works to engage young children with ceremonial traditions as creative director of the Milpirri Festival at Lajamanu. The children wear USB wrist bands—in colours corresponding to kinship rights and responsibilities—which read, "Track a footprint; track a wordprint." Like Yolŋu ceremony, Warlpiri ceremony is about following established patterns for life bestowed upon each generation. Patrick also teaches in a course at the Australian National University, challenging students to respond to this epistemology, which begins with the land as the primary text of ancestral creation:

> Out of the land, our sounds become our words. Our words become our stories. Our stories become our songs. Our songs become our ceremonies. Our ceremonies become our teachings. Our teachings become our beliefs. Our beliefs become our Law, and through that, we are strong and know who we are wherever and whatever we are doing.[3]

The attribution of agency to the land, the idea that it generates words and stories, songs and life, shows the excess of meanings that extend from a primary point of creation. The inception of life is prolific and ongoing; the actions, relationships and songs of *yolŋu* (people) today attest to this original creative action as expansive. Therefore, individuality and personal agency are not subsumed by creative ancestral action but affirmed as necessary to the complexly interwoven expression of life.

In the movements of life, relationships with others and with the land—in hearing, thinking, smelling, eating, laughing, growing, dancing, and

---

3   Wanta Jampijinpa Patrick quoted in Corn, "Indigenous Australian Music and Media".

dying—*yolŋu* (people) are enfolded into original ancestral creativity. Ceremonial narratives indicate toward ecological patterns, birds and animals, people and human activities, that can be read as a text, the tangible traces of ancestral creativity. A sense of contiguity between present life and ancestral creation is often conveyed in stories of the land and animals as a speaking, vocative presence. This *ancestral text*, the presence of original, creative action, can be felt in the breeze and heard in the cry of a *biywik* (cuckoo). People are a part of the living ancestral text, in which they hear, smell, think, live, and sing. Daniel Wilfred remembers learning about *manikay* at his homeland Ŋilipidji:

> When we were little, we went down to the river [at Ŋilipidji], and we sing this song, "Wata" [Wind]. And this wind was blowing. And then we heard a bird coming towards us. The bird called like this: *ki-ol ki-ol, ki-ol ki-ol*. And we stop for a little while and listen, and he's still coming, that bird. And we have to run back home [scared!]—when we were kids. And when we went up in the hills, Justin [Nunggarrgalug] had to run, get my shirt, pulling me back, "Don't run, listen to this bird." And we went back there to sit and start singing again, the wind.[4]

The enduring forms of *manikay*, sustained over countless generations, convey a comprehensive ancestral creation that continues to shape life. Performance of ceremonial expressions supposedly reveals patent truths that, as Stanner claims, "no one in his right mind would have thought of trying to bring to the bar of proof."[5] Because *manikay* is underpinned by this orthodox imperative to transmit and retain, it becomes a means of holding present generations to account. This is inherently political and strategic: the performance of *manikay* becomes a means of asserting the validity of present decisions and shaping conversations around issues related to education, cultural authority and leadership, and responsibilities in land ownership. Here, *manikay* provides an interesting insight into cultural identities: distinction and autonomy are emphasised by songs that are rightfully owned and performed by Wägilak alone. Yet songs also embody connections and cooperation with other families and homelands, as relational—even *diplomatic*. As an ancestral institution concerned with the identity and relationality, it is no wonder that Yolŋu refer to *manikay* and ceremonial performance as the equivalent of "schools and universities",[6] and sometimes even "Parliament" or a "chamber of law".[7]

As well as shaping identities and connections, the narratives in Wägilak *manikay* concern perennial human questions of death and identity (see Chapter

---

4   Daniel Wilfred, interview with the author, Ngukurr, 13 July 2011.
5   W.E.H. Stanner, "Some Aspects of an Aboriginal Religion", *Colloquium* 9, no. 1 (1976): 19.
6   Trudgen, *Why Warriors*, 123.
7   Banduk Marika, "The Story Behind the Project", *Yalangbara: Art of the Djaŋ'kawu*, National Museum of Australia, http://nma.gov.au/exhibitions/yalangbara/about/

Four). Amid the seeming cacophony of free jazz improvisation in *CRB*, Wägilak sustain these core images through directions given to play like the wind, or in imitation of the *birrkpirrk* (plover). *Manikay* is flexible and poetic in the creation of meaning: creativity is essential to musical performance if core principles of tradition are to be carried or received in new contexts. The *manikay* tradition is not an object of history transposed into contemporary contexts, like a stone artefact carried through time in the cradle of a museum display. It is imagination and the living breath of creativity that bring existential insights and questions to light through performance.

Supported by the forms and patterns of song and dance, *manikay* performers respond creatively to life, and allow life to be illuminated by song (Chapters Four and Five). Just as rippling water throws off reflections in a myriad of angles, ancestral patterns carried in music are always animate and renewing, shimmering with an abundance of life.

Footprints

> The country is the songs; country got the songs. And even the rivers got the songs. Dogs, no matter what animal, got songs. Songs coming out from your land and from your walk. Songs coming out from your ground. Songs coming out from water, and from the ground, and from the spirit—no matter where, songs can come out. Culture is really strong. So you have to hold your culture strong like me.[8]

We sing and dance because sound and movement exist. Singing is heard because the tangible text of existence is a song: "The country is the songs; country got the songs." The performance of *manikay* gives voice to the dynamic ancestral text, which is read from the land, ecology, animals, *raŋga* (sacred objects) and people—those tangible traces of creative action.[9] It is a text also carried in human bodies, relationships and ceremony. This text is a track to be followed.

Maḏayin (ancestral law and ceremony) is sacred in that it draws individuals towards ŋalabuluŋu rom (correct living), following the patterns bestowed to the people by the great *waŋarr* (creative beings).[10] *Maḏayin* shapes human actions

---

8   Benjamin Wilfred, "Digital Audio Technologies".

9   Frances Morphy writes of the "layer of sacred geography [that] is ontologically prior and underpins all else". Frances Morphy, "(Im)mobility: Regional Population Structures in Aboriginal Australia", *Australian Journal of Social Issues* 45, no. 3 (2010): 368. F. and H. Morphy consider human relationships "fitting into pre-existing footprints (*djalkiri, luku*) visible in the landscape". Frances Morphy and Howard Morphy, "Tasting the Waters: Discriminating Identities in the Waters of Blue Mud Bay", *Journal of Material Culture* 11, no. 1 (2006): 69. See also Roland Berndt, "An Adjustment Movement in Arnhem Land, Northern Territory of Australia", facsimile edition of *Oceania Monograph 54* [1962] (Sydney: University of Sydney, 2004), 64.

10   Cf. Corn's discussion of *rom* (law) in ceremonial performance. Aaron Corn, "Ancestral, Corporeal, Corporate: Traditional Yolŋu Understandings of the Body Explored", *Borderlands* 7, no. 2 (2008):

and relationships in line with the footprints of these *waŋarr*. *Manikay* (song), *buŋgul* (dance), *miny'tji* (design), and *yäku* (sacred lexicon) are all component forms in the continuation of *maḏayin*. These forms are entwined together, a woven amalgam encoding knowledge of *gurruṯu* (kinship) proprieties and responsibilities; *riŋgitj* (*bäpurru* alliances) and Ŋärra' (restricted chamber of law); diplomatic and trade procedures; land ownership; and rules for conservation, hunting, and resource management.[11]

Writing about ancestral, corporeal, and corporate bodies in *manikay*, Aaron Corn considers the variety and diversity of Yolŋu experience as an abundant manifestation of "eternal blueprints."[12] Like the *manikay* tradition passed down the generations, performed and understood creatively, these *blueprints* are not monochromatic. The ancestral text is not archived in dead permanence but lives through heterophonic expression in multiple bodies and generations. Similarly, human bodies cannot be separated from the performance—the articulation and continuation—of *maḏayin*. Ceremonial performance is not static: in many different places, many different bodies perform in many different ways.

To follow in the *ḻuku* (footprints) of generations past by performing traditional repertoires is to shape lives in reflection of the ancestral past, to extend efficacious precedence. Marika-Munuŋgiritj explains this view:

> The part of a Yolngu education described as *lundu-nhäma* means identifying the pattern and the style of the past. This refers particularly to our forebears, our ancestors, but also to the elders of the present day. First we must recognize what has gone before and know exactly how it fits in with the whole way of meaning which makes Yolngu life—*dhin'thun* [to track; follow].[13]

As a tradition, *manikay* opens a person's eyes to the ancestral footprints all around them. Marika-Munuŋgiritj continues, "We can see all those things because we can read them in the land, and they have been passed down to us through their songs."[14] The world is saturated with tangible traces of the *waŋarr* (creative beings). Yolŋu read—they see, hear, feel, and smell—an excess of meaning from an engaging ancestral text. Using metaphors that show understanding always to be situated within linguistic and cultural traditions, W.E.H. Stanner puts it eloquently: "Most of the choir and furniture of heaven and earth are regarded

---

1–17; Corn, "Land, Song, Constitution", 85.

11 The translations used here are clearly drawn from Western history and structures of polity and law. Translation is always imperfect. However, metaphors such as "alliance" and "parliament" do open new possibilities of understanding. Djiniyini Gondarra, "Assent Law of the First People: Views from a Traditional Owner", *National Indigenous Times*, 3 March 2011; Trudgen, *Why Warriors*, 13.

12 Corn, "Ancestral, Corporeal, Corporate", 14.

13 Marika-Munuŋgiritj and Christie, "Yolngu Metaphors", 61.

14 Ibid.

by the Aborigines as a vast sign-system. Anyone who, understandingly, has moved in the Australian bush with Aboriginal associates becomes aware of the fact. He moves, not in a landscape, but in a humanized realm saturated with significations. Here 'something happened,' there 'something portends.'"[15]

Equivalence

The Yolŋu world is shaped by pedagogical sequences built upon stages of access to ceremonial knowledge. The Yolŋu world is one in which people always "learn deeper meanings as they pass through life."[16] Between *garma* (public) and *ŋärra'* (restricted) interpretations, an individual is located along a continuum of rights to knowledge. Levels of initiation govern access to esoteric knowledge and sacred manifestations of the ancestral text.[17] The more knowledgeable an individual becomes, the more layers of meaning he or she can read into outside, *garma* (public) expressions such as *manikay*.

Manikay is a public tradition that is open to all. Yet the narratives and images in *manikay* precede and allude to deeper, inside meanings that are restricted and sacred. When new interpretations of song are revealed through experience or information, another layer of meaning is read onto the basic, public narrative. Such secret, sacred meanings do not supplant public ones; mundane images are essential in establishing a context and language for the revelation of more abstract meanings.

There are many layers of meaning in *manikay*. But they start with *garma* (public) themes and images, like Djuwalpada making the string. "You can learn about string. That's why he is making a string: making a line, to go fishing."[18] Fishing is the public version and even the Balanda (non-Indigenous people) know that one. Everyone can dance *raki* (string). But it is not just about fishing. *Raki* is a basic idea of responsibility that everyone needs to know. "Accountability

---

15 W.E.H. Stanner, "Religion, Totemism, and Symbolism", in *Aboriginal Man in Australia: Essays in Honour of Emeritus Professor A.P. Elkin*, ed. R. M. Berndt and C. H. Berndt (Sydney: Angus & Robertson, 1965), 227.

16 Howard Morphy, *Becoming Art: Exploring Cross Cultural Categories* (Sydney: University of New South Wales Press, 2008), 109.

17 Keen outlines different Yolŋu age-gender designations. While female categories tend to relate to the reproductive cycle, men's categories include: *gadaku* (uncircumcised male); *gurrmul* (bachelor and circumcised male); *wurrwiliny* (mature man, in his thirties or forties); *yindi yolŋu* or *ŋalapalmirr(i)* (big man, grey-haired man), and *liya-ŋärra'mirr(i)* (learned and wise with restricted knowledge). Ian Keen, *Knowledge and Secrecy in an Aboriginal Religion: Yolngu of North-East Arnhem Land* (Oxford: Clarendon Press, 1994), 92. Frances Morphy adds that *ŋalapalmirr(i)* also includes grey-haired women; grey hair connotes wisdom, which is not gender specific (pers. comm., 2013).

18 Daniel Wilfred, comment during a dance workshop, Melbourne, 29 May 2014.

is represented in ritual feather strings that are fashioned for each clan and worn when dancing the journeys of the first ancestral creators."[19]

The Wägilak song "*Guku*" (Honey) illustrates this hermeneutic. The song imagines the flight of a bee toward the honey in its hive. The bee flies from the outside to the inside, mirroring an individual's growth and orientation in life (see below). Similarly, in carving a pair of *bilma* (clapsticks), the outer layers of bark or flesh are whittled away to reveal the core—the hidden *ŋaraka* (bones). Everything in the Yolŋu ceremonial world is shaped by this movement from the mundane to the sacred. The sacred is always anticipated in public narratives.[20]

Identifying tangible evidence of ancestral creation in the land and society, Yolŋu speak with metonymic equivalence. For example, the sandbank in the coastal shallows "*is* the body" of the ancestral shark, Buḻ'manydji. Daniel Wilfred points to the hills in the distance and says, "See where that lightning struck? That *is* the snake. My wife has that song, it's her country."[21] The land and society are always present and can be seen by all, a pervasive text carrying deeper meanings. The tangible world provides a poetic and abundant language for song and narrative.

The name *Lärra* provides just such an example. Lärra identifies Ŋilipidji as "stone spear country". You can walk through this country, smelling it and feeling it; you can hear this country in song. The name Lärra is equivalent to the country, which itself is a text: the boulders in the ground are the fat of a kidney in the earth; these boulders are also pregnant as they give birth to ŋambi children (stone spear-tips), which are in turn fashioned into a finished *lira* (tooth), also known as penetrating *gurrka* (penis) spear tips.[22] Thus the word *Lärra* is a tangible thing and its *meaning* is only known through the experience of that country, the manufacture of stone spears and their use in hunting.

The term *metonymic equivalence* conveys something of this sense of direct correspondence between text and experience, with which Yolŋu speak about ancestral reality. A signifier in metonymic expressions is a direct transposition of the essence of the signified, for example, the *leg* of a chair. This is not mere representation, simile, or metaphor, suggesting tiers of literal/non-literal meaning: For example, reading this chapter is a *breeze*. Leading

19 Fiona Magowan, "It Is God Who Speaks in the Thunder: Mediating Ontologies of Faith and Fear in Aboriginal Christianity", *The Journal of Religions History* 27, no. 3 (2003): 303.

20 H. Morphy elaborates on the place of creativity within this scheme. Howard Morphy, "Yolngu Art and the Creativity of the Inside", in *Aboriginal Religions in Australia: An Anthology of Recent Writings*, ed. Max Charlesworth, Francoise Dussart, and Howard Morphy (Aldershot, Hampshire: Ashgate, 2005), 159–70.

21 Buku-Larrnggay Mulka Centre, *Saltwater: Yirrkala Paintings of the Sea Country* (Yirrkala, NT: Buku-Larrnggay Mulka Centre, 1999), 91; Daniel Wilfred, in discussion with the author, 2012.

22 Rhys Jones and Neville White, "Point Blank: Stone Tool Manufacture at the Ngilipitji Quarry, Arnhem Land, 1981", in *Archaeology with Ethnography: an Australian Perspective*, edited by Betty Meehan and Rhys Jones (Canberra: Australian National University, 1988), 51–87.

Australian anthropologist Howard Morphy presents this challenge: "The use of *representation* would suggest a gap between signifier and signified that is not consistent with Yolngu ontology."[23] Perhaps the use of *metonymic equivalence* might account for the substantial congruence between tangible experience, narrative, and signifier in Yolŋu hermeneutics.

Metonymy grounds language and concepts in experience: the sweetness of honey is law. Exploring the function of metonymy in thought, culture, and religion, Lakoff and Johnson characterise metonymy as "not merely a referential device; it also serves the function of providing understanding."[24] In *manikay*, metonymic equivalence allows complex significations to splice together like fibres in a string, entangling meaning with materiality rather than clarifying meaning from material complexity.

At a mundane level, the bee collects pollen and produces honey—just one narrative from Wägilak *manikay*. This is a necessary, literal foundation for additional meanings. Further interpretations suggest that the bee's stinger is phallic; another layer again and the honey produced by the bee comes to signify knowledge itself. Public songs about the mundane bee are therefore is necessary to deeper meanings. The flight of the bee is a visible, public text that can be followed to more secret, sacred meanings. The bee can be tracked from the outside to the inside of the tree, where it's honey *is* the law.

Similarly in artistic design, where a particular geometric figuration might simultaneously convey fire, heat, glimmering water, and glistening honey.[25] These basic narrative subjects or figurations form a "core mnemonic that can generate a series of alternative images".[26] This figurative core—bee, fire, and heat—is a basic and stable text, read from the land, ecology, and society, yet it produces an excess of heterophonic meanings.

Because each *bäpurru* identity extends from a unique ceremonial figure, journey and place, each *bäpurru* possesses different ceremonial repertoires. Wägilak follow the tracks or the "songline" of Djuwalpada, which incorporates numerous events and objects from the story of his travels. Benjamin Wilfred explains, "We always sing about Wild Blackfella [Djuwalpada] when we walk: follow that track, where the elders in the olden days went, we follow them."[27] Weaving together unique threads of different languages, stories, and country, greater Yolŋu society is a complementary amalgam (Chapter Two). The performance of ceremony within this greater society is a responsibility to

---

23 Morphy, *Ancestral Connections*, 189.
24 George Lakoff and Mark Johnson, *Metaphors We Live By* (Chicago: University of Chicago Press, 1980), 36.
25 Morphy, *Becoming Art*, 94. See also Howard Morphy, "From Dull to Brilliant: The Aesthetics of Spiritual Power among the Yolngu", *Man* 24, no. 1 (1989): 21–40.
26 Morphy, *Becoming Art*, 78.
27 Benjamin Wilfred, interview with Daniel Browning, "Crossing Boundaries".

maintain unique knowledge essential to the vibrancy of this whole, to "hold culture strong".

In chorus, a multitude of voices respond to the complex, layered brilliance of existence. In community, each individual sings with their own voice, with unique inflection and contour. Equivalent but distinct, the present is shaped by the forms of the past. Performers are drawn into the ongoing articulation of an abundant ancestral text, heard as it is animated in song and dance: "No matter where, songs can come out."[28]

Revealing Existence

Wurrpu dilyunayi, dhaŋarra bädun,
Buluwulu gupurranayi, milimili bädun dilyunayi

Flowers are starting to come out, white Eucalyptus flowers
Seeds falling down, flowers withering and dying

("Dhaŋarra" White flower song text)

As the seasons turn and the *dhaŋarra* (white eucalyptus flowers) start to bloom, boys begin their formal entrance into the life of *maḏayin* (ancestral law).[29] They follow the bee's flight from the flower to the hive, the outside to the inside— external phenomena to sacred law. The bees sing, buzzing toward the pollen, before carrying it back to the hive where they make sweet honey.

Brave young boys are brought into a circle of men, their chests painted with the white-dot *dhaŋarra* design. Voices singing the *gumurr* (chest; see Chapter Five) of the song "Dhaŋarra" surround them, combining in heterophonic unity. The boys stand strong, holding their spears high, ready to throw, about to begin hunting for themselves.

Dhapi (male circumcision) marks the initiation of a boy into a covenant of law and responsibility. Ḻiyagawumirr artist Albert Djiwada explains, "Just like grade one when you go to school, *dhapi* is the first step" into men's secret religions knowledge.[30] This is a living relationship to law involving the whole body. Ancestral precedence comes to be known as it is followed and understood, as an individual realises the relevance of law within the events of life. *Dhapi* is not just a record of law left on the body but is an orientation in life sustained through ceremonial performance, carried by singing, dancing bodies. *Dhapi* projects forward through life as becoming.

---

28 Benjamin Wilfred, "Digital Audio Technologies".
29 At least this is the narrative; circumcisions may occur at any time of year.
30 Albert Djiwada, quoted in Caruana and Lendon, *Painters of the Wagilag Sisters*, 72.

The following words from Gupapuyŋu elder and academic Joe Neparrŋa Gumbula name numerous *manikay* which shape to Gupapuyŋu life. These narratives move the singer toward a more comprehensive identity, finally to be found in death, in which an individual's identity is subsumed by ancestral reality. This passage originated in a 2001 lecture on the Garma Festival, given at the University of Melbourne:

> In life, I am Neparrŋa Gumbula, but in death, I am already named by *waŋarr* (ancestral progenitors). My feet and legs are those of the *wurrpan* (emu). My knees are fruit from the *ṉarraṉi* (native apple) tree. My front is that of the *mokuy* (ghost) hunter, Muyarana. My back is the *djaḻumbu* (hollow log coffin). My heart beats as *wurrpan's* (emu) and my stomach, like his, is *butulak* (yellow). My spine is the *waymamba* (pathway) worn in the scrub by the *guwak* (koel cuckoo). My mouth is the entrance to the beehive. My nose is beeswax. My eyes are nuts from the *warraga* (cycad palm). My hairs are the fine roots of the *mayku* (paperbark tree) and the *wuḻu* (white foam) that they produce in the swamp at Djiliwirri. My head and my knowledge are *guku* (honey) from the *waŋarr* Birrkuḏa (short-nosed bee). In death, my name is no longer Neparrŋa. It is Birrkuḏa.[31]

In the human body, as in the land, ancestral presence is seen, felt, and known tangibly through corporeal embodiment. Ancestral presence is sustained in the bodies of Yolŋu who are more than collections of signifiers—of ears, eyes, hands, and feet. Standing on the ground, my feet firmly planted, my elbow strong, and my spear sharp. In this place, looking, feeling, and thinking. Encircled by brothers, fathers, and uncles, my own body is evidence of a past—my chest beats with the same blood as elders who have lived before me. I originated, a bud on a branch. I started to grow, my life manifest in new contexts—the life of the *waŋarr* (creative beings) also finding expression. My body lives within *maḏayin* (ancestral law).

Budding

Long before the separation of girls and boys through *dhapi* (male circumcision), children learn to understand the world through *manikay*. They begin this education in the first few years of life. Learning by participation and imitation—in between energetic play on the *buŋgul* (dance) ground—children dance alongside older men and women, or sit listening intently to their parents' songs and stories. Boys often play *biḻma* (clapsticks) made from twigs or small *yiḏaki* (didjeridu) about a metre long.

As they grow older, gender distinctions come to the fore. Boys learn to sing *manikay* and its accompanying *yiḏaki* (didjeridu) patterns, while girls

---

31 Neparrŋa Gumbula, quoted in Corn, "Ancestral, Corporeal, Corporate", 1.

learn *ngäthi* or *milkarri* (crying/keening songs). Benjamin and Daniel Wilfred remember learning *manikay*:

> Benjamin Wilfred: When I was growing up, I didn't think I'd be doing this stuff [leading ceremony]. I didn't know what I was gonna be … As soon as my uncle and grandpa showed me a ceremony, here [in Ngukurr], then I think. When I saw the one ceremony, that made me come into the …
>
> Samuel Curkpatrick: Find a purpose?
>
> BW: Yeah. Soon as I saw men's ceremony, then I just keep going from there. That was on my mind. From that day I was on my toes, following my grandpa [Sambo Barabara]. Just following him, following … They go sing, my grandpa always go and I sit down one-side to him. I reckon I wouldn't get this knowledge …
>
> I really respect my grandpa, what he did. I thought I can't teach [learn] properly, but he just touched my heart and I was with him: all the time, every day, singing. I just kept going. Sit down one-side and hear him, and keep singing. And I put my ears to him, singing.[32]
>
> Daniel Wilfred: And we were making noise when we were kids. And my dad used to chase me with a stick, "Alright, go get your didj and clapping stick, start singing!" And then we went down to the big shade and sat. I had to ask my little uncle to play me didj, and I asked my two sisters, "You want to come? We'll sing songs and you two dance." And my sister asked me, "What are we going to sing?"
> "I'm going to sing. You know how to sing?"
> "Yeah, I know how to sing. What song?"
> "This song called Djuwalpada. He's pointing with his elbow."
> And my uncle got the didj and we played, and my sister listened. "Hey, when you grow up, maybe we will listen to you leading these songs."
> "Yeah," I said, "When I grow up you can listen. We can do a recording when we're singing," I told my sister.[33]

Children dance and sing in all public ceremonial contexts, learning the basic narratives of *manikay* songs like "Raki" (String) or "Birrkpirrk" (Plover). The metonymic layering of narrative allows young children to internalise and engage with ancestral law through its exoteric stories. These are established as prior tenets that, one day, become the basis for more profound interpretations.

---

32 Benjamin Wilfred, interview with the author, Ngukurr, 19 June 2011.
33 Daniel Wilfred, interview with the author, Ngukurr, 13 June 2011.

Even as deeper significances are understood by older performers, children can still dance like the *wäkwak* (black crow) looking for a feed, or laugh at the *waṯu* (dog), who buries the fire after a smoking ceremony.

Emerging

As new generations emerge along the *yarraṯa* (string line) of their *bäpurru* (father's group; agnatic descent), the ancestral text is sustained through new performances. Through performance, *manikay* remains connected to its deep foundations; to perform is to follow the tracks of the past, known as *ŋaḻabuluŋu rom* (correct living; following law).

Speaking about his father's father, Wägilak elder Peters states, "He was giving me story for culture side, for skin, for ceremony. Gave me a lot of experience to understand my foot-tracks from my father—old days."[34] Likewise, Daniel Wilfred recounts his older brother Barabara's words about passing ceremony on:

> You have to hold this song: when you grow up and when you're married, and when you find your kid. And your kid can follow your track. Like you're following my track. I'm giving you all the words for the songs, and for the bush tucker [food] and bush medicine. Keep telling them.[35]

To diverge from the tracks of previous generations and break the continuation of *manikay* performance is to rupture the *yarraṯa* (string line) that connects father to son, a disavowal of the past that shapes the present in its image. Anthropologist Nancy Williams conveys this concept as it was explained to her: "*Bäpurru* is something important in our lives; it is like the soul, you can't see it. It means something we share before we are born and keep on sharing during our lifetime and after we die."[36]

In applying neat, categorical thinking about tradition as an observable process of continuity and change, our understandings of Yolŋu ceremonial practices are bound to be confused. Narritjin Maymuru, leader of the Maŋgalili in the 1970s and 1980s, challenges such thinking: "You want to show us that our art has changed, we will show you that it has not."[37] Yet performances occur in an ever-changing world. As Marika-Munuŋgiritj explains further, ceremonial performance is "reworking the truths we have learned from the land and from the elders, into a celebration of who we are and where we are in the modern world."[38] In performance, ancestral presence emerges through

---

34 Andy Peters, interview with the author, Ngukurr, 12 July 2011.
35 Daniel Wilfred, interview with the author, 13 July 2011.
36 Williams, *The Yolngu and Their Land*, 66.
37 Narritjin Maymuru, quoted in Morphy, *Ancestral Connections*, 182.
38 Marika and Christie, "Yolngu Metaphors", 61.

situated, contextual experience. New significances are always emerging from the footprints of the past.

From the singing, dancing body emerge interpretations that point to meanings beyond mundane symbols and signifiers—meanings hidden to those without the requisite knowledge. *Maḏayin* (ceremonial law) is dynamic, moving from dull to brilliant, raw to cooked, *garma* (public) to *ŋärra'* (secret).[39] Like an unfolding story, the profound beauty of existence is sequentially uncovered.

Experience of this knowledge—like the country at Lärra—fills out the basic forms of *manikay* (introduced in Chapter Five). The outline of musical structure is filled by performance: bodies are compelled to dance, excitement builds, and the deep names held by a *bäpurru* are intoned. Past, present, and future entwine together as new generations join the ancestral song.

Flowering

Nyalk, galkanan nyalk
Gumurr nhäwurlanapu
Gel-gel-gel ḻikanangayi nyalk
Balaŋayi nyalk mala

Rain, falling down
I see the clouds forming
The rain is coming, cooling rain
Falling on the country

("Wukuṉ" Clouds song text)[40]

Manikay extends beyond the iteration of legal, cultural, and religious precepts. Through *manikay*, Yolŋu learn to read existence as an abundant, expansive ancestral text. *Manikay* enriches experiences of the world and the world is experienced through the sounds of *manikay*.

In *manikay*, ecological knowledge is constituted through song, and song in ecological knowledge. After learning the dance for "Wäkwak" (Black crow) and hearing the vocal interjections imitating the sound of a crow—the name is onomatopoeic, like many bird names in Yolŋu languages—I always think of crows as *wäkwak*. Wherever I am, the name and song, particularly its strutting rhythms, are ingrained in my experience of that bird. Ethnomusicologist Fiona Magowan writes of this process as becoming "disciplined into a sensory

---

39 Morphy, "From Dull to Brilliant"; Aaron Corn, discussion with the author, 2010.
40 Translation completed with Andy Peters, Ngukurr, 2012.

habitus that relates to the ancestral law."[41] For Yolŋu, there are many complex associations embedded in their experience of the world.

Manikay also maps onto specific country and places, although it is important to be aware of our assumptions about cartography when thinking about this. *Manikay* carries a library of history concerning ownership of estates, and *yäku* (sacred lexicon) convey the physical and genealogical connections between different places and peoples. In song, sequences of proper names mirror ancestral tracks, forged by the journeys of figures like Djuwalpada or the shark Bul'manydji. These *songlines* are visible in the landscape, in rivers, mountain ranges, and vegetation.

Manikay evokes and creates place in Yolŋu minds.[42] Such knowledge is learnt through the tangible experiences of human bodies in the environment. Consequently, to sustain the *manikay* tradition is to sustain human connection with the land and specific places.[43] Daniel Wilfred discussed this very attribute in an interview with ethnomusicologist Aaron Corn:

> DANIEL WILFRED: I was staying back at Ŋilipidji … From Ŋilipidji to Walker River we walked. Carried the *yidaki* [didjeridu] too. I had a small *yidaki*. And we used to play, when we were kids; play, singing, dancing. We made a little corroboree [ceremony] and then my dad started to listen to what we were singing. We were singing that song, Yolŋu [Djuwalpada], that's where my dad told me to start up. And when we were finished we walked, shooting birds with a shanghai. But we didn't stop singing. Walking, shooting birds, keep singing song. That's what I learnt about—and I listen.

> AARON CORN: The *manikay* really do tell you how to move through the country itself?

> DW: Yeah, that's right.

> AC: The *manikay* almost take you where you're going, because they point out places.

---

41 Magowan, *Melodies of Mourning*, 15.

42 Aaron Corn and Peter Toner both consider the power of *manikay* to evoke and create place through performance, despite the physical location of the singer. Aaron Corn, "Nations of Song", *Humanities Research* 19, no. 3 (2013): 145–60; Peter Toner, "Sing a Country of the Mind: The Articulation of Place in Dhalwangu Song", in *The Soundscapes of Australia*, ed. Fiona Richards (Aldershot, Hampshire: Ashgate, 2007), 165–84.

43 Magowan considers the detrimental effects of declining access to the hereditary estates for many Yolŋu people: "Decreasing degrees of intimacy with the environment has had serious ramifications for the reproduction of song knowledge as all songs entail a critical understanding of the intricate sounds, movements, smells and feel of ecological forms." Magowan, *Melodies of Mourning*, 37.

DW: Yeah, that's what I learnt about.[44]

The seasons billow and roll over the country. Moving indiscriminately over different homelands, the seasons connect families and places. Important *manikay* narratives are related directly to seasonal patterns, which "characterise all Dhuwa and Yirritja songs beginning with winds that bring either rain or dry heat, each associated with a particular flora and fauna."[45] The Wägilak songs of Ṉilipidji are know n collectively as the wind songs, linked to the walma "build-up" season (November–January) when guku (wild honey) is abundant and the *gadayka* (Stringybark tree) flowers with white dhaṉarra. Peters' country at Wuḻku is connected to Wägilak from Ṉilipidji through his *wukuṉ* (cloud) songs. These clouds form out to sea before being blown inland by the Wägilak *wata* (wind), as Peters explains:

> I'd like to tell you one more story. I started off [singing] from my country right back at Wuḻku. And we can see Gumurrnama Waltjaṉa [rainy season], we see that cloud coming towards us. And the cloud make himself rain fall down. *Wukuṉ* [clouds] come from Luṯunba [in Blue Mud Bay] towards my country, to Wuḻku … *Wata* [wind] comes from Luṯunba, comes through Ṉilipidji way, goes to *riŋitj* country [connected by alliance]. Then to my place, Wuḻku, then Djilpin.[46]

This ecological cycle can be elaborated: clouds form above the smoke from the fires burning on the country. These clouds are blown by the wind, later to fall as rain. The rain causes floods to spread freshwater out of the billabongs and into the streams and rivers. Running toward the sea, the freshwater becomes brackish as it mixes with saltwater in the estuaries, before eventually flowing back out to sea.

Other branches of narrative extend from this sequence. During *nyalkthaŋ'puy*, the heavy rains (January–March), the *birrkpirrk* (plover) and Djuwalpaḏa search for yams, *impregnated* into the earth by the rain. To get to the *duyṉambi* (yams), Djuwalpaḏa must find their white flowers, *baṉbalarri*. Later in the year, when the *birrkpirrk* (plover) is nesting, it is the right season to start burning-off the country. This produces smoke, then clouds, which are blown again by the wind that comes before the rains.[47]

Manikay brims with ecological knowledge, directly informing a person's being in the world. As ancestral law is progressively revealed, the world blossoms with beautiful complexity and variety; the world comes alive as a text to be read.

---

44 Daniel Wilfred, interview with Aaron Corn and the author, Ngukurr, 13 July 2011.

45 Magowan, *Melodies of Mourning*, 46.

46 Andy Peters, interview with the author, Ngukurr, 12 July 2011.

47 Ibid.; Ngukurr Language Centre, *Ritharrngu/Wagilak Seasons*, unpublished chart, Ngukurr, NT, Australia.

In the looming thunderclouds and fresh breeze, creative ancestral action is seen and felt. When the life-giving rains break, the waterholes fill and flood the land. The original creative action of ancestral beings continues to sustain life through each new generation.

Withering

As Wägilak elder Barabara was nearing death, he passed on to Benjamin and Daniel Wilfred the authority to continue performing Wägilak *manikay*. Benjamin recalls the night Barabara died: "Sambo came in my dream and gave me that clapping stick."[48] In the space left by death, something new comes out.

Creative ancestral action is dynamic and pervasive, and death is a part of it. As the *dhaŋarra* (eucalyptus flowers) wither and die, seeds fall down. Yet one day, nurtured by the soil and rain, something new will emerge. In the song "Mädawk" (Friarbird), the red haze of *wärrarra*, the blood of the setting sun, seeps from the west. Djuwalpada looked west to find his home, throwing his spear in that direction. In an open space or clearing, also called *wärrarra*, a new generation will gather to dance. New shoots will come up and they will sing the songs of old with fresh, lively colour.

Adjustment

Wägilak elder and ceremonial leader Sambo Barabara grew up "in the bush". A skilled painter and musician, his life was shaped by *madayin* (ancestral law). Today, Wägilak look back to this lifestyle and see it as productive and healthy. But after moving to live in the Ngukurr community in the 1970s, Barabara witnessed drastic health problems, cultural disintegration, and violence— communities spiralling out of control. Like many others, his unfortunate death was just one consequence of these wider social problems.

Recent decades of social and economic problems—or symptomatic conditions—in Arnhem Land are grim. The disempowerment of John Djatjamirrilil has been too common a reality: "We sit with sad faces, with nothing to do except watch the Balanda [non-Aboriginal people] running around doing everything for us."[49] After decades living and working for Yolŋu in Arnhem Land, Richard Trudgen writes in the new-millennium of once-great warriors, leaders, intellectuals, politicians, tradesmen, and linguists, overwhelmed by a void of redundancy: "Yolŋu then have almost totally lost control of their lives and living environment as the dominant culture has moulded them to fit its own reality. Some are coping very well against the odds, but the majority are

---

48 Benjamin Wilfred, interview with Jane Ulman, "Cultural Crossings".
49 John Djatjamirrilil, quoted in Trudgen, *Why Warriors*, 158.

collapsing from the unrelenting strain."[50] Similarly, traditional languages and ceremonial practices have been strained, some to near-extinction.

Difficulties of communication continue to separate Yolŋu and Balanda in Ngukurr. Neither the government nor school teachers speak Kriol or other indigenous languages. Cultural literacy and understanding are also limited. Even as Indigenous visual art has become highly successful in mainstream Australia, much meaning is lost to "fascinated" outside audiences, who consume "the primitive as a complicated delicacy".[51]

Still Yolŋu persist in communicating with the outside world through art and performance. Outsiders who desire greater understanding and relationship are welcomed, and new forms of technology embraced. Collaborations such as *CRB* arise: in many ways, these are appropriated by Yolŋu as outreach programs to the *kinless, country-less* masses running mainstream Australia.[52] In response to new situations, Yolŋu cultural protocols are continually adjusted to face destructive gaps in understanding and to deal with ever new challenges to defining Yolŋu autonomies both essential and relative.[53]

Through creative projects that incorporate traditional knowledge into contemporary forms and forums, Yolŋu leaders have responded to the pressures impacting their systems of knowledge and society. They aim to create awareness of the ongoing value of Yolŋu culture. The annual Garma Festival at Gulkala on the Gove Peninsula is a prominent example of this. Engagement with outsiders is also a strong political assertion that ancestral constitution—carried in cultural traditions—continues to shape Yolŋu lives today and is not just something relegated to a pre-colonial past.

Howard Morphy considers the "Elcho Island adjustment movement" as the earliest attempt to reveal to outsiders some of the deeper, secret meanings of Yolŋu culture: "In 1957 at Elcho Island (Galiwin'ku) in North East Arnhem Land, a set of carved and painted sacred objects were erected in a public place alongside the church." The display of these *raŋga* (sacred objects) belonging to many different groups demonstrated a "united front in their [the Yolŋu's] negotiations with Europeans."[54]

This event at Galiwin'ku is considered by Yolŋu elders as "the first and only time these law symbols have been revealed," a radical demonstration of Yolŋu

---

50 Ibid., 220.

51 Marcia Langton, "Culture Wars". in *Blacklines: Contemporary Critical Writing by Indigenous Australians*, ed. Michele Grossman (Melbourne: Melbourne University Press, 2003), 81.

52 Aaron Corn, pers. comm., 2013.

53 For Frances Morphy and Howard Morphy's consideration of *relative autonomy*, see "Anthropological Theory", 176.

54 Howard Morphy, "Now You Understand: An Analysis of the Way Yolngu Have Used Sacred Knowledge to Maintain Their Autonomy", in *Aborigines, Land and Landrights*, ed. N. Peterson and M. Langton (Canberra: Australian Institute of Aboriginal Studies, 1983), 110–11. See also Berndt, "An Adjustment Movement", 64.

law that is ongoing and relevant. Yolŋu hoped that recognition and an equal meeting of representative legal figures from both cultures, Balanda and Yolŋu, "might end up in some form of a legal treaty or a statutory harmonisation of both legal systems." This act preceded decades of struggles for land rights and high-profile legal clashes between mining companies and Yolŋu.[55]

Decades later, Rirratjiŋu artist Banduk Marika, discusses the significance of widening performance contexts—into presentations, performances, exhibitions and publications—for the continuation of Yolŋu culture. She refers to a national art exhibition, *Yalangbara: Art of the Djaŋ'kawu*, which has travelled around the country since 2010.[56] Yalangbara is one of the most important sites for Yolŋu of the Dhuwa moiety. It is the place where the Djang'kawu *waŋarr* (ancestral beings), a brother and his two sisters, landed at the coast after their voyage from the spirit island Burralku. Marika outlines her motivations for this exhibition:

> This is our country, our inheritance, and our responsibility, and we must look after it. This is our law and our strength. You could say that by showing the art, we're entering into our parliament—the Rirratjingu people's parliament. We are giving public access to information that has been forbidden for thousands of years because it's time to show the public that Yalangbara is important … And so we want to tell their stories properly now and hopefully through this exhibition Yalangbara will get the protection and the recognition that it deserves.[57]

The *Saltwater National Tour* (1999–2001) was an earlier exhibition by Yolŋu *bäpurru* from Blue Mud Bay that sought to educate outsiders through art. This exhibition was formed in direct response to the desecration of sacred sites by illegal fishermen in 1996—just one such invasion in a long history of destructive ignorance. Wäka Munuŋgurr and Djambawa Marrawili, a community leader at Bäniyala, led local artists to produce close to one hundred bark paintings, expressing the significance and ownership of tracts of sea, coast, waterways, and intertidal zones.

The exhibition revealed "the sacred designs (*miny'tji*) of the area in order to educate strangers about the law that Yolŋu live by."[58] A catalogue containing detailed narratives documenting the ancestral law and sacred sites of different *bäpurru* of the area was also published. This included knowledge concerning an important *riŋgitj* (embassy) site for the Wägilak, Luṯunba (see Chapter Four). All of the painted designs can also be found in *manikay* repertoires.

---

55 Gondarra, "Assent Law", 26. See also Howard Morphy, "Art and Politics: The Bark Petition and the Barunga Statement," in *The Oxford Companion to Aboriginal Art and Culture*, ed. Sylvia Kleinert and Margo Neale (Melbourne: Oxford University Press, 2000), 100–103.

56 West, Margie, ed., *Yalangbara: Art of the Djang'kawu* (Darwin: Charles Darwin University Press, 2008).

57 Banduk Marika, "The Story behind the Project".

58 Buku-Larrnggay Mulka Centre, *Saltwater*, 6.

The *Saltwater* exhibition was a performative response to a political issue—sitting down and painting ancestral narratives for completely new contexts.

Howard Morphy considers this characteristic interdependence of Yolŋu art and politics: "Yolngu do not neatly separate the functional purposes of rituals from the performative—art from political action … Yolngu use ceremonial performance as a means of setting the agenda or conveying an important message."[59] By asserting *maḏayin* (ancestral law) in new contexts, Yolŋu retain control of their expressions. This demands political and artistic creativity, matched by a desire to retain traditional identities and meanings.

For the past half-century, political-cultural assertions made by Yolŋu have sought a respectful hearing from an Australian polity and public who, despite much good will, seem to overlook the significance of such deputations. Within this context, it is significant that in 2005, the AAO came to Ngukurr with open ears and minds, wishing to collaborate with Wägilak musicians. Their openness to being led into something new allowed Wägilak autonomy and leadership within the collaboration.

The AAO began the process of learning about Wägilak culture by joining in a *buŋgul* (dance), hearing the songs and connecting rhythmic forms with the narrative subjects. This was carried out with a respectful seriousness, characteristic of a liberal conscience, which happened to coincide with a Yolŋu oriented frame of learning by imitation and participation—"by way of slow osmosis and orchestrated dissemination of knowledge".[60]

Under the quiet guidance of Barabara, Benjamin Wilfred taught the actions of the Wägilak dances to the AAO. His expressed desire, to "keep culture strong" by performing with the AAO, resonated with the orchestra's desire to create a new and respectful collaboration, while enriching their own perspectives on music and culture. Benjamin occasionally chastised those who forgot any element of these dances too readily; without the correct sequence of songs, the collaboration could not claim legitimacy as a performance of *manikay*.

During that trip to Ngukurr, Barabara gave his formal permission for the AAO to continue working with Wägilak musicians, approval that was consummated by an outdoor ceremonial performance in which Barabara participated. The AAO musicians had not only been accepted into a new aesthetic world, but one of inherent responsibilities to kin, country, and ceremonial practice. More than capable of withdrawing his support, Barabara desired engagement that would carry Wägilak ceremonial practices to new audiences; he wanted to promote mutual understanding and a better future for all. Ngukurr elder Kevin Numamuḏiḏi Rogers reflects:

---

59 Morphy, *Becoming Art*, 79.
60 Andrew Blake, quoted in Buku-Larrnggay Mulka Centre, Saltwater, 8.

The Wägilak were chosen because they had taught the performances [*manikay* and *buŋgul*] and because of their openness and willingness to go and venture into setting up a new kind of real Australian music. This is not talking bull, if you know what I mean. This is the kind of music we've been looking for and by getting together, understanding each other, respecting each other, it's bringing music and people together—understanding each other.[61]

The ongoing legacy of concerts, workshops, masterclasses, and annual lecture-demonstrations has carried Barabara's desire to educate the wider Australian public about Wägilak ceremony. In a way, this book too has come out of that first meeting in Ngukurr. Of course, as in any human endeavour, there is a degree of posturing that goes alongside public exposure. Benjamin Wilfred often praises *CRB*, which has provided him with a platform to continue to assert a sense of authority derived from ceremonial tradition:

And I love my job when I do it, sharing my knowledge in community and in the city. That's why I do it. I have never let my grandpa down. So I told Paul and the orchestra, I will just go for it. No matter where I tour with the orchestra, I will share my culture and talk—no matter where I go. We toured last year from Darwin, right up to Broome. Then flew over to Perth, played in the Perth Concert Hall with my grandpa's painting [projected on-stage]. We talked about him and his stories; what he did … Whenever I sing, Grandpa is there; he always follows on my back.[62]

Today, the AAO's awareness of the Yolŋu world deepens as they become more familiar with the significance of Wägilak narrative and musical forms. The Yolŋu hermeneutic of narrative expansion makes collaborations such as *CRB* possible, as core meanings are retained through the interpolation of new performances and relationships. This is something that is necessarily involved, as outsiders step into performance with an openness to "be known" by the songs. Daniel Wilfred reflects on the process of collaboration during the Australian Art Orchestra's *Creative Music Intensive* (a two-week long residency in Tasmania): "I share the song with them. But the song doesn't change, it just travels further. Listen carefully to the song. If you step back then the song won't know you [Roper Kriol: *sabi yu*] … You have to go straight ahead like that *raki*. If you go forward, the song will know you."[63] While the aesthetic forms of *manikay* have been engaged with nuance and complexity by the AAO (Chapters Six and

---

61 Kevin Numamudidi Rogers, forum discussion on *CRB*, University of Melbourne, 16 April 2009.

62 Benjamin Wilfred, "Digital Audio Technologies".

63 Daniel Wilfred, in *Djuwalpada* (film), Ngukurr Story Project, directed by Daniel Wilfred and Nicola Bell, (Ngukurr, NT: Ngukurr Arts Aboriginal Corporation and Ngukurr Language Centre, 2019).

Eight), the time, distances and costs involved in travelling between Melbourne and Ngukurr have prevented frequent visits by the AAO, and therefore exposure to *manikay* within its highly relational context amid everyday life. The development of *CRB* as a collaboration has largely occurred within formal settings: in time-constrained rehearsals, recording studios, and concerts at high-profile venues. Interestingly, it has been during informal settings and travel that the layering of new meanings into Wägilak *manikay* has occurred most readily. When camping on tour near One Arm Point in Western Australia, for example, Daniel composed a new version of "Wäkwak" (Black Crow), incorporating the instruments of the AAO into his rendering of the traditional *manikay* subject (see Chapter Five).

In accepting the need to learn about *manikay* with appropriate deference to the unknown, the AAO participate in the continual expansion of ancestral narratives into new iterations and relationships. This process is at the heart of sustaining culture in the Yolŋu world. *Manikay* is reinvigorated as it is carried into new times and places, "no matter where". The ancestral past resounds through the present and the world is brought to life through *manikay*.

Floodwaters

Gularri is the name given to bodies of Yirritja moiety floodwaters.[64] *Gularri* illustrates our connection with the past as it intimately configures our lives, giving us an orientation within present praxis. David Wilfred explains that, through *gularri*, Yolŋu are connected to everything "from old times".[65]

Gularri (floodwaters) are the lifegiving freshwaters that fill rivers, tributaries, and billabongs during the wet season, quenching the dry country. Like the *wata* (wind), these waters spread across the land, connecting different people, languages, and homelands together. Mandawuy Yunupingu, a Gumatj elder and celebrated frontman of the band Yothu Yindi, explains *gularri* as "one way of imagining how we can bring our pasts into our futures".[66] Over time and great distance, this ever-moving flow of water courses from flood to stream, and from river to ocean.

This narrative is a fitting illustration of tradition as effective history: the present exists within the flow of the past, a moment in a stream, supported by the water that surrounds it. Daniel Wilfred elaborates, "*Manikay* was a long time ago and it's still here today: what those elders hand over still going to be there for the young people."[67] *Manikay* flows from the past, into the present and

---

64 Frances Morphy, in discussion with the author, 2013.
65 David Wilfred, in discussion with the author, 2012.
66 Mandawuy Yunupingu, "Vision for the North: Bringing Our Pasts into Our Futures" (keynote address, Charles Darwin University, 21 May 2013).
67 Daniel Wilfred, interview with the author, Ngukurr, 13 July 2011.

future; what is sung today is unique, yet it is supported by everything that has gone before. Performance is both creative and constituted. In a similar way, Yunupingu continues:

> *Gularri* is about bringing our pasts into futures according to certain principles. One of these principles is the unity in diversity ... There are many Yolngu clans with many different lands. We are connected and also made separate by our languages and our *gurruṯu*—our kinship with people and places. There are many Aboriginal peoples with their own unique places. We as Yolŋu are separate from them, because we are connected to them. And we keep making new connections and new separations ... *Gularri* shows us that connectedness in separation is not contradictory. But to understand this we need to get a correct view of history.[68]

For Wägilak elder Andy Peters, the *ŋaḻabuluŋu rom* (following law) is similar to the concept of *gularri*. *Ŋaḻabuluŋu rom* is following the patterns of ancestral precedence—tradition—through ceremony, a life-giving connection that extends through the generations. *Ŋaḻabuluŋu rom* gives a person orientation and responsibilities in the world, locating them within patterns of land, society, kin, and history. An individual is dependent on these identities that constitute their being, carried and animated by the flow of the past.

Muḻkurr, the "flowing water", is a concept that can "truly express the uniqueness of our place and time".[69] Frances and Howard Morphy have written on the multiple meanings of *muḻkurr*. *Muḻkurr* "is the top part of a person's head in a general sense, including the temples".[70] Other compound words that use *muḻkurr* refer to states of mind, such as *muḻkurr-gulku* (head-many; indecisive). For Yolŋu, mind is located in the fluid just below the frontal region of the skull and this *water* is associated with the source of a "knowledge and the place to which the spirit returns".[71] This fluid is equivalent to the *gapu mangutji* (sacred waterholes) at the focal centre of Ŋärra' (secret-sacred law) ceremonies and a group's *djalkiri* place (foundational site of ancestral knowledge).[72] In the wet season, these sacred waterholes are flooded, "spreading ancestral *mind* (knowledge) over the land to replenish it."[73]

Through the performance of ceremony, ancestral knowledge is spread through the generations. *Manikay* carries ancestral creativity into the present;

---

68 Yunupingu, "Vision for the North".
69 Yunupingu, "Vision for the North".
70 Frances Morphy and Howard Morphy, "'We Think through Our 'Marwat' (Paintbrush)': Conceptualising Mind Cross-Culturally" (research paper, Australian National University, Canberra, 29 May 2013).
71 Ibid.
72 Ibid.
73 Frances Morphy, pers. comm., 2013.

manikay is living, effective history. Just like the natural word, it "is many pasts brought into many futures". With creative minds, Yolŋu carry the ancestral text into new contexts, filling the present with the lifegiving floodwaters of the past.

4

NARRATIVE CONSTELLATIONS

The abundance of the natural world is an indelible manuscript of ancestral creation, a rich constellation of narratives interwoven in song. Living, walking, thinking, laughing, and having children in this world, *yolŋu* (people) are an inseparable part of the stories they sing, their lives and interactions caught up in the world as an ancestral story.

Every performance of *manikay* begins with tangible images and events experienced in daily life, movements of environment and society. These images—such as the wind, the plover, and the spear—are animated by deeper, existential concerns. On stage in Melbourne or in the dust of Ngukurr, *manikay* draws singers and musicians together in community, pulling them through life and enfolding them within the movements of the ancestors. "I can feel it on my mind. I can feel the old people. The *raki* is still there, pulling me."[1] *Manikay* is a complex network of living stories and events, and through this abundance the presence of Djuwalpada emerges. Layered meanings and complex nodes of connection in song can be traced like a constellation in the night sky, one songline "from the top to the bottom."[2]

Any understandings of *manikay* narrative are always emerging amid expanding layers of allusion—in the Yolŋu hermeneutic there are always further complexities (Chapter Three). Mixing my own words with the those of my Wägilak teachers, this chapter offers a basic narration of just some of this rich story. The criss-crossing references of image and narrative come out of the story of Djuwalpada, a story belonging to Wägilak from Ṉilipidji. In many

---

1 Daniel Wilfred, in *Djuwalpada* (film), directed by Daniel Wilfred and Nicola Bell.
2 Ibid.

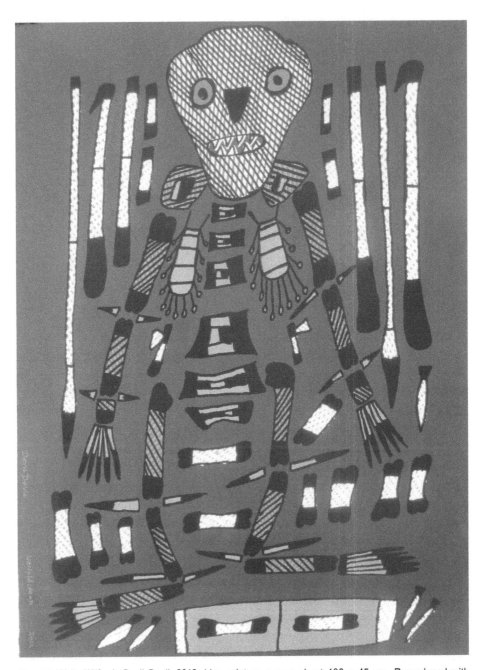

Fig. 4.1. Wally Wilfred, *Devil Devil*, 2012. Lino print on paper, about 100 x 45 cm. Reproduced with permission.

ways, parts of the story of Djuwalpaḏa's journey also extend into the narratives of other *bäpurru* and homelands.

Sung and danced by many creative individuals, in many different times and places, Wägilak *manikay* shapes a world permeated by an abundant and lifegiving ancestral reality.

Wata—Purification

Djiŋala gurru yalagarayi Mawululayi
Gumurr-wuma wäkura dädutj-manayi
Gumurr yabalayi gumurr-wuma gumurr-gumirrila balayi

He's going up to Ŋilipidji
Pulled to the country by his chest
Walking back to his place

("Wata" Wind song text)

Walking with his spear, Djuwalpaḏa heard the wind rustling in the trees. He was frightened. The wind was much bigger and more powerful than he was. It was blowing from far out at sea. As it picked up, he thought he had better throw his spear, to find a home. There, at that place, he could go into the ground. "He always lives there. He got a hole there; *mokuy* (ancestral ghost) at Ŋilipidji."[3]

Mokuy (ancestral ghosts) like Djuwalpaḏa are central to the *manikay* narratives of many Yolŋu *bäpurru*: they give public law, ceremonial responsibility, and title to land—especially for inland areas of scrubby, eucalypt forest. Outside of the *ŋaraka-wäŋa* (bone-country) that is their home, *mokuy* are unruly and malignant—"cheeky" or evil. Not only will they make a "mess in the kitchen while you are asleep",[4] they might cut the fuel line on the boat when you are out at sea. "He'll bite you too."[5] Sometimes *mokuy* are dangerous; at other times, benign (fig. 4.1; see also fig. 1.1).

Like contemporary Wägilak painter Wally Wilfred, Barabara frequently painted this character. The name *Devil Devil*, given to many paintings of Djuwalpaḏa, not only reflects the influence of mission station English, but something of Djuwalpaḏa's disposition. Barabara vividly describes Djuwalpaḏa as a

fighting man with blades on knees and middle place on his arm. They can rip you open. Also, feet can kick you. He fights with blades on

---

3   Daniel Wilfred, "Digital Audio Technologies".
4   Justin Nunggarrgalug, in discussion with the author, Ngukurr, 2 September 2010.
5   Benjamin Wilfred, interview with the author, Melbourne, 19 March 2011.

elbows and knees—to kill whitefella or blackfella. The claw hands are same way used as weapons, they can tear away the ribs. And the teeth and the feet—they can cut. When he gets you by the ears you can't know anything.[6]

After death, *mokuy* embody the lingering presence of a person's ghost.[7] Caught in an ambiguous state between life and death, a purification ceremony is the only way to "finish it", "to send that *mokuy* away".[8] At Dhuwa moiety funerals in Ngukurr, Wägilak singers begin with the songs of Djuwalpada's journey to establish Ṉilipidji. Before they finish with the celebratory song "Birrkpirrk" (Plover) a few hours later, a ceremonial smoking is performed to the song "Wata" (Wind). In this song the *mokuy* is sent away. This sequence characterises all performances.

During funeral singing, the song "Wata" (Wind) begins sparsely. Led by the *biḻma* striking slowly, only a breeze is felt, the first tickling movements of a forceful hurricane (audio example 4a).[9] It gradually picks up in speed and intensity, conveyed in the rhythmic constructions (see Chapter Five; table 5.2). This is the same wind that blows the *wukuṉ* (clouds) forming out at sea beyond Luṯunba inland; it blows across the country and peoples connected to Luṯunba:

> DANIEL WILFRED: That wind there. See it blowing? Just the wind [pointing to breeze]—come up from nowhere. Cyclone.

> SAMUEL CURKPATRICK: And it starts blowing when someone passes away?

> DW: Yeah. Blows through all that country—*riŋgitj* [*bäpurru* alliance].[10]

Audio example 4a. "Wata" (Wind), beginning with the *slow* mode and then shifting into the *strong wind* mode. The YWG leading a funeral in Ngukurr, 18 August 2010.[11]

The song *wata* is carried on the singers' voices, by human breath which is like the wind. The *yiḏaki* (didjeridu) is played with the same breath, a wind which rushes through the *ḏupun* (hollow log coffin), the container for the bones—the prototype

---

6   Quoted in Bowdler, *Colour Country*, 62.

7   Morphy, *Ancestral Connections*, 280.

8   Benjamin Wilfred, "Digital Audio Technologies."

9   Cf. Corn and Gumbula's description of ancestral presence sensed in ecological movements. Corn and Gmbula, "Formal Flexibility," 124.

10 Daniel Wilfred, interview with the author, Ngukurr, 13 June 2011.

11 Toner names these modes as *bulnha* and *yindi* respectively. See Peter. G. Toner, "Form and Performance: The Relations of Melody, Poetics, and Rhythm in Dhalwangu *Manikay*", in *A Distinctive Voice in the Antipodes: Essays in Honour of Stephen A. Wild*, edited by Kirsty Gillespie, Sally Treloyn, and Done Niles (eds) (Canberra: Australian National University Press, 2017), 110–12.

of the *yiḏaki*. As the singers call the sacred *yäku* (names) of places on Djuwalpada's journey to Ŋilipidji, the dancers place green *many'tjarr* (leaves) on small campfires surrounding the *buŋgul* (dance) ground. These are the same leaves that Djuwalpaḏa swished back and forth as he danced, to keep away the flies.

> Wata buthun marayi
> Läplap mirriŋani
> Djulgarram buma
> Mokuy mali nhaŋgu
> Gangul gangul butthun marayi

> The wind is blowing
> The *mokuy* is walking with the wind
> He is dancing on the ground
> He is looking at the shadows
> The *mokuy* flies now

> ("Wata" Wind song text)

Billowing white smoke engulfs the yard of the deceased's house where the singers, dancers, and family have congregated. Flour tins full of smouldering leaves are taken through and under the house itself, as well as into the Toyota Landcruiser that carried the coffin. The body had already been buried earlier that day, and as the wind blows the smoke away, the *mokuy* is dismissed.

Likandhu-ŋupan—Connections

> Likandhu-ŋupan Djuwalpaḏa
> Djuwalpaḏa, Ŋirriyiŋirriyi, Dhawal-wal duy'yun

> Djuwalpaḏa, with elbows pointing
> Djuwalpaḏa, Ŋirriyiŋirriyi, walking across the country

> ("Djuwalpaḏa" song text)

As Djuwalpaḏa was searching for honey, his elbows were bent, raised to eye level, pointing where his eyes searched. Dancers mimic this action in the songs of Djuwalpaḏa. The phrase *likandhu-ŋupan* (with elbow pointing) is a prominent reference in the text for these songs, situated at the beginning of most *gumurr* (chest) sections—the large structural segment of *manikay* song items defined between rhythmic cadences (in the musical sense of cadence as a structural "punctuation"). Frequently, this is also the text sung at the end of each *l̲iya-waŋa* (coda) (see Chapter Five).

More widely, *l̲ikan* is a term best understood as *connection*, just like the elbow joint. It also refers to the junction between branch and trunk, the crescent shape of the moon or bay, or the bend in a river.[12] As opposed to the embedded, secret *ŋaraka* (bones) of a *bäpurru*, *l̲ikan* express extended relationships between family groups. Yol̲ŋu also speak of ancestral descent as branching off, different groups connected to a common *waŋarr* (ancestral being), "quite literally like the branches or *l̲ikan* (elbows) of a tree or a river system".[13]

In song, *l̲ikan yäku* (elbow names)—names that connect—are invoked over *bil̲ma* (clapstick) striking rapidly and energetically. Multivalent *l̲ikan yäku* are shared names that invoke public connections between different but related *bäpurru*, and the co-identification of people, places, and ancestral figures. In Wägilak funeral ceremonies, *l̲ikan yäku* are often intoned rhythmically over the top striking *bil̲ma* when the body of the deceased is moved into the coffin or from the morgue. The caller of these names is known as the *djirrikay*.

When being photographed on stage or for publicity during *CRB* tours, the YWG assert their connection to ancestral law and the country at Ŋilipidji by pointing their elbows. The elbow-pointing dance and songs connect Wägilak directly to the *mokuy* Djuwalpada, who journeys to establish this homeland and law. Further, by invoking sacred names in song, a singer demonstrates their ongoing rights of ownership over particular country—authority given by the bestowal of these sacred *yäku* (names) and *manikay* repertoires to that individual.

Birrkpirrk and D̲ud̲ut̲ud̲u—A Duet

As he was looking for a home, Djuwalpada heard the voice of the *birrkpirrk* (plover), carried on the wind and crying, "Yawilila, yawilila". Someone else heard the *birrkpirrk* too. The *d̲ud̲ut̲ud̲u* (night owl) heard its song. He was sitting in his country, not that far away, another Wägilak homeland that Djuwalpada founded—but that is another story.[14]

D̲ud̲ut̲ud̲u's country is north of Ŋilipidji at a place called Wul̲ku—where the rain starts falling. You remember the clouds that the wind blew inland? Well they fell down as rain at Wul̲ku. And there, that is where the *d̲ud̲ut̲ud̲u* heard

---

12 Corn, "Ancestral, Corporeal, Corporate", 2.

13 Ibid., 11. See also Ian Keen, "Metaphor and the Metalanguage: Groups in Northeast Arnhem Land", *American Ethnologist* 22, no. 3 (1995): 511.

14 The *manikay* of Andy Peters, which precedes the sequences relating to Ŋilipidji, tells of Djuwalpada's search for his deceased "mate—dead body, bones hanging in that tree, hang up in that table [platform]", after he sets out from Butjulubayi. "And he is going to cry when he sees [those bones]. For smoking ceremony, to open that house. Maybe he's going to put it in that hollow log, the *larrakitj* [hollow log coffin]. Paint him up." Andy Peters, interview with the author, Ngukurr, 12 July 2011.

the *birrkpirrk* crying. Frightened by the wind, the *birrkpirrk* flew away from Djuwalpada. And he met the *dudutudu*, and they started to sing together.

Today, the Wägilak of Ṉilipidji and the Wägilak of Wuḻku sing a duet together. Giving their individual voices into song, the *birrkpirrk* and *dudutudu* collaborate in a a close relationship of reciprocal responsibility.

The *birrkpirrk* and *dudutudu* represent two distinct patrigroups within the Wägilak, which own different homelands and ceremonial repertoires. This connection is formalised and remembered in song. Peters is one custodian of the country and songs of Wuḻku and stands in the relationship of *märi* (mother's mother's brother) to Benjamin and Daniel Wilfred, the closest type of relation in Yolŋu *gurruṯu* (kinship) outside of direct agnatic descent. Reciprocally, Benjamin and Daniel are Andy Peter's *gutharra*, his (sister's) daughter's children.[15] The song "Birrkpirrk/Dudutudu" connects two different branches of *manikay* extending from the same trunk.

The "Birrkpirrk/Dudutudu" duet (audio example 4b) is based on a *biḻma* (clapstick) mode that is shared by Wägilak *bäpurru* from the homelands of Ṉilipidji and Wuḻku: the rhythmic mode for "Birrkpirrk" singing is basically the same as the mode used by Andy Peters for "Dudutudu". The only difference lies in the cadence (terminal punctuation) of each (see table 4.1).

"Birrkpirrk/Dudutudu" is structured in two large sections or *gumurr* (chests). The first repeated section is the song "Birrkpirrk", bound by its particular rhythmic cadence; the second section is the song "Dudutudu". Underpinned by a common groove, these birds find cohesion in rhythmic form. In song, these two birds meet—separate but together, their distinct voices combine (audio example 4b).

> ANDY PETERS: This one, that *birrkpirrk* and *dudutudu*, owl, night owl. Those two have to face together, and those two have to play together.

> DAVID WILFRED: Dance together. This is a double one [with two *gumurr* "chests"]. Different—it changes. *Dudutudu*, change, *Birrkpirrk*. You have to listen.

(Discussion on audio example 4b)

Audio example 4b. "Birrkpirrk/Dudutudu" (Plover/Owl) duet. Andy Peters and David Wilfred (*yiḏaki*). Ngukurr, 12 July 2011.

---

15 Frances Morphy suggest that this distinction, between what might be termed the upper and lower Wägilak—different *bäpurru*—most likely came about as the clan grew and natural fission occurred along the *märi-gutharra* line (pers. comm., 2013).

Table 4.1. *Biḻma* (clapstick) modes and cadence patters for "Birrkpirrk/Ḏuḏuṯuḏu" (Plover/Owl) (audio example 4b).

Time code	Section of song (Ghost)	*Biḻma* mode (around 66 beats/minute)	Cadence pattern
00:00	Birrkpirrk from Ŋilipidji	*(clapstick notation)*	*(cadence notation)*
00:54	Ḏuḏuṯuḏu from Wuḻku	*(clapstick notation)*	*(cadence notation)*
01:16	Birrkpirrk from Ŋilipidji	*(clapstick notation)*	*(cadence notation)*

The ceremonial ground where the *birrkpirrk* and *ḏuḏuṯuḏu* met a long time ago is a site where Wägilak from different homelands today might meet on common ground. Although living in Ngukurr, Numbulwar, Donydji and other towns around Arnhem Land, the continuation of song sustains the pattern of this relationship between different Wägilak *bäpurru* (father's groups). The law of respectful collaboration—*riŋgitj* (embassy; alliance)—exists between these groups. "Birrkpirrk/Ḏuḏuṯuḏu" teaches ongoing cooperation.

The term *riŋgitj* designates the satellite camps and preparation grounds of different *bäpurru* around the periphery of a Ŋärra' ceremonial ground. This ground is a central point where different groups come together for important ceremonial and political activity. In seeking to better communicate Yolŋu social and political structures, *riŋgitj* has been translated as "embassy" by Yolŋu people and Ŋärra' as "parliament", reflecting a desire to interpret their cultural, legal and ceremonial practices in ways that assert equivalences with the social and political structures in Australia.[16] The Yolŋu epistemology of expanding reference and connection—like branches on a tree—permits such translation.

Benjamin Wilfred explains how the law of *riŋgitj* expressed in "Birrkpirrk/Ḏuḏuṯuḏu" extends beyond the Wägilak. *Riŋgitj* links together greater narratives of clouds, wind, and rain that codify productive international cooperation. There are common clapstick modes that are always shared between *bäpurru* with *riŋgitj* connection:

BENJAMIN WILFRED: When *ḏuḏuṯuḏu*, night owl, and plover bird [*birrkpirrk*] met one another, from there they found a song.

SAMUEL CURKPATRICK: Yeah, that's where Ŋilipidji meets Wuḻku?

16　For example, by Banduk Marika, "The Story Behind the Project", n.p.

BW: Yeah, that's where Wägilak meet Wuḻku mob. From there they sung rain, from there. Right up to my place [Ŋilipidji]. All the way down [across the country]. From there, from Wuḻku it started, that rain. That's where Andy [Peter's] starts from, where that night owl and plover bird met together.

SC: Before Andy's songs, where does that *wukuṉ* [cloud] come from? From Blue Mud Bay?

BW: Yeah, travels through there. Come up, right to top. All the way from the coast, right up to the fresh water; all the way down … Nunydjirrpi and Maŋgurra mob, and Djambarrpuyŋu mob: we all meet together then when the two birds meet. All the totems now, from those two animals—that song spread from there. And all the elders and old people just keep travelling and sing along from those two animals. From there, all the songs spread out, from each animal's totem. From each clan.[17]

Guku—Direction

Lirrawar' banburr mayipa
Guyu-guyu, guyu-guyu, ahhhh, ohhhh
Rawarrararay, bulunyirri dalgumirri

The toothed bee is flying, starting to make a hive
Buzzing, buzzing, ahhhh, ohhhh [sound of the wind]
Like the wind, it flies a long way to make another home

("Guku" Honey song text)

The bee Lirrawar' enters the beehive through its entrance tunnel known as *dhapi*, a term which also names the important rite of male circumcision. This ceremony begins with the song "Dhaŋarra" (White flower), from which the bee collects pollen: "That flower for Stringybark tree, those white flowers make the honey too. The bee goes to eat them flowers and then he flies. He goes to make that sugarbag [honey], makes that nest. Makes one there, makes one there, camp [home] for the sugarbag. Then he flies back, feeds more. Then he makes the song [*manikay*]" (audio example 4c).[18]

---

17 Benjamin Wilfred, interview with the author, Ngukurr, 19 July 2011.
18 Benjamin Wilfred, interview with the author, Melbourne, 19 March 2011.

Audio example 4c. "Guku" (Honey). The YWG singing at a funeral; Andy Peters sings the coda. Ngukurr, 18 August 2010.

Benjamin Wilfred continues to explain how the bee also moves across *bäpurru* and language boundaries, joining groups together for the business of initiation into *maḏayin* law: "This sugarbag [bee] flew from the other place. He hung around there [Ŋilipidji]. Sometimes he goes to Yirritja country. There is a different Yirritja honey-fly too. Dhuwa and Yirritja got sugarbag; for men's business, men's ceremony."[19]

The *guku* (honey) inside the beehive is sweet sustenance, good law for living: "Honey (*guku*) and [the bee's] hive teach us how to live … A bees' hive is a symbol of excellence that can be achieved both in individual and community life."[20] In the Wägilak narrative, Djuwalpaḏa finds the *guku* and carries it with him in his dillybag.

For the Wägilak, the bee Lirrawar' begins its journey at Ŋilipidji and finishes at Raymangirr in Arnhem Bay, where the Marraŋu have their traditional homeland. The bee's flight through various tracts of country connects Dhuwa moiety *bäpurru* in relationships above the immediate family level: the bee brings these *bäpurru* together within a greater polity established through initiation and circumcision. The song text "*gaŋga-mäwulmirr*" is a *ḏikan yäku* (elbow name) that identifies these relationships, a shared Dhuwa-moiety name for honey sung throughout the Wägilak Djuwalpaḏa song subject.[21]

At funerals in Ngukurr, a length of *raki* (string) or rope is tied around the perimeter of the house of the deceased. The family remain outside of this until the *wata* (wind) purification is complete. This string represents the journey of the bee. Cloth tassels are tied along its length, interspersed by around one metre intervals. Corresponding to the flight of the bee, these are the different places and stages of life through which a person travels.[22] Another *raki* made from the hair of deceased relatives is also placed in the house until the smoking ceremony is complete. Within that *bäpurru*, the ceremonial leader for *manikay* is responsible cares for this hair-string and keeps it safe.

When the house is smoked, the perimeter string is taken down. This is the end of one journey; the bee has reached its destination in the hive. The women dance around, elbows pointed, buzzing around with bee-like wings. After the song "Birrkpirrk" (Plover) has been sung, the ceremony is finished; the *birrimbirr* (soul) has been pulled back into the deep, profound waters, sweet like honey.[23]

---

19 Ibid.
20 Corn, "Dreamtime Wisdom", 106.
21 Ibid. appendix 3.77.
22 Magowan, "It Is God Who Speaks", 304. Williams, *The Yolngu and Their Land*, 32.
23 Cf. Magowan, "It Is God Who Speaks", 305.

Raki—Baskets and Bags

> Malka dil'yun marrayi bulunyirri
> Rrr, rrr, rakirri; Rrr, rrr, gawudju

> That string bag—now we are painting up
> Rolling that string; rolling and making it longer

> ("Malka" String bag song text)

Around Djuwalpada's neck hung a *galpan* (dillybag), a type of woven basket on a long string; on his shoulders hung woven *Malka* (string bags) (see figs. 1.4, 4.1). These were full of his possession, as well as secret and sacred *ranga* (objects) representing the law.

Djuwalpada made string himself. When he was hungry, he made a fishing line to catch some fish. He wove his string bags too. First, he found the right *djirrpal* (bark fibres) from the *balgurr* (Kurrajong tree). The choreography of "Malka" (audio example 4d) depicts Djuwalpada swishing the bark in the air to dry and pounding it to separate the fibrous strands. The fibres are then rolled together, using an open palm on the dancer's thighs, intertwining each individual strand into the whole. The string is extended, becoming longer. The danced actions of rolling string accompany the song.

Audio example 4d. "Malka" (string bag), *dancing* mode. Jim Wilfred leading the YWG in a funeral in Ngukurr, 18 August 2010.

Ceremony has a texture just like string. Different forms like dance and design are like the fibrous strands of string, woven together, twisting into a unified expression. Each singing voice is also like one strand that contributes to the complex, interwoven whole. Every performance of *manikay* entwines into an ongoing tradition that began when Djuwalpada started to roll his string (see Chapter Seven).

Further, *manikay* repertoires have been passed on down the Wägilak *yarrata* (string line) of agnatic descent, father to son, for generations. In *mamarru* exchange ceremonies, this is represented by a string held over the head of a procession. This string is suspended at each end by the *djungayi* (ceremonial manager), connecting all of the family underneath. Individuals take on the responsibility of sustaining their *bäpurru*'s (father's group's) distinct narrative elements within the greater ceremonial whole, a Yolnu-wide expression of *madayin* (sacred law). New generations join in the action of rolling the *raki*, like Benjamin Wilfred's children:

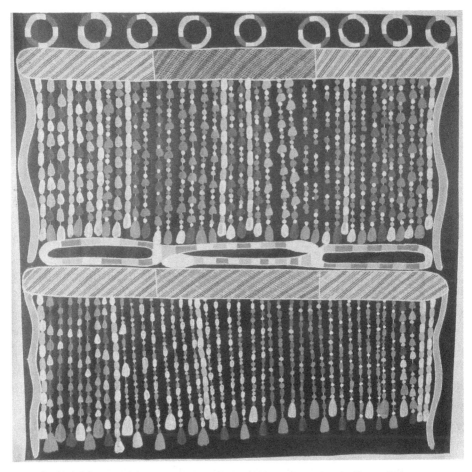

Fig. 4.2. Wally Wilfred, *Dancing Gear*, 2012. About 120 x 120 cm. Reproduced with permission.

My little boy, he's going to be a didj man, like me. And he's a dancer. Even Daniel's sons, they all dance, and they respect the culture. So we are giving them culture, when they are young. And I know that my kids [will] just keep rolling it, and they want more knowledge from me.[24]

By his acts of stalking prey and spear throwing, Djuwalpa<u>d</u>a is associated with traditionally male characteristics. "Yet men explain that the profoundest and most sacred meanings of many of the spirit-beings are female or else have an important characteristic (or property or activity) that is associated with women."[25] In Wägilak *manikay*, Djuwalpa<u>d</u>a's femininity is revealed in rolling the string and carrying the *Malka* (string bag), typically women's activities in Yolŋu tradition.

24 Benjamin Wilfred, interview with Daniel Browning, "Crossing Boundaries".
25 Williams, *The Yolngu and their Land*, 50. Berndt and Berndt contrast the feminine *mokuy*, associated with flesh and blood, with the masculine *birrimbirr*, which is associated with bone and semen. Roland M. Berndt and Catherine H. Berndt, *The World of the First Australians: Aboriginal Traditional Life Past and Present* (Canberra: Aboriginal Studies Press, 1988), 213.

In *CRB*, the YWG often wear *balku*, belts made from red, yellow, and black wool, hanging down to their knees in long tassels; sometimes they wear simple armbands around their biceps, known as *ŋanbak* (fig. 4.2). Likewise, the Djaŋ'kawu Sisters—important Dhuwa moiety *waŋarr* (creative beings)—were adorned with strings decorated with bright feathers. These sisters performed the first Ŋärra' ceremony, connecting Dhuwa moiety *bäpurru* together. As the Djaŋ'kawu Sisters travelled around the land, plunging their digging sticks into the ground at many different locations, they formed the different Dhuwa language groups, named places, plants, and animals, and gave birth to the inhabitants of these places.[26]

The woven *galpan* (dillybag) hung around Djuwalpada's neck also has feminine characteristics associated with the Djaŋ'kawu Sisters. The Sisters carried their *raŋga* (sacred objects) in a woven mat rolled up like a cone—the same shape as the *galpan*. This *ŋanymarra* (woven mat) was a container of life, a womb. The *raŋga* inside were taken out and plunged into the ground at certain places, creating the wells from which conception spirits emerge.

Just as the foundational *raŋga* (sacred objects) are hidden in the ground of a group's *ŋaraka-wäŋa* (bone-country), Djuwalpada's dillybag carries secret-sacred aspects of law. In Wägilak *manikay*, the dance of the *watu* (dog) mimics the covering over of the Wägilak *raŋga*: at the close of the smoking ceremony, the *watu* (dog) scuffs over the fire, putting it out but also burying the *raŋga* in the ground. Knowledge of these *raŋga* are protected by the most senior elders, even as they are carried through public songs like "Galpan" and "Malka".

Luṯunba—Deep Waters

Yawilila yawilila
Moyŋu moyŋu
Birrkpirrk ŋäthi Luṯunba
Wäŋa Gawirrinydji

Plover crying, plover crying,
Djuwalpada dancing, Djuwalpada dancing
Plover crying for Luṯunba
[And] the country Gawirrinydji

("Birrkpirrk" Plover song text)[27]

---

26 Benjamin Wilfred's totem is the *bidjay* (goanna; sometimes *djanda*), a manifestation of the Djaŋ'kawu Sisters.

27 This translation was begun by Aaron Corn, 26 May 2010.

The plover, *birrkpirrk*, cries for a dead relative. In chorus, the Wägilak group also cry "*Yä wäwa, yä märi'mu*" ("Oh brother, oh fathers' father") and call out the name Luṯunba, where Dhuwa-moiety *birrimbirr* (souls) of the dead return to the deep, sacred water. As the wind picks up "that spirit flies; it's going home now".[28]

The multiple *bäpurru* who share close ceremonial relationships with the Wägilak are all connected to Luṯunba through their songs, a sacred site of profound significance for many Yolṉu groups. Near Luṯunba, there is a Wägilak *riŋgitj* (embassy; alliance) site in proximity to a secret and restricted Ŋärra' ceremonial ground. Many days' walk from Ṉilipidji, this site is looked after by one of the Wägilak's *djuŋgayi* (manager), in this instance the Maḏarrpa.[29]

Luṯunba is the sacred name given to the northern side of the Baygurrtji River mouth and the saltwater beyond.[30] This river enters the Gulf of Carpentaria in the northern waters of Blue Mud Bay at a cove known as Fowler's Bay. At Luṯunba there are multiple *riŋgitj* (embassy; alliance) sites, common in highly significant meeting places and at the location of restricted ceremonial grounds. The Dhuwa moiety *bäpurru* Gupa-Djapu[31] and Marrakulu also have rights and responsibilities to similar *riŋgitj* sites near Luṯunba, within the boundaries of the Dhuḏi-Djapu estate.

For the Dhuḏi-Djapu, the waters at Luṯunba are protected by Mäṉa, an ancestral saltwater shark and her small children, some growing inside her *djukurr* (liver) and some already born.[32] Djutjadjutja Munuŋgurr, a Gupa-Djapu man, cautions, "Mäṉa hunts around here then goes into his *wäŋa* [home]. *Martaŋa* (boats) do not go too close to here—it's *yindi bathala* (too big). If the shark takes your hook you must cut the line or a bad accident will result by you being there."[33] Sacred locations are protected by potential dangers for those coming too near.

Wägilak name this ancestral shark Buḻ'manydji—*mäṉa* is a generic Yolṉu-matha term for any man-eating shark.[34] Benjamin Wilfred tells of Buḻ'manydji swimming inland and forming Wuṉungirrna, the Walker River.[35] On the upper reaches of this significant waterway, the Wägilak *ŋaraka-wäŋa* (bone-country)

---

28 Daniel Wilfred, comment during recording session for *CRB*, Melbourne, 19 March 2011.

29 Andy Peters, interview with the author, Ngukurr, 12 July 2011.

30 Referred to on maps as the Baykultji River [alt. Baygurrtji; Baiguridji]. "Baykultji" is actually the name of one location on this river, which belongs to the inland Maḏarrpa (Frances Morphy pers. comm., 2013). See also Buku-Larrnggay Mulka, *Saltwater*, 29.

31 Gupa-Djapu was Barabara's *märi* (mother's) group.

32 Mäṉa also protects areas belonging to the Gupa-Djapu and Djambarrpuyŋu.

33 Djutjadjutja Munuŋgurr, quoted in Buku-Larrnggay Mulka, *Saltwater*, 29.

34 Zorc, David R., *Yolṉu-Matha Dictionary* (Batchelor, NT: Batchelor College, 1996).

35 Walker River is named differently at various locations, beginning as Wunungirrna at Ṉilipidji, then Marrkalawa about 15 kilometres from the coast where it broadens and becomes mixed with salt water. The estuary and river mouth are known as Anhdhanaŋi.

is located. After forming this river and other freshwater steams and waterholes, Bul'manydji returned to the coast and "goes into the ground" at Luṯunba.[36]

Just like the *yarraṯa* (string line) which represents a person's ancestry, Bul'manydji is often depicted in paintings connected to her subterranean world by a sacred rope, *bundhamarr*. This pulls Bul'manydji and any returning *birrimbirr* (souls) back into Nambatj'ṇu or Rinydjalṇu, her place of origin in the deep, profound waters of Luṯunba.[37]

At Luṯunba, *birrimbirr* (souls) cross the boundary between the world of humans and the world of the *waŋarr* (ancestral beings). Luṯunba is the destination of these *birrimbirr* after they travel from a person's body and through their *ŋaraka-wäŋa* (bone-country). "Travel from Raymangirr, past Dhuḏi-Djapu, go through Luṯunba, all the way down."[38] *Birrimbirr* enter the brackish water, the medium of this crossing through which this soul is released from worldly embodiment and constitution back to its original conception state. The amorphous, liminal state of salt and fresh water mixing at Luṯunba—forming brackish water—is known as *dhä-weka-nha-mirri,* "giving taste to each other".[39]

In ceremonial performance, *birrimbirr* (souls) are pulled by their connection to the deep waters, represented by the *garram* or *balku* (rope; string waist band). A ground sculpture representing Luṯunba is sometimes made in the sand. "We put a stone in middle. Draw circle [around it] now. And everyone sits in that hole and make clear for self [purification]. Called Luṯunba now; later on, we do that smoking."[40]

Luṯunba is an ultimate meeting place where fresh and salt water meet, where human lives return into ancestral reality. This conduit is a destination of life, the essential orientation and meaning of the Wägilak's *wata* (wind) *manikay* series. It all "finishes at Luṯunba. We sing along from here [the beginning]; finish at Luṯunba."[41] At Luṯunba, all outside referents and significations in Wägilak narrative and ceremony come together. It is an orienting *telos*, the end of an existential journey: "This is the end of the story. Everything stops there."[42]

In song, the name Luṯunba is called out, directing the *birrimbirr* (soul) to the sacred waters. On the wind, the *birrkpirrk* flies, sent on its final journey into the sweet *guku* (honey).

---

36 Bul'manydji also formed a sandbar near to the coast at Luṯunba, where it basked in the shallow water. Other accounts expand this narrative, telling of the ancestral shark travelling to Groote Eylandt and Umbakumba. Buku-Larrnggay Mulka, *Saltwater*, 91–2.

37 Ibid., 29, 90.

38 Benjamin Wilfred, interview with the author, Melbourne, 19 March 2011.

39 Morphy and Morphy, "Tasting the Waters", 76.

40 Daniel Wilfred, interview with the author, Ngukurr, 13 July 2011.

41 Benjamin Wilfred, interview with the author, Ngukurr, 19 July 2011.

42 Daniel Wilfred, "Digital Audio Technologies".

5

SINGING BONES:
"THOSE CLAPPING STICKS HAVE A SONG"

Bilma (clapsticks) are living, singing *ŋaraka* (bones). This pair of hardwood clapsticks is fashioned by whittling away the outside skin and flesh of a hardwood tree to reveal its *ŋaraka* (bones). *Bilma* are individually identified as *bäpa/gäthu* (father/child) or *wäwa/yapa* (brother/sister), the larger stick being either the father or brother of the pair. Sometimes painted with a white clay, *bilma* are a simple technology that underpin vocal improvisation and complex *yidaki* patterns. They are so simple that *bilma* might be fashioned from whatever material is at hand, including sticks, coke bottles, or rubber thongs. Daniel Wilfred surmises: "Clapping sticks, they are the main ones. You have to follow them. Everything comes out of the clapping sticks: you think they are just sticks but they have a song."[1]

Bilma inspire action. Leaping into movement, dancers are carried by the persistent momentum of these sticks striking with an extraordinary resonance. Caught in the groove, the *yidaki* (didjeridu) player elaborates the basic rhythmic structure with complex syncopations that display virtuosity and dexterity. Illustrating Yolŋu notions of tradition, the *bilma* animate musical forms that have been carried through the generations: the *bilma* carry song by their pervasive groove, which opens out, draws in, and moves along.

Even in its poetic and abundant layering of image and meaning, *manikay* grasps at stability through the generational perpetuation of recurrent musical forms. This could be taken of an illustration of the Yolŋu concept of history: the

---

1   Daniel Wilfred, interview with the author, Melbourne, 6 March 2011.

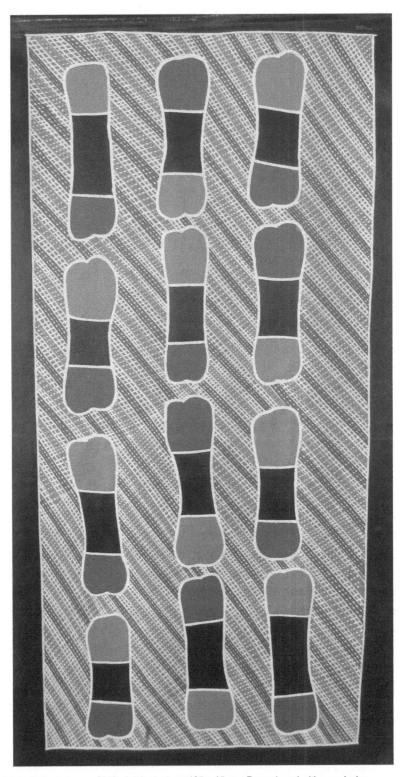

Fig. 5.1. Wally Wilfred, *Bones*, 2012. Original, about 125 x 45 cm. Reproduced with permission.

present extends from "pre-existing footprints (*djalkiri*, *luku*)" of the past.[2] The past is carried in the perpetuation of orthodox *ŋaraka* (bones), the structural components of a legitimate *manikay* performance, which are tied inseparably to important social and legal interests, to family groupings, land, and sea ownership, and hereditary rights and responsibilities (fig. 5.1). These *ŋaraka* (bones) also carry central tenets of the Wägilak narrative.

This hermeneutic is often expressed in phrases like "keeping culture strong" and "following your elders' tracks." Just as *yothu* (children) are connected, by virtue of their very existence, to their *bäpa* (father) and *ŋändi* (mother), so too does Wägilak *manikay* extend backwards as a musical form established in the ancestral past, "found" or first conceptualised, sung, and danced by Djuwalpada, whose tracks across the country are an inscription of the grooving *bilma*.

For Yolŋu, continued performance demonstrates "that things are as they have always been: the authority of their forbears is confirmed" through the "performance of that authority".[3] The creativity of improvisation and energy of performance that brings *manikay* to life reveals the continued efficacy and relevance of its structuring bones. Howard Morphy expresses this idea in relation to Yolŋu art:

> The ancestral form, however, is an idea that only exists through its replication, and the criterion by which the success of a replication is judged is that it is a recognizable token of its type: for example that it has the correct clan designs, that it is an effective encoder of ancestral meanings and that it conveys the power of the ancestral past through the aesthetic affect of its infill.[4]

Manikay is not an archaic body of irrelevant, primeval knowledge that is preserved as archive through performance, which is more than a curatorial process. In the realisation of musical forms, *manikay* draws performers into a way of being in the world, of belonging to a homeland and to kin, and following the tracks of their ancestors. *Manikay* draws people into an active, living ancestral law that sustains people and place. Brought to life by the present generation of Yolŋu, the bones of *manikay* sing.

Essential Bones

Pervasive Western concepts of tradition as mere custom or inherited pattern can ring hollow in the Yolŋu world. The term *tradition* insufficiently encapsulates the ceremonial corpus of *maḏayin* (the sacred system of social and religious law), of which *manikay* is a component, and *rom* (way of life; correct living).

---

2   Morphy and Morphy, "Discriminating Identities", 69.
3   Caruana and Lendon, *Painters of the Wagilag Sisters*, 26.
4   Morphy, *Becoming Art*, 153.

Manikay is a performed with a sense of responsibility toward generations past, present, and future.

Rather than tradition, Wägilak speak of ancestral precedent, manifest through *maḏayin* (ancestral law) and *rom* (proper living) and through which all life moves and functions. Ancestral precedent might be described as *effective history* that is not relegated to a temporal past; it is a history which Françoise Dussart considers "immune to the deceptive rigor of carbon dating or the tyranny of the time line".[5] Djiniyini Gondarra asserts, "Our Madayin law comes from time immemorial, and was handed down to us from the *Waŋarr*, the Great Creator Spirits." It is the "defining standard and law that we all live by. So Yolngu people are ruled by the rule of Madayin Law, not by man."[6]

The work and creativity of celebrated artist Narritjin Maymuru is also directed by the laws of *maḏayin*:

> We can't follow a new way—the new way I cannot do that—I go backwards in order to work. I cannot do any new things because otherwise I might be making up a story—my own thoughts, you see— and people over there, wise people, would look at my work and say, "Ah! that's only been made up by him."[7]

In *maḏayin* law, the past is not supplanted by creative innovation; rather, the ancestral past irrevocably pervades all creative impetus; the past is very much active in the present. Corn and Yunupingu explain: "Not only are the Yolŋu the direct descendants of the original *waŋarr* (ancestral beings), they are also mirrored physical consubstantiations of the original *waŋarr* presences that remain eternal and sentient in country."[8] The original *waŋarr* remain present in human creativity. Likewise, the *ŋaraka* (bones) or forms handed down through ceremony, such as the rhythmic structures of *manikay* or figurative patterns of art, are brought to life as they are filled out with fresh vibrancy and colour. *Manikay* remains effective as it is filled with creativity. Reflecting on his recent collaborations with Korean musicians, Daniel Wilfred explains: "If you go forward, the song will know you"[9] (see Epilogue).

Manikay can therefore be considered one means of articulating the *maḏayin* (ancestral law) embedded in musical structures. As in painting, *manikay* is "a reiteration of origins, of place, of ownership, authority, and identity through

---

5 Françoise Dussart, Introduction to Part 3: "Sacred Places", in *Aboriginal Religions in Australia: An Anthology of Recent Writings*, ed. Max Charlesworth, Françoise Dussart, and Howard Morphy (Aldershot, Hampshire: Ashgate, 2005), 113.

6 Gondarra, "Assent Law", 24.

7 Narritjin Maymuru, quoted in Morphy, *Becoming Art*, 148.

8 Corn, "Land, Song, Constitution", 86.

9 Daniel Wilfred, in *Djuwalpada* (film), directed by Daniel Wilfred and Nicola Bell.

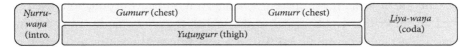

Fig. 5.2. The different sections of a *manikay* song.

the rendition of a particular narrative."[10] In performing *manikay*, one becomes accomplished in knowledge of *rom* (correct living). This is a source of pride and strength, as Benjamin Wilfred announces emphatically: "I'm proud of the songs Grandpa gave me … these songs are keeping me strong."[11]

In the correct, lawful progression of song subjects, a narrative unfolds through performance, bringing to awareness the knowledge necessary to interpret the tangible, living world of ecology and society. *Maḏayin* knowledge embedded in *manikay* includes "corporate clan rights; processes of parliament and dispute resolution",[12] as well as title to land, and rules governing hunting, resource harvesting, and kinship (Chapter One). *Manikay* and *buŋgul* (dance) are not mere cultural pleasantries: the performance of ceremony becomes a political assertion of authority and legitimacy under the *maḏayin* law. Conceptualisations of the *manikay* tradition as mere custom, myth, artefact, or ritual are anathema to *maḏayin*. Gondarra challenges, "These ideas [concerning *tradition*] do not fit or make any sense to us; in fact they are repulsive."[13]

Fleshing Out

Every performance of *manikay* consists of numerous iterations of short song items, anywhere from twenty seconds to two minutes in length. These are often repeated and progress through a series of rhythmic modes and narrative subjects (see below). Each discrete song item is made up of three basic sections, which might be thought of as the *introduction*, *body*, and *coda*. The descriptive nomenclature *ŋurru-waŋa* (nose-speech), *yutuŋgurr* (thigh), and *liya-waŋa* (head-speech) is here used to describe these sections, following Corn's documentation of Gumatj *manikay* (fig. 5.2).[14] Wägilak only use *yutuŋgurr* descriptors, as well as common term *gumurr* (chest; see below); the other terms are used for ease of discussion. These sections structure a performer's selection, elaboration, and improvisation of different rhythmic and melodic elements characteristic of a *manikay* repertoire (see below).

---

10 Caruana and Lendon, *Painters of the Wagilag Sisters*, 36.

11 Benjamin Wilfred, "Digital Audio Technologies".

12 Gondarra, "Assent Law," 24.

13 Ibid.

14 Corn, "Ancestral, Corporeal, Corporate", 8; Aaron Corn, *Reflections and Voices: Exploring the Music of Yothu Yindi with Mandawuy Yunupingu* (Sydney: Sydney University Press, 2009), 152.

The *ŋurru-waŋa* (nose speech) is a short, hummed introduction, used by the lead singer to orient the pitch and establish the *biḻma* mode of the coming song subject (audio example 5a). This is a very informal opening and might go unnoticed during the general chatter, tea drinking, and cigarette smoking—also an important part of ceremony as a gathering of family. *Manikay* is, of course, fundamentally about relationships. Songs emerge out of living community.

Audio example 5a. "Dhaŋarra" (White flower). The YWG singing at a funeral in Ngukurr. This example begins with an extended ŋurru-waŋa (nose-speech; introduction). 8 July 2011.

The *ŋurru-waŋa* is akin in freedom and fancy to what might be hummed while walking along, thinking about a song. The lead singer taps out a *biḻma* mode on the ground, establishing speed in relation to previous songs. By the strength of their voice, the intensity of the singing to follow is indicated. Once a starting pitch is located, the leader breaks into song, drawing the other singers into a performance that emerges from convivial social interaction, without rigid demarcation between song and life.

While the overall order of songs and their subjects is fixed, the lead singer selects each subject depending on the context—like selecting a few books from an alphabetised shelf while keeping them in order. The exception to the rule is during *buŋgul* (dance) for pure entertainment, such as at festivals, when song selection is more flexible and items are chosen out of sequence for the enjoyment of the dancers.

In the *yuṯuŋgurr* or *makarr* (thigh) of a *manikay* item, dancers leap into action. This is also the segment of a song in which the singers improvise independently within the established modalities of rhythm and pitch. The *yuṯuŋgurr* may be divided into multiple *gumurr* (chests), usually segmenting the *yuṯuŋgurr* into two repeated halves. Songs with two *gumurr* are described as "double" songs. In *manikay*, the *gumurr* "leads you, pulls you towards country".[15] In these "double" modes, the first half is usually tapped with the *biḻma* on the ground, the second half with the clapsticks striking together (audio example 5b). Different *gumurr* are separated by a rhythmic cadence.

Audio example 5b. "Djuwalpaḏa," *brother and sister* mode. Daniel Wilfred leads Benjamin Wilfred, Roy Natilma, Andy Peters, and David Wilfred plays *yiḏaki*. Ngukurr, 8 July 2011.

In the *yuṯuŋgurr* (thigh), individuals weave their own melodic line at will, the multiple strands of voices coming together in dense heterophony, lending the aural texture a certain vibrant brilliance (see Chapter Seven). In a descending cascade of sound, each singer extends their own string of words, rhythms, and pitch, expressing poetically the underlying narrative, its significations, and images. The best singers and dancers are renowned for breaking out of the

---

15 Daniel Wilfred, interview with the author, Melbourne, 6 March 2011.

typical forms maintained by the performing group around them, introducing new variations and rising over the top of the group (see audio examples 6i and 6j).

Within a performance, singers usually draw on an established stock of texts or *yäku* (sacred lexicon) appropriate to a song subject. Phrases are somewhat fragmentary and form "cryptic strings of names and archaic words that can be ordered quite differently with each new performance". The variety of textual images is constituent of a greater, heterophonic narrative running through the entire *manikay* series.[16]

The table below shows Daniel Wilfred's elicitation of the text for "Djuwalpada" *walking* mode in the first column.[17] The second and third columns show the different texts sung simultaneously by Daniel and Benjamin Wilfred in a performance of the same song (audio example 5c; see table 5.1).

Audio example 5c. Different text selections in a recording of "Djuwalpada." Ngukurr, 8 July 2011. Example is in four parts (see table 5.1).

   a.   Daniel Wilfred speaking the text of "Djuwalpada" (column 1);
   b.   Daniel Wilfred singing "Djuwalpada", *walking* mode (column 2);
   c.   Benjamin Wilfred singing "Djuwalpada", *walking* mode (column 3);
   d.   The overall mix with b) and c) overlayed.

Table 5.1. Text use in a recording of "Djuwalpada" (audio example 5c).

Text of Djuwalpada spoken by Daniel Wilfred	Text of Djuwalpada sung by Daniel Wilfred	Text of Djuwalpada sung by Benjamin Wilfred
Djuwalpada name of Wägilak *mokuy*	likan-dhu, likan-dhu elbow-with [repeated]	likan-dhu elbow-with
Ŋirriyiŋirriyi name of Wägilak *mokuy*	Djuwalpada name of Wägilak *mokuy*	Djuwalpada, Djuwalpada name of Wägilak *mokuy*
dhawal-wal duy'yun arriving at his home place	dhawal-wal duy'yun arriving at his home place	Ŋirriyiŋirriyi, Ŋirriyiŋirriyi name of Wägilak *mokuy*
ŋopurr-ŋopurr wrist or forearm	likan-dhu, likan-dhu, likan-dhu elbow-with [repeated]	Djuwalpada, Djuwalpada name of Wägilak *mokuy*

---

16 Corn, "Land, Song, Constitution," 9. Toner explains that the rich and descriptive poetry of song texts form "not only a *description of* a place, but also a sense of *belonging to* a place, an inalienable and populated landscape." Toner, "Sing a Country," 176.

17 Completed with suggestions by Frances Morphy (2013).

Burrwanyila name called by *mokuy*	Djuwalpaḏa name of Wägilak *mokuy*	Nyagulnyagul name for Mäḏawk (Silver crowned friarbird)
ḻikan-dhu elbow-with	Garrayaŋa, garrayaŋa place where Djuwalpaḏa walked	Butjulubayi place where Djuwalpaḏa began walking
garrarr'yun dance	Wakura place where Djuwalpaḏa walked	ḻikandhu-ŋupan with elbow-pointing
Mokuy-u, Mokuy Ghost [ergative]	Gurrumirri place where Djuwalpaḏa walked	Djuwalpaḏa name of Wägilak *mokuy*
ŋupana follow, pointing	Dulumirri place where Djuwalpaḏa walked	ŋäkirri, ŋäkirri cover [fresh meat in ground oven]
dhawal-wal ḏuy'yun arriving at his home place	gumurrmirri chest-having	dhawal-wal ḏuy'yun arriving at his home place
Gandjalala name of Wägilak *mokuy*	Wakura place where Djuwalpaḏa walked	ḻikan-dhu elbow-with
Mokuy-u, Mokuy Ghost [ergative]	Gurrumirri place where Djuwalpaḏa walked	Djuwalpaḏa name of Wägilak *mokuy*
ŋupana follow, pointing	ḻikan-dhu elbow-with	Ŋirriyiŋirriyi, Ŋirriyiŋirriyi name of Wägilak *mokuy*
Ŋirriyiŋirriyi name of Wägilak *mokuy*	gara'yun spear	
dhawal-wal ḏuy'yun arriving at his home place		

The final cadence by the *yiḏaki* (didjeridu) and *biḻma* (clapsticks) signals the singers to stop. The song then closes with a *ḻiya-waŋa* (head speech), a sung melismatic coda. In the *ḻiya-waŋa*, the lead singer improvises a solo reiteration of the important song words and the *ḏämbu* without accompaniment (audio example 5d). As in this example, multiple voices can continue into the *ḻiya-waŋa*, but these eventually drop out leaving only one solo voice. The coda sometimes makes up half the length of the overall song and allows for an extended demonstration of virtuosic ability. The *liya-waŋa* (coda) extends the song item with the same energy as the *yuṯuŋgurr*, keeping it strong and powerful, holding the audience's attention and drawing them on to further songs with cries of "*Yo, manymak!*" (Yes, good!).

Audio example 5d. "Guku" (Honey). An extended *liya-waŋa* (coda), finished by Benjamin Wilfred. With Daniel Wilfred, Roy Natilma, Andy Peters, and David Wilfred playing *yiḏaki*. Ngukurr, 8 July 2011.

Rhythmic Bones

Performances of *manikay* progress through a narrative which is outlined by rhythmic modes, the patterns played by the clapsticks which underpin a song and its dances: "Everything comes out of the clapping sticks."[18] Within the subject "Gara", for example, there are three different rhythmic modes that are typically used; each of these are usually repeated a few times, before the lead singer indicates a shift to the next mode. Between different song subjects, such as "Gara" (Spear) and "Raki" (String), there are similarities between the rhythmic modes used. The table below (5.2) gives an idea of how different rhythmic modes (identified as mode a, mode b, etc.) might be used over the course of a *manikay* performance.

Table 5.2. The performance of *manikay* consists of repeated songs on different rhythmic modes, and within a narrative progression of song subjects.

Song subject	Rhythmic modes used	Indicative number of repetitions
"Djuwalpaḏa" (Ghost)	Mode a	5
	Mode b	6
	Mode d	3
"Gara" (Spear)	Mode a	3
	Mode d	2
	Mode e	2
"Raki" (String)	Mode b	4
	Mode d	3
	Mode e	5

18   Daniel Wilfred, interview with the author, Melbourne, 6 March 2011.

Fig. 5.3. Approximate notation of the Wägilak _ḏämbu_ (audio example 5f).

Djuwalpaḏa, the first subject in the Wägilak narrative, is first accompanied by the _walking_ mode, a pattern that is, throughout the entire song series, associated with Djuwalpaḏa travelling through the countryside, naming plants and animals (see table 5.3). The dance actions are performed in synchronicity with this repetitive rhythmic structure, translating sound into movement and bringing narrative action to life.

Each rhythmic mode is characterised by its speed and length: "For Djuwalpaḏa, first that long one [_biḻma_ mode], then the short one, then double one. Then Woomera ["Gaḻpu" Spear thrower]: first that long one, then the short one, then double one."[19] When the rhythmic mode changes to the _stalking prey_ mode, Djuwalpaḏa—and the dancers—stalk prey with a spear; when Djuwalpaḏa finds the _guku_ (honey), his celebratory dance is accompanied by the _dancing_ mode. In the _running_ mode, the more frequent the alterations between the different rhythmic components, the closer Djuwalpaḏa is to reaching his country. The beginnings of all subsequent subjects or events in the narrative action of _manikay_ are clearly identified by a change in the _biḻma_ mode, and climaxes are anticipated with building momentum.

The following table (table 5.3) represents the rhythmic modes used by Wägilak in Ngukurr for smoking ceremonies. The modes typically performed in _CRB_ (sixteen of the thirty-four modes documented here) are indicated with an asterisk. The transcribed cadence patterns are used to demarcate the _gumurr_ (chests) segments within a song within the song or conclude the _yuṯuŋgurr_ (thigh). "Double" indicates two _gumurr_ are performed. The ordering of modes below remains consistent in performance.

---

19 Ibid.

Table 5.3. *Biḻma* modes used in Wägilak smoking ceremonies
* indicates the rhythmic modes heard on the first *CRB* album (AAO 2010)
† indicates the songs that are *yuṯa manikay* (new songs; see section below)

	Biḻma mode	Rhythmic patterns used	Cadence pattern	Typical speed (beats per minute)
Djuwalpada	Walking*			106
	Walking (ii)—getting closer to Ṉilipidji			106
	Stalking prey*			88
	Dancing—double*		Syncopated vocal interjections	102
	Running—double*			86; 94
	Brother and sister—double†			102
Gara	Throwing*	(Unmeasured; fast)		112
	Dancing*		Syncopated vocal interjections	98 or 120
	Running			96; 106

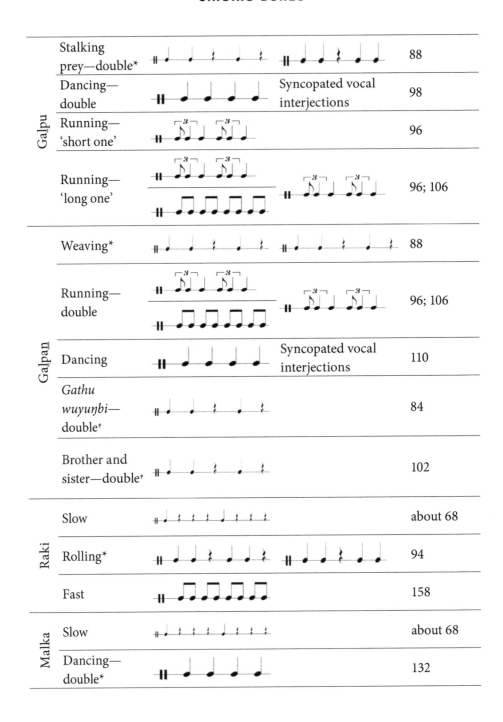

Galpu	Stalking prey—double*			88
	Dancing—double		Syncopated vocal interjections	98
	Running—'short one'			96
	Running—'long one'			96; 106
Galpan	Weaving*			88
	Running—double			96; 106
	Dancing		Syncopated vocal interjections	110
	Gathu wuyuŋbi—double†			84
	Brother and sister—double†			102
Raki	Slow			about 68
	Rolling*			94
	Fast			158
Malka	Slow			about 68
	Dancing—double*			132

Wata	Gentle breeze*	♩ notation		about 68
	Picking up strength— double*	notation	notation	about 68 or 108
	Strong wind*	notation	Syncopated vocal interjections	102
Birrkpirrk	Slow	notation		about 68
	Looking for yams	notation		46
	Walking	notation		66
	Singing	notation	notation	66
	Dancing*	notation	Syncopated vocal interjections	112
	Mother— double*	notation	notation	126–134
	Brother and sister†	notation	notation	112
	Goodbye— double*† (or "Märi'mu")	notation	notation	66

There are startling consistencies to be found in comparing *bilma* tempo between contemporary performances by the YWG and the earliest known recordings of Wägilak song. Listening to Jeffrey Heath's 1976 recording of Sambo Barabara at Ngukurr, it seems that the *bilma* modes used have barely changed at all; many of them consistent to the exact beat-per-minute (audio example 5e).[20] This clearly shows that traditional means of transmission were and are highly stable. In the decades since this recording, Wägilak have not learnt *manikay* with consistent reference to any recorded audio or notation, despite the occasional use of cassette recordings and now mobile phones. Learning *manikay* continues to be done through active listening and participation, under the careful attention of the *djungayi* (ceremonial manager).

---

20 Jeffrey Heath, "Texts Recorded in the Numbulwar Area", tapes 4803–4 (HEATH_J04), Ngukurr, 1975, Australian Institute of Aboriginal and Torres Strait Islander Studies Audio Visual Archives.

Fig. 5.4. *Brother and sister biḻma mode of Daniel Wilfred's yuta manikay.*

Audio example 5e. "Djuwalpaḏa," *walking* mode. In two parts: a) Sung by Sambo Barabara with Roy [Natilma] playing *yiḏaki*, Ngukurr, 1975 (courtesy of Jeffrey Heath); b) Sung by Benjamin Wilfred and Roy Natilma, with David Wilfred playing *yiḏaki*, Melbourne, 13 April 2009.

Such consistency is probably reinforced by the sharing of *biḻma* modes between *bäpurru* with close *riŋgitj* (alliance) connections. Despite having different *manikay* narratives, closely related *bäpurru* all dance to the same *biḻma* groove. While performing Marraŋu *manikay* at the Ngukurr Festival in 2010, David Wilfred explained: "Same: this one isn't different—*biḻma* are the same." The Marraŋu living at Gapuwiyak use a set of *biḻma* modes similar to the Wägilak. Song subjects are also shared, such as "Guku" (Honey).[21]

Peter Toner's documentation of Dhaḻwaŋu *manikay* shows how an underlying set of rhythmic modes is transposed into different *manikay* narratives. Toner notes five important categories used to label *biḻma* modes: *bulnha* (slow); *yindi* (big; important); *gumurr wanggany* (chest one; regular); *gumurr marram* or *baṉtja* (chest two or arm); *yuṯa manikay* (new song).[22] If it is used, the *bulnha* mode always comes at the beginning of a song subject and accompanies slow narrative action, such as a gentle breeze or water bubbling up from the ground.[23] The *yindi* mode always uses a fast, non-metrical pattern, similar to Djuwalpaḏa *running*. *Gumurr wanggany* (chest one) and *gumurr marram* (chest two) provide dancers with "two rhythmically distinct versions of a song subject to dance to," and might correspond to the various *walking* and *stalking* modes of Wägilak *manikay*.[24] Wägilak often refer to a faster, second rhythmic variation—usually the *dancing* mode, a mode with short *gumurr* (chests) that energises the dancers—added to a performance as a "double one", which seems comparable to Toner's *gumurr marram* (chest two). While these Dhaḻwaŋu terms are generally understood by Wägilak in Ngukurr, they are not the descriptors used, despite obvious similarities.

---

21 A mobile ringtone commonly heard in Ngukurr is the Marraŋu version of "Guku" (Honey).

22 Toner, "Form and Performance", 79–81.

23 Peter Toner, "When the Echoes Are Gone: A Yolngu Musical Anthropology", PhD diss., Australian National University, 2001, 85.

24 Toner, "Form and Performance", 96.

Melodic-Harmonic Bones

Each set of *manikay* songs is also based on a melodic and harmonic pattern specific to each *bäpurru*.[25] There are more than sixty distinct *bäpurru* in Arnhem Land and each has its own repertoire of *manikay*, which uses a unique *ḏämbu* (head)—a term used to refer to the pitch structure of the entire song series.[26] Individual *ḏämbu* are instantly recognisable, leading those schooled in Yolŋu ceremony to identify the particular *bäpurru* (father's group) to which the songs belong. *Ḏämbu* is a unique musical signature, synonymous with the narrative, lineage, and estate belonging to each *bäpurru*. Andy Peters' songs from Wuḻku use a different *ḏämbu* than the songs from Ŋilipidji (audio example 5f).

Similarly, while the Marraŋu and Wägilak share *manikay* narratives, each uses a different *ḏämbu*. Daniel Wilfred tells the story: "Djuwalpaḏa was chasing a really wild man across the country. He cut down a large *gaḏayka* (Stringybark Tree) which fell across the land, reaching all the way to the saltwater at Raymangirr."[27] Djuwalpaḏa then sung to the Marraŋu people, passing his words on to them. "They use those words today, got them from the Wägilak, but they have a different song [*ḏämbu*]."

Voices improvise independently around the *ḏämbu*, weaving words and phrases selected from the song text into a melismatic cascade of sound. Improvisations begin at the top of the pitch series and trend downwards over the course of one *gumurr* (chest) segment (see fig. 5.2). A song item usually has one or two *gumurr* between the introduction and coda, and these multiple *gumurr* make up the main *yutuŋgurr* (thigh) of the song. The *ḏämbu* (head) is simultaneously melodic and harmonic, in that the pitches are set to text horizontally (melodically) by the individual voice, and vertically (harmonically) through the combination of voices singing different pitches (audio example 5f). *Ḏämbu* is a set of intervals fixed relative to a starting pitch: no matter what note the song begins on, the intervals remain consistent in their span as the song unfolds.[28] The starting pitch generally tends higher over the course of a performance, rising as singers become more energetic toward the climax of a ceremony.

Audio example 5f. Two different *ḏämbu* (head) patterns: a) "Wäkwak" (Black crow) from Dilipidji. Benjamin Wilfred, Daniel Wilfred, and David Wilfred (*yiḏaki*). Ngukurr, July 8, 2011; b) "Dhaḻara" (King Brown snake) from Wuḻku. Andy Peters and David Wilfred (*yiḏaki*). Ngukurr, 11 July 2011 (see fig. 5.3).

---

25 See Chapter One for a more detailed discussion of *bäpurru*.

26 Corn, "Ancestral, Corporeal, Corporate", 8; Steven Knopoff, "Yolngu Clansong Scalar Structures", in *The Garland Encyclopaedia of World Music, Australia and the Pacific Islands*, vol. 9, ed. Adrienne L. Kaeppler and J. W. Love, 141 (New York: Garland Publishing, 1998); Peter Toner, "Melody and the Musical Articulation of Yolngu Identity", *Yearbook for Traditional Music* 35 (2004): 69–95.

27 Daniel Wilfred, interview with the author, 1 February 2019.

28 See Toner, "Melody and the Musical Articulation".

Represented in a scale, the _ḏämbu_ unique to the Wägilak might approximate to the following (fig. 5.3). Within _CRB_, the sound of the AAO's equal temperament instruments invariably shift the singers' voices toward a pentatonic scale, even as the AAO musicians adjust their tuning with micro-tonal inflections. In local performances, the intervals here represented as a minor third (F–D; C–A) are somewhat flexible and often much narrower.

The pattern of _ḏämbu_, passed down the generations, allows freedom for creativity through inflection and improvisation. Significantly, a singer might decide to sing with the voice of an elder past—an imitation of timbre and improvisatory style—often an elder who was an important teacher or ceremonial leader. Daniel Wilfred joined the _CRB_ tour after Roy Natilma decided he was too old to keep on going. Daniel frequently imitates Natilma's voice when singing, regarding it as nuanced and beautiful. So too Sambo Barabara's voice, which is lower than his own. In 2017, Daniel began using the voice of his young son, Isaiah Wilfred, which is higher and more nasal, obviously the voice of a young child:

> I got different voices. I got a voice for Sambo [Barabara]. [Did] you hear me? I sing with Sambo's voice. I sing with Roy's [Natilma] voice. I got my own voice too. Sometimes I go high, sometimes I go low ... You have to sit next to those elders. They have to sing right into your ear, first left, then right. You have to sing with them and you learn that voice—right into your head.[29]

Through the _ŋaraka_ (bones) of song sequence, rhythmic construction, pitch, and vocal timbre, _manikay_ is carried down the generations as an expression of pervasive ancestral presence. Singing _manikay_ correctly means singing with due regard to its orthodox elements of musical form, the structuring _ŋaraka_ that begin with the _biḻma_. This stability provides _manikay_ with a continuity that justifies estate ownership, _riŋgitj_ obligations, and kinship relations. More than a cultural tradition, _manikay_ engages the current generation with aspects of _maḏayin_ law as they substantiate present life and society and the _garma_ (public) manifestations of ancestral precedent.

While highly significant, the _ŋaraka_ (bones) structuring _manikay_ require improvisation to be realised: melodic improvisation, the use of individual vocal timbres and text selections made by every singer. Through set patterns of _biḻma_ modes, the intervallic _ḏämbu_ and fixed narrative sequences, diverse individuals are held together in a unified body of song, pulled by the _gumurr_ (chest) toward Ŋilipidji.

"Productive ambiguity", a term borrowed from Gadamer, refers to structural space or indeterminacy that allows for a renewing play of movement, allowing a work of art continually to become new event.[30] The _ŋaraka_ of _manikay_ structure

---

29 Daniel Wilfred, interview with the author, Ngukurr, 18 August 2010.
30 Gadamer, _Truth and Method_, 198, 498.

performances with spaces of "productive ambiguity", allowing individuals the discretion and creativity to realise a particular song in their own way, with reference to the forms of tradition and the voices of others. Ethnomusicologist Sally Treloyn explores a similar concept in her discussion of "Songs that Pull", in research on Junba song from the Kimberley region of North West Australia:

> Patterns of interaction that are laid down by ancestral beings are manifested in song conception—in a mutual *pull* between composers and the song-giving spirits of their deceased relatives. This *pull* is shown to draw in wider groups of people through song transmission and performance, maintaining and re-invigorating connections between people and country.[31]

The *ŋaraka* of *manikay* also come to be known through active participation: the realisation of conceptual patterns requires creativity, drawing an individual into the momentums song. As no single vocal line dominates the aural canvas, productive ambiguity exists also for the listener, whose attention is drawn this way or that, free to shift between points of interest or follow individual voices or lines within the ensemble. *Manikay* is heard through active listening.

In painting, the different colours of ochre—taken from the ground—are used to create a body of ancestral presence: red ochre for the blood; black for the skin; yellow for the fat; white for the bones.[32] *Manikay* songs also have a body that sings and dances. The *gumurr* (chest) pulls a song toward country through text and melody; the *yutuŋgurr* (thigh) inspires dance and action through rhythm and syncopation; the ŋurru-waŋa (nose speech) leads the song, perhaps as the nose leads the body; the *ḏämbu* (head) provides a structural patterns for elaboration; *ḻikan yäku* (elbow names) connect a song with people and country. *Manikay* song is a living organism that comes out of its structuring *ŋaraka*, bringing Wägilak narrative to life.

New Songs

Manikay lives and breathes the rhetoric, "What we do today is nothing new, we only do what the elders have done before us." Importantly, such statements do not contradict the practice of *yuṯa manikay* (new songs), which are composed—"found" or "dreamed"—in response to contemporary situations.

One interesting Wägilak *yuṯa manikay* (new song) was "found" just before the Ngukurr Bulldogs competed in the Big Rivers Football League grand final.

---

31 Sally Treloyn, "Songs that Pull: Jadmi Junba from the Kimberly Region of Northwest Australia", PhD diss., University of Sydney, 2006, i.

32 These equivalences (red ochre is blood, etc.) were presented in a graphic display at the National Museum of Australia, in an exhibit of ochre in the Gallery of First Australians, 2014. The information was recorded by Steve Fox, and probably based on his discussions with Yolŋu artist Narritjin Maymuru.

Daniel Wilfred sung a version of "Mädawk" (Friarbird) with a new text, its skipping rhythms and pace imitating the chant "Come on the Bulldogs" (audio example 5g). This song was again heard a few days later, incorporated into a local funeral.

> Nyagulnyagul wärrarra dunbirriyunayi
> "Ŋarra dhu bulyun, ŋarra dhu bulyun"

> *Mädawk* flies through the red sunset
> "I want to play [football], I want to play"

> ("Mädawk" Friarbird, *football* mode song text)

 Audio example 5g. "Mädawk" (Friarbird), *football* mode. Benjamin Wilfred, Daniel Wilfred, and David Wilfred (*yidaki*). Ngukurr, 26 May 2010.

Yuta manikay are poetic, juxtaposing new meanings onto old songs; contemporary events and relationships are spliced into ceremonial repertoires. *Yuta manikay* fit into established *manikay* series, elaborating the basic narratives by altering or reinterpreting elements such as text, rhythmic form or structure.[33] For example, the "Mabulmabul" (Marble) song from 2014 reinterprets the circular dance of "Galpan" (Dillybag) and is a musical response to children playing marbles in a circle at school. These children kept their marbles in a bag around their neck, like Djuwalpada's *galpan* (dillybag).

> Dillybag [*galpan*], it's a bush bag. Where Djuwalpada put his beef, honey—sugarbag from the tree. He put in the bag. But we made a song. We saw our kids playing with marbles: they were playing and we start changing around the song. You have to stand around, circle. That's the *mabulmabul* (marble) song.[34]

In this way, the bones of *manikay* are passed down the generations as they are transposed into new situations. *Yuta manikay* are understood as a legitimate expression of ancestral narratives; they are not new but come from past generations, as Benjamin Wilfred explains:

> New songs come in the dream and Grandpa is always following me, no matter where we go. He's always following and telling me new songs. No matter where I go, he's always there. My grandpa, he was the head

---

33 For a detailed exploration of new songs, see: Steven Knopoff, "'Yuta Manikay': Juxtaposition of Ancestral and Contemporary Elements in the Performance of Yolngu Clan Songs," *Yearbook for Traditional Music* 24 (1992), 138–53; Peter Toner, "When the Echoes are Gone".

34 Daniel Wilfred, comment during a dance workshop, Melbourne, 29 May 2014.

leader with the most knowledge and the most songs, and the most spirit in his life. We go everywhere with him, his spirit and his songs. Connection to the land and country, and families.[35]

The "Mabulmabul" song was also based on a new rhythmic mode that came to Daniel Wilfred "in a dream" in late 2010. Known as the *brother and sister* mode, this *bilma* pattern was the basis of several *yuta manikay*. At Daniel's insistence, one of these songs was recorded for the first time with his non-Yolŋu brothers as the opening track for the second *CRB* album. The *brother and sister* mode recounts of the travels of two siblings, represented by the pairing of two *bilma* strikes (fig. 5.4):

> Yolŋu brother and sister. Double one. Brother walking with spear; sister walking with *many'tjarr* (leaves), hitting bushes and dancing. I just woke up, dreamed a new one. Went down to do ceremony, and I asked David [Wilfred], "Hey, you want to play with me a new song?"[36]

New *bilma* modes are almost always performed as *double modes*, consisting of two or four *gumurr* (chests), with the first half of the song tapped on the ground. New modes always slot into a *manikay* series after the established modes for a song subject have been performed, and before the next subject begins. Indeed, it makes a lot of sense to think of *yuta manikay* as new modes of existing song subjects, which are enriched through juxtaposition and invention.

Frequently, *yuta manikay* add a unison *chorus* section to the end of each double *gumurr* (chest). Chorus sections usually consist of new text spliced into a traditional *manikay* item, which remains otherwise unaltered. For example, the phrase "*Yä wäwa, yä märi'mu*" (Oh brother, oh father's-father) is added to the usual text for "Birrkpirrk" (Plover), creating the new "Goodbye Song" (audio example 5h).

Audio example 5h. Unison chorus from the "Goodbye Song". Benjamin Wilfred, Daniel Wilfred, Roy Natilma, Andy Peters, and David Wilfred (*yidaki*). Ngukurr, 8 July 2011.

When Barabara died in 2005, Benjamin Wilfred "found" the "Goodbye Song", which has become a poignant tribute often performed at the end of Wägilak funerals. As family members stood on the airstrip at Ngukurr, looking up at the light plane carrying Barabara's coffin to its place of burial at his mother's country, "all the faces looked out the window. And they were sad. And they started to move, like this [waves goodbye]."[37] Poignantly, this song drew on text and rhythmic patterns from "Birrkpirrk" (Plover), whose cry is heard carried on the wind, when someone dies, the *birrimbirr* carried back to country. Through

---

35 Benjamin Wilfred, "Forum on CRB", panel discussion, Melbourne University, 16 April 2009.
36 Daniel Wilfred, interview with the author, Melbourne, 6 March 2011.
37 Benjamin Wilfred, in discussion with the author, 2012.

yuṯa manikay, the essential narratives carried by ceremony are brought to life through real situations and emotions.

Worry is a very visceral, present emotion, and in the act of "finding" *yuṯa manikay* in response to troubling situations, the *manikay* tradition becomes directly relevant to contemporary lives:

> And in my mind when I sing, I cry. You listen to me, when I change my voice, I'm crying. Today, when I'm singing, I'm a bit changing. Always singing this song; always thinking about my brothers, sisters, all my nieces, nephews. When I sing this song, it's always in my mind, make me cry. Maybe you listen and hear my voice changing: that's me crying.[38]

The "Goodbye Song" is also a powerfully *present* song musically: its sections of unison chorus is rich with vocal timbres. A dozen men can be standing, huddled in a circle around a smoking fire, their voices charged with emotion—heard in their fluctuating vocal timbre and vibrato. And at the very end of the ceremony, the "Goodbye Song" brings their voices together, merging into one unison expression that moves from sadness to celebration. The *yiḏaki* (didjeridu) is held up high, bell in the air, and if there are any lingering sorry feelings or worry, these are externalised in song with great vigour and energy.

The "Goodbye Song's" chorus, "Yä wäwa, yä märi'mu" (Oh brother, oh father's-father), is a cry also carried through performances of *CRB* placed at the end of "Birrikpirrk" (Plover) to conclude performances and often repeated as an encore. During this song, the AAO musicians leave their instruments and come to the front of the stage, participating in the dance actions: large side-to-side swaying with two hands in the air—like the faces seen in the plane windows—waving goodbye to the audience at the end of a tour, ready to journey home. Daniel introduces this encore: "I'll sing you one song. I'm saying to all you mob, goodbye. I'm saying goodbye to everyone here … And I'm saying thank you mob to dance my songs, thank you mob. Hope I'll see you again."[39]

This is not a trite, audience-pleasing farewell. The "Goodbye Song" is a summation of the *CRB* collaboration, an expression of reaching out but returning home, and of newfound kinship between performers—heightened by melodic and rhythmic unity. "When we were singing today, I was saying goodbye to my friends, the orchestra. In my heart, just crying, you know. I'm leaving tomorrow morning … when we stop, we have to sit quiet."[40]

There is an underlying parallel between the disquiet in funeral *manikay* for the *birrimbirr* (soul) of the deceased and a characteristic theme of *warwu* (sorrow, homesickness, worry), expressed in many *yuṯa manikay*: "Concern for

---

38 Daniel Wilfred, comment during a dance workshop, Melbourne, 29 May 2014.
39 Daniel Wilfred, comment during a performance of *CRB*, Melbourne, 27 May 2014.
40 Daniel Wilfred, interview with the author, Melbourne, 6 March 2011.

birrimbirr (souls) of the recently deceased, or sorrow for one's own or another's absence from kin or country."[41] Other *yuṯa manikay* composed by the YWG include "Gathu Wuyuŋbi" (My Son Is Lost). It was sung by Roy Natilma when Benjamin Wilfred went missing on a *CRB* tour in Melbourne, in 2007. Another was composed by Daniel Wilfred when feeling homesick on a trip to Hong Kong.

Yuṯa manikay are "the same, not different" in their continuation of ancestrally given narrative and musical elements. This is not anathema to creativity: new songs flesh out the legitimate, orthodox skeleton of *manikay*, expanding core narrative sequences with contextual relevance. Through *yuṯa manikay*, the forms of the past speak into the present.

Conservation and innovation are necessary to any tradition's ongoing, dynamic presence in contemporary lives: these things are not binary opposites. Howard Morphy writes, "Yolngu art has always been diverse, dynamic and changing, despite an ideology of conservatism, and Yolngu on the whole have been the main agents of change."[42] While *yuṯa manikay* can be considered as creative innovation and contextualised understanding, for Wägilak they are essentially expressions of the ongoing power, relevance, and efficacy of the past. *Yuṯa manikay* are not simply made up: they come in dreams and are there to be found.

Through *yuṯa manikay*, tradition emerges as something more vocative—spoken and heard—than any representation of essential forms might allow, singing into present lives and contexts. In performance, the forms of the past are fleshed out, sustained by the creativity of individuals. In *yuṯa manikay*, the present is shaped in conversation with the past. Reverberating down the generations, the bones of *manikay* are always singing.

Living Voice

The performance of *manikay* is not the technical reproduction of old forms and narratives; through performance, new vistas of meaning emerge. Individual creativity and improvisation animates this process and is at the roots of cultural sustainability. "To be situated within a tradition does not limit the freedom of knowledge but makes it possible."[43]

Orthodoxy does not preclude change. Like the painter, the *manikay* singer "isn't just keeping Yolngu culture unchanged like a museum piece. He has learned to create something that is especially his own, but quite consistent with the past."[44] To speak with authority into contemporary life, tradition changes to stay the same; tradition is understood from new situations and must be made

---

41 Corn, "Dreamtime Wisdom", 157. Explored further by Corn, "Land, Song, Constitution", 89; Knopoff, "Yuṯa Manikay", 144.

42 Morphy, *Becoming Art*, 72.

43 Gadamer, *Truth and Method*, 354.

44 Marika and Christie, "Yolngu Metaphors", 62.

relevant to situation if ancestral patterns are to become meaningful today. The bones of *manikay* must sing with a living voice.

Sustaining the *ŋaraka* (bones) of ancestral law requires creativity. As integral structures are maintained through the generations, these structures entail productive ambiguities, allowing individuals to be pulled into the animate play of performance. Set in motion by the *biḻma*, the living voice of *maḏayin* (ancestral law) is infused with personality through: the unique characters of those who are pulled into performance; the grain (timbre) of an individual's voice and stylistic vocal inflections; choices of words and textual images; vocal improvisation around the *ḏämbu* (head); contextualised song and rhythmic mode selection; the composition and juxtaposition of *yuṯa manikay*.

This can be seen in a *yuṯa manikay* composed by Daniel Wilfred, as a part of the *CRB* collaboration. In late 2013, Daniel was on tour with members of the AAO, travelling some four-thousand kilometres between Darwin and Perth, and giving concerts and workshops at Aboriginal communities along the way. At One Arm Point, a community north of Broome, Daniel dreamt a *yuṯa manikay* that was immediately incorporated into tour performances. Uniquely, the AAO musicians were the inspiration of this *yuṯa manikay*, their instruments and improvisations envisaged in place of the *biḻma* and *yiḏaki*, enfolded into the *manikay* tradition. Daniel tells the story:

> We went up to One Arm Point. We had a concert in the night—we went to do the sound-check. We had to go back, stay in the tent, the bush. Nice place: good view, good saltwater. In the night, we went back [to camp] to start eating the saltwater turtle, we call *miyapunu*, and to go to sleep … And I saw five crows coming towards me, from the sea. And I was asleep. And I started singing, singing. In my back [behind me], I listened: bass, lead, drum, keyboard. They were playing. And when it stopped, I woke up, and I look around. And I saw a bird under the tree, talking: "Wäk wäk wäk" [crow calling]. And I went up to tell David [Wilfred], "Hey, I dreamt last night. I saw five crows come towards me. And I heard it all start up from those [AAO] instruments.
>
> And then we went up to One Arm Point to have the concert at night, and I told them boys, Paul [Grabowsky] and all them other fellas, "I made a song, crow song." And we start playing. Steven, the lead player, started to make the sound. No didjeridu, no clapping sticks. It just came up from nowhere, from the instruments. And I follow the instruments when I sing.[45]

The new voices and contexts that *CRB* introduces do not diminish the *manikay* tradition. Instead, they generate new movement and energy. This is no

45 Daniel Wilfred, story told during a dance workshop, Melbourne, 29 May 2014.

juxtaposition of the contemporary with the classical. Instead, the AAO have become entwined within the movements of *manikay* as a living process, an intricate network of connections and narratives. The *ŋaraka* of *manikay* are always on the move. "I share the song with them. But the song doesn't change, it just travels further."[46]

---

46 Daniel Wilfred, in *Djuwalpada* (film), directed by Daniel Wilfred and Nicola Bell.

6

GROOVING TOGETHER:
THE CROSSING ROPER BAR COLLABORATION

This thing can make song. Everything comes out of the clapping sticks.

—Daniel Wilfred
Interview with the author, Melbourne, 6 March 2011

We drive down the Roper Highway towards Ngukurr, on the way back from a performance of *CRB* in Darwin—the launch of an exhibition of paintings from Ngukurr at the Museum and Art Gallery of the Northern Territory.[1] It is a hot, muggy afternoon. The tarmac has ended and the dust from the vehicles in front envelops our view.

Silence sits like the heavy humidity, except for the occasional verbal punctuation as various creeks, hills, old cattle stations, and roads—veering north into Arnhem Land or south into Alawa country—are identified. In our minds, we each sing our own song, amorphous fragments that twist around, emerging and disappearing like the water glimpsed through the trees that race by. Sounds from the previous night's gig linger in our minds, fragmentary strings, tracking with us as we make our way toward Ngukurr.

Outside of our thoughts, our bodies are drawn along together. In unity, we all tap a *biḻma* (clapstick) mode. No one can avoid this infectious groove. Although lifting only one finger to expend as little energy as possible, we are carried along, connected by pulse. Methodical rhythm accompanies our travel;

---

1   See Bowder, *Colour Country*.

our thoughts, the landscape, and our interactions with one another are pulled together in a common groove.

The core of *manikay* is the groove of the *bilma* (clapsticks). To those predisposed to hear only primitive pulsation, or who seek validity in the complexity of structure, the repetitive forms of *bilma* conceal a rich depth of meaning. Redundancy of invention—repetition—is stable.[2] The *bilma* do not change whimsically but carry *manikay* through many different seasons. The simplicity of these sticks is foundational to an abundance of possibility.

Groove is form in motion. It is performance breathing life into structures; structure substantiating performance.[3] Groove is felt in the body, physical sensation pulling an individual into community. Groove engages us on a fundamental level. Caught in a groove of expected regularity, bodies are committed. Experience is central: where groove is not felt, it is not groove. Conversely, there is no groove where there is no underpinning form, reliable and regular.

Groove articulates the paradox of tradition: form and experience, object and subject, inheritance and continuance, are indivisible. To perceive the repetitive forms of tradition is to conceptualise history at a distance, objectively removed from the experience of encounter—law, rule, or principle, separated from the bodily experience of performance and hearing. Musical form is known in the event of structures becoming manifest and realised with creativity. Object and subject collapse; tradition is known as present event.

Performance carries ideas into situation. When the *bilma* strike, the structural forms of *manikay* come to life—Djuwalpada starts to walk. Form is contiguous through multiple iterations even as the present experience of form is unique to every individual. Conversely, creativity within a tradition is contingent on the repetition of elements of that tradition, structuring individual expression (see Chapter Five).

In *manikay*, underpinning structures animate performance. These forms are necessarily in transit, impelling movement and participation. The orthodox musical structures of *manikay*, the *ŋaraka* (bones) that encode important patterns concerning land, relationship, and identity, are encountered; understanding is effected through action.

Contrary to notions of historical reconstruction—the reproduction of musical form as the end goal—this chapter looks to musical form as a possibility for new beginnings. Form is the foundation of exploratory engagement

---

2   Charles Keil writes: "Repetition and redundancy, which to most people is a bore, is music's glory. That's where a groove comes from … the repletion and redundancy of information with minor but frequent variations." Charles Kiel and Steven Feld, *Music Grooves* (Chicago: University of Chicago Press, 1994), 23.

3   Cf. Steven Feld's comments on groove as "style as process, a perception of a cycle in motion, a form or organizing pattern being revealed". Keil and Feld, *Music Grooves*, 109.

through imitation and response, a back-and-forth play of understanding. *CRB* is approached as a living tradition in which musical structure sets in motion new relationships and ways of engaging with Wägilak ceremony. Further, *CRB* illuminates *manikay* as a vibrant tradition sustained within ever widening contexts of expression.

Reclaiming Groove

Primitives are those fantastical savages constructed in the romantic gaze of many Western minds. They are those who can do nothing but groove, unable to break out of a seemingly redundant, superseded past. The perceived lack of developed syntactical systems in music among *primitive* peoples—systems which academies obsessed over throughout the twentieth century—was understood as a disability to evolve beyond the immediate gratification of the basest of all affecting experiences: the throb of repetitious rhythm pulsating through bodily flesh.[4] Developing his *information theory* of musical aesthetics in 1957, celebrated composer and author Leonard Meyer perpetuates the myth of the primitive: "Because the primitives themselves do not make musical creation a self-conscious endeavour, they have neither a theory of music nor even a crude 'aesthetic' which might serve to connect their musical practices to their responses."[5]

In his extensive study published in 1893, *Primitive Music: An Inquiry into the Origin and Development of Music, Song, Instruments, Dances, and Pantomimes of Savage Races*, Richard Wallaschek wrote the following of Indigenous Australians:

> The character of Australian music depends a good deal on its rhythm, which is strongly marked … music excites his anger, with it he rushes into the fray, hurries off to the dance or the hunt, or willingly resigns himself to his master's orders. For these different circumstances the native seeks out the definite rhythm which best fits his case, quick for the dance, slow and solemn for love, wild and pathetic for mourning.[6]

Implicit assumptions of primitivism often surface in popular culture. The primitive is often seen as a direct connection to nature, contrasted with the complexities of *developed* culture. Charles Chauvel's classic Australian film *Jedda* depicts the inner conflict of a young Aboriginal girl named Jedda,

---

4   Steven Feld also writes of "the unabashed reproduction of primitivism" on a global level and which characterises much recent music identifying with the label *world music*. Steven Feld, "A Sweet Lullaby for World Music," *Public Culture* 12, no. 1 (2000): 154.

5   Leonard Meyer, *Emotion and Meaning in Music* (Chicago: University of Chicago Press, 1957), 289.

6   Wallaschek, *Primitive Music: An Inquiry into the Origin and Development of Music, Song, Instruments, Dances, and Pantomimes of Savage Races* (London, Longmans, Green & Co., 1893), 39.

raised on a cattle station in domestic European culture.[7] In one scene, Jedda is practising the piano. Epileptically, she suffers a portrayed bout of primitivism, her repressed but true primitivism slipping to the surface. As she plays, the music slips out of the syntactical constructs of European classicism and tonality, and she begins to bash frenetically on the keyboard.

Romantic notions of the primitive can also be found in orchestral representations of Indigenous Australian cultures: these compositions and their performances can have little to do with the Indigenous people they represent, or the complex structural and aesthetic intricacies of ceremony. Within the classical orchestral tradition, composer Peter Sculthorpe is often heralded as having developed an original style reflective of Australian landscape—that is, the popular images of huge expanses, small country towns, and a rich Indigenous history. Leaving aside Sculthorpe's characteristic approaches to textural, rhythmic, and melodic invention, perhaps the most important means of creating Australia in music was his use of external programmatic descriptions.

While Sculthorpe seeks to celebrate Australia's Indigenous people and heritage, he also betrays an affinity with the concept of primitivism, conceiving of Aboriginal people as primal and *in tune* with the earth: "A bogus national identity and its commercialisation have obscured the true breadth of our culture … Perhaps we now need to attune ourselves to this continent, to listen to the cry of the earth, as the Aborigines have done for many thousands of years."[8]

Sculthorpe imagines a return to a more natural state where people are unconsciously synchronised with the land and ecology, a position in which culture is derived from nature and strives for an affecting connection with these roots. In holding such views, Sculthorpe himself is culpable of fostering a "bogus national identity", evident in compositions such as *Mangrove* (1979), *Earth Cry* (1986), and *Kakadu* (1988)—iconic works studied in Australian musical history courses.[9]

These compositions have little to do with Aboriginal people, groups, or traditions they represent. Instead, they romanticise the primitive through easy but false representations. For example, *Kakadu* is dominated by a relentless, repetitive drumming, something quite foreign to the song and dance of the West Arnhem region. Rather, *Kakadu* foregrounds the experience of direct, rhythmic sensation, unadulterated by the formal complexities of developed musical syntax. As we will see, the complexity of *yiḏaki* patterns in *manikay* shows such understandings of simple, repetitive grooves to be false. Similar romantic notions are expressed by some jazz and popular music students who

---

7   Charles Chauvel (director), *Jedda* (California: Columbia Pictures Industries, 1955).
8   Peter Sculthorpe cited by Graeme Skinner in CD liner notes. *The Music of Peter Sculthorpe: Sydney Symphony Orchestra* (Australian Broadcasting Corporation, ABC Classics, 1989).
9   Sculthorpe had not been to Kakadu when he wrote his orchestral work by that same name. He "knew the place only from books and photos and, perhaps most importantly, in his imagination." Deborah Hayes, "Review: Sculthorpe's 'Kakadu'", *Notes* 52, no. 3 (1996): 1029.

attend the AAO's *Creative Music Intensive*, who begin with vague motivations to become attuned to the ancient *vibe* of the land—an immanent sensation of belonging prior to any complexities of culture and history. That is, before two weeks of performance workshops with Daniel and David Wilfred lead them toward a more relationally involved and technical astute awareness of *manikay*.

There are few recent examples of orchestral engagements which are responsive to the internal complexities of Aboriginal song. Paul Stanhope's *Jandamarra* (2014), with a libretto by Steve Hawke, extends the *junba* tradition of the Kimberley region of the Northern Territory into an expansive work for orchestra, choir, soloists and *junba* singers. It was created in collaboration with the Bunuba people, with whom Hawke had worked closely over some decades, and involved numerous workshops between musicians from the Sydney Symphony Orchestra, who travelled to the Kimberley to sit and listen to *junba* singers.

A very different work by Erkki Veltheim, *Tract*, was first performed in 2010 by the London Sinfonietta with the Young Wägilak Group and questions the very process of scoring a work that incorporates Indigenous tradition. Veltheim had worked closely with Wägilak singers for five years and has a developed appreciation for the rhythmic and tonal complexities of *manikay*, having recorded and transcribed many *manikay* items and *yidaki* patterns. Although an orchestral score, *Tract* avoids any synthesis or intentional musical framing of *manikay* through composition. Instead, the orchestral score and *manikay* are performed simultaneously without foregrounding any process of engagement. These two traditions intentionally clash. The work is as much an ethical statement as it is an aesthetic one. Rejecting the tradition of orchestral arrangements of Indigenous music, *Tract* holds Wägilak *manikay* up as an equal partner, comparable to the most advanced, complex Western art music traditions. While *Tract* shows a great deal of respect for *manikay*, outside of the composers own personal relationships with the *manikay* singers and history of working with *CRB*, any conversational interplay in this work seems to be left to one side. The ethical statement remains primary and explicit.

Veltheim's later work scoring orchestral parts based on *yidaki* rhythms for Gurrumul Yunupingu's final album, *Djarimirri (Child of the Rainbow)* (2018), perhaps shows the positive development of the ethic promoted in *Tract*. This collaboration was the inspiration of Skinnyfish Music producer Michael Hohnen, who also produced *Muyngarnbi: Songs from Walking with Spirits* along with Tom E. Lewis. The score replicates the highly complex patterns of Gumatj *manikay* with great attention to detail, rather than simplifying these patterns into a basic, pulsating groove.

Kalkadungu is a composition from 2007, for orchestra, voice, didjeridu, and electric guitar, by didjeridu virtuoso William Barton and composer Matthew Hindson. It is based upon songs written by Barton when he was fifteen years old and depicts some of the bloody contact history between the Kalkadungu people and the Queensland police. Barton is given much freedom to shape his solo singing and didjeridu improvisation—although, as a composed piece, what we hear is Hindson's musical response to Barton, rather than a dialogue between the musicians on stage. An album featuring *Kalkadungu* won the 2012 Australian Record Industry Award for best classical album.[10]

Alongside many praiseworthy aspects of this work, there is perhaps an unintentional recourse to notions of primitivism in the program notes. Hindson states that the electric guitar was included in the score to create a "link with the present day", and with "contemporary culture".[11] The didjeridu is described as forming a "primal duet" with the bass drum in "Spirit of Kalkadungu", the fifth and final movement of the composition. These comments may reflect the promotional appeal of melding the *ancient* and *modern* together. While it would be sensible to assume that Hindson and Barton have a respectful and valuable personal relationship with one another, these comments indicate to a general problem with language among Australian musicians that should be addressed.

If notions of primitivism persist in mainstream understandings of Indigenous song, many rich performance traditions like *manikay* will continue to be positioned as *otherwise* to complex and developed contemporary culture. These traditions have for too long been deployed to either conjure an imminent and indeterminable spiritual depth to supposedly vacuous contemporary culture, or to display the liberal, progressive credentials of artists and composers seeking to engage with Indigenous people or content. Representations that emphasise the pulsating throb of the didjeridu rather than the complexities of rhythmic construction separate these traditions from their intricate musical forms and narratives. The complex connections encoded in these forms and narratives are lost.

An obverse illustration might be made in relation to academic ethnomusicology. As the discipline of ethnomusicology emerged in the mid-twentieth century, formalism was still an important current within Western musicology and composition. Formalism seeks meaning in complex syntactic arrangements, in the intricate, mathematical processes of musical form. Like primitivism, formalism is reductionist, in the sense that a formalist view reduces the rich, phenomenological excess of *manikay* to pattern and system.

Alan Merriam, a central figure in the founding of the modern ethnomusicological discipline, posits "precise", "statistical" approaches to the study of music as the "greatest possible contribution" that the discipline can make to

---

10 William Barton, *Kalkadungu: Music for Didjeridu and Orchestra*, CD (Australian Broadcasting Corporation, ABC Classics, 2012).

11 William Barton and Matthew Hindson, "Kalkadungu (2007): programme notes," http://hindson.com.au/info/kalkadungu-2007/ (accessed 9 January 2013).

cultural history.[12] Merriam sees the analysis of objective form—"through techniques of historic documentation and archaeological investigation"—as an end and not a means, a position rooted in the scientific rationalism of Descartes and the Enlightenment. Largely, this "worldview still holds sway, and assumes itself to be the language of authority and legitimacy in the modern age".[13] By this measure, the *biḻma* in *manikay* are primitive, two simple sticks playing basic patterns and not much else.

Many leading musicologists in the late-nineteenth and twentieth century denied that music had any existence outside of "autonomous beauty" and absolute "tonally moving forms",[14] a conceptualisation of music which stems from Kant's aesthetics of "disinterested contemplation".[15] To Meyer, Hanslick, and other formalists, musical emotion was constructed in the formal arrangements of sounds perceived by the "auditory imagination", which "enjoys in conscious sensuousness the sounding shapes, the self-constructing tones, and dwells in free and immediate contemplation of them."[16] It was maintained that, outside of objective constructions in sound, "extraneous comparisons are deeply detrimental to our understanding" of music.[17] In the university environment, ethnomusicology grew amid inherited orthodoxies of empiricism and formalism. Much early research is characterised by complex transcriptions into Western notation and the documentation of song texts (this book preferences recorded audio examples rather than transcription).

The concept of *groove* underpinning this chapter moves beyond both primitivist and formalist views, which have variously characterised Australian ethnomusicology and engagement with Indigenous musicians. In the performance of groove, both experience and form, sensation and process, tangible bodies and abstract concepts, are held together. Groove draws us into a community of complex, interactive individuals. Further, an inherited corpus of tradition is realised as presently efficacious. These seeming contradictions splice together in the event of performance

Reggae grooves, funk grooves, heavy-rock grooves, and Ṉilipidji grooves contain a wealth of information: they are specific to history and culture, representing distinct musical traditions. But they also extend through and

---

12 Alan Merriam, *The Anthropology of Music* (Evanston, Ill.: Northwestern University Press, 1964), 301.

13 Chris Lawn, *Gadamer: A Guide for the Perplexed* (London: Continuum, 2006), 5. Similarly, Aaron Corn attempts to expand on empiricist approachs to ethnomusicology in "Nations of Song", *Humanities Research* 19, no. 3 (2013): 147.

14 Eduard Hanslick, *On the Musically Beautiful*, trans. Geoffrey Payzant (Indianapolis, IN: Hackett, 1986), 29–30.

15 Peter Kivy, *Introduction to a Philosophy of Music* (Oxford: Oxford University Press, 2002), 55.

16 Hanslick, *On the Musically Beautiful*, 30.

17 Wayne Bowman, *Philosophical Perspectives on Music* (Oxford: Oxford University Press, 1998), 134.

across different cultures: *manikay* singers from Ngukurr imagine a basic country-rock groove as backing to the *yuṯa manikay* "Wäk Wäk" (Black Crow) (Chapter Five).

The success of *CRB* has depended on groove, enabling the structural perpetuation and experience of engagement with *manikay*. In *CRB*, groove "forms a musical basis, understood by all musicians, regardless of tradition and heritage", permitting a conversation between traditions in which understanding emerges through performance.[18] The AAO render the various grooves of Wägilak *manikay*—Djuwalpaḏa walking, running, and dancing—in a complex way, building new musical syntax and idioms onto these underlying forms. These legitimate *biḻma* modes are retained as they allow musicians to groove together, beginning a conversation of musical voices.

When two hardwood *ŋaraka* (bones) from the core of a tree strike together, something happens: an event, a meeting of people, a new relationship, and conversation come into being. As dancers leap into action, there is a shift from rhythm to groove: form becomes experience; song becomes life. "When I sing, the clapping sticks leading me. And he got all the song, that clapping sticks."[19] Relationships are animated in song; many feet leave overlapping tracks in the dust. Wägilak narrative is carried into the relationships that constitute present life in contemporary Australia—Balanda and Yolŋu; this is *ŋaḻabuluŋu rom* (following law), the realisation of ancestral patterns in the present. As the forms of the *biḻma* are animated in performance, the *ŋaraka* (bones) continue to groove; *manikay* is living.

The Early Sessions

When musicians from the AAO arrived in Ngukurr in July 2005, they came with an agenda. Based on highly developed listening skills honed through jazz performance and improvisation, they desired to forge a new model of musical engagement with Aboriginal musicians. They wanted to comprehend technical and aesthetic complexities of *manikay* through listening and performed engagement. This was in line with the general approach to collaboration taken by the AAO in other projects (see below). Paul Grabowsky, who had previously travelled to Ngukurr to seek initial permission for collaboration, reflects:

> It is with this spirit of serious collaboration that we went to Ngukurr. Benjamin [Wilfred], Roy [Natilma] and the others sat down with our ensemble ... They began to sing and explained that this was a song called "Black Crow" [Wäkwak]. Our musicians asked to listen to it a number of times and then played back to them. This was a moment

---

18 AAO drummer Niko Schäuble, interview with the author, Melbourne, 13 October 2011.
19 Daniel Wilfred, interview with the author, Melbourne, 6 March 2011.

Fig. 6.1. Sambo Barabara (centre) and Benjamin Wilfred (centre left) leading a *buŋgul* (dance) with AAO musicians, Ngukurr, July 2005 (courtesy of Jeff Wassmann and the AAO).

etched into my memory forever. The look of surprise and delight on the faces of our hosts, the fact that here were whitefellas sitting at their feet, wanting to learn their music and actually making a version of it, which they recognised as being close, in spirit at least, to what they actually do—not some Western version of it with all the microtonal inflections and gritty textures removed …

So great was the enthusiasm of the Wamut [skin name] mob, that the senior songman was summoned, the great artist Sambo Barabara. And he too gave his approval. We were then told that we had all become members of the Wamut clan, and that our responsibilities to that status would begin immediately. We were taught some dance steps and then told to perform them at a *buŋgul* [dance]. Everyone did it; this was all part of the collaboration.[20]

Like children learning a language, the AAO approached this strange and foreign music through listening and imitation (fig. 6.1). Grabowsky continues: "This is the thing about being improvising musicians—we listened very, very carefully, asked them to play it a number of times, and played it back to them

---

20 Paul Grabowsky, "The Complete Musician", paper presented in the Australian National University's public lecture series as part of the H.C. Coombs Creative Artist Fellowship, Australian National University, Canberra, 14 October 14, 2010.

as best we could."[21] The AAO musicians were looking for ways *into* the music, not to create a new, synthetic iteration of *manikay*, but to enter into performed musical dialogue alongside the Wägilak singers. Considering histories of non-engagement and appropriation of Indigenous cultural material in Australia, this process was far from any norm. "Just to feel that the paradigm was being reversed for once, God! I can't tell you what a moment that was. It was profound."[22]

Over the coming days of workshops and rehearsals, all the musicians sat down together, learning through conversation both musical and verbal. Listening to recordings of these early sessions, it is possible to hear the AAO musicians developing a basic feel for the music, first by imitating what they heard and then by playing these impressions together with the singers. Discussion and recalibration followed each attempt as greater resonance with the *manikay* style was found. Saxophonist Julien Wilson reflects on the first days of collaboration: "There are so many different things going on at once that I'm not accustomed to ... trying to work out what to remember first when we're learning pieces. There's a lot of steps."[23]

Manikay is complex, as trombonist James Greening observes: "It's hard to understand from a Western point of view, their differences in subtle variations and developments. It's not really overt. It's a language ... to learn it takes years and years and years."[24] Faced with such complexity, rehearsals began by seeking points of musical cohesion, most obviously in rhythmical forms. Barabara gave his approval for the AAO to start by learning the song "Wata" (Wind), a song carrying themes of meeting and dialogue, different groups and individuals blown together in song. Everyone tapped along to a demonstration of "Wata" by Barabara, Natilma, and Benjamin Wilfred.

Later that afternoon, the AAO had develop a basic approach to playing *manikay*: the drums followed the *biḻma*, maintaining the form but elaborating it with infill; the trombone followed the *yiḏaki*, trying to imitate its complex rhythms and cadence patterns; and the violin, soprano saxophone and guitar followed the voices, seeking to reproduce the characteristic intervallic framework. The song "Birrkpirrk" was then demonstrated by Barabara and imitated by the AAO with this same approach (audio example 6a).

 Audio example 6a. "Birrkpirrk" (Plover), *walking* mode. The first *CRB* rehearsal. Ngukurr, 27 July 2005.

As the musicians got a better feel for sounds and rhythms that matched those in the *manikay*—coming to grips with the structures of an unknown language—a groove slowly started to emerge. This allowed the momentum of

---

21 Grabowsky, "The Complete Musician".

22 Ibid.

23 Quoted in Australian Broadcasting Commission and Murray McLaughlin (reporter), "Orchestra Collaborates with Top End Musicians," *7.30 Report*, 2 August 2005.

24 Quoted in Ibid.

the *manikay* song items to carry into improvisations when the voices dropped out between songs. In these spaces, the imitators could begin developing voices of their own, with reference to the established frames of *manikay*.

Like the song "Birrkpirrk/D̲ud̲ud̲u" (Plover/Night Owl), which employs a shared rhythmic foundation to carry *riŋgitj* (parliamentary) relationships (Chapter Four), musical integration in *CRB* began with the shared language of groove. Over the past decade of collaboration, this has been a persistent foundation underpinning musical dialogue. The *bil̲ma* have always been recognised as core to the narrative of *manikay* and a natural point of cohesion.

The very first concert of *CRB* was held on an outdoor stage in Ngukurr on 28 July 2005, with interested and somewhat perplexed locals looking on (audio example 6b). Benjamin Wilfred introduced the concert and the songs to be performed, "Birrkpirrk" (Plover) and "Wata" (Wind): "This first one is Birrkpirrk. Everybody should know that. They [the orchestra] put that music together; they follow me. Copy us mob. It's for my culture, from Wägilak *buŋgul* [ceremony]." The performance was, for Benjamin, yet another opportunity to assert the authority of Wägilak as important ceremonial leaders in Ngukurr (see Chapter Two).

Audio example 6b. "Birrkpirrk" (Plover), *walking* mode. The first concert of *CRB*, introduced by Benjamin Wilfred. Ngukurr, 28 July 2005.

The performance began with the YWG, followed immediately by the solo improvisation of one of the AAO musicians; an iteration of the *manikay* song was then improvised by the full complement of the AAO. This pattern, repeated with each successive *manikay* item, allowed the AAO musicians to first hear *manikay* on its own terms before responding to it. Over time, more integrated modes of presentation developed, while allowing Wägilak singers to retain independence in their own musical direction and creativity (Chapter Eight).

Renowned Aboriginal singer-songwriter Archie Roach, who had travelled to Ngukurr with the AAO, reflected on the first performance: "I'm really, really excited. It nearly made me cry one time because professional musicians are actually playing the music from the people, rather than musicians arranging music for didj or clapsticks."[25] Grabowsky too: "We did that with seriousness of purpose, albeit total ineptitude. I was talking to one of the elders this morning and he said it was enormously significant that we did that last night. It was a sign to them that we were willing to go wherever, do whatever, be whatever."[26]

In the first few years of collaboration, the musicians involved slipped into a productive conversational groove, using performance opportunities at the Garma Festival and other concerts in Melbourne to experiment with ways

---

25 Quoted in Ibid.
26 Quoted in Ibid.

of playing that would be cohesive but also allow for something new to be created. As a back-and-forth conversation between interlocutors, this musical dialogue sought to avoid blatant appropriation. It was understood that the provisional understandings and anticipations of musicians would shift within a performance and over time as the collaboration developed. For the AAO, a key aim of improvisation and musical creativity is to continually develop a unique voice—a distinct sound and process that becomes their own. While this openness seems almost opposite the Wägilak notion of persistent *ŋaraka* (bones), it does allow all musicians involved the space to develop their own voices within a performance, and therefore sense a of ownership.

In *CRB*, the freedom to improvise with and around *manikay* is due, in part, to the apparent simplicity of the *biḻma* modes and the *ḏämbu* (melodic structure), when compared to the musical traditions underpinning other AAO collaborations (see Chapter Eight). If the *biḻma* continue to lead performances, almost any musical input will be tolerated around this narrative core. For highly trained improvising musicians, the *ḏämbu* also offers many possibilities for harmonic and melodic invention, especially as *manikay* foregrounds improvisation based on pitch modification, the interplay of individual vocal lines with the whole, and subtle timbral and pitch inflections.

Yet despite an easy coincidence of *biḻma* forms with AAO improvisations, the *yiḏaki* patterns remain confusingly complex to most AAO musicians. Without dedicated time spent building specific rhythmic capacity in this area— as AAO musicians Christopher Hale and Simon Barker have done with Korean traditional music and *hohŭp* rhythmic patterns[27]—there seems little likelihood that these aspects of *manikay* will become a part of the musical language of *CRB*.

That differing agendas for performance hold together within *CRB* is both coincidental and a result of the AAO's approach to collaboration and the exploration of different musical traditions through improvisation. Most importantly, Wägilak continue to collaborate because they retain a genuine sense of direction, and the *manikay* narratives and *biḻma* modes remain a persistent feature structuring performance. For Benjamin, this has largely meant the continued assertion of cultural authority, whereas for Daniel Wilfred, the mutual exchange of ideas and relationships between musicians has been given greater prominence (see Epilogue). As the collaboration has matured, those musicians who have developed friendships and regular communication with one another have been the ones to continue to explore new directions for performance.

In any cultural context, one can never completely comprehend experience from another vantage point: to claim authority of understanding would be to

---

27 See Christopher Hale, "Ritual Diamonds and Bass Hohŭp: Strategies for Cross-domain Creative Engagement and Influence with Korean Traditional Rhythm," PhD diss., University of Sydney, 2019.

commit to an act of pure fantasy. This is the case in a collaboration like *CRB*, as it is within our own traditions of expression, as Gadamer concludes: "I must allow tradition's claim to validity, not in the sense of simply acknowledging the past in its otherness, but in such a way that it has something to say to me."[28] Grabowsky outlines a similar approach to *listening* as the basic premise of the collaboration:

> The way that we improvising musicians learn is not that dissimilar from the way that these [Wägilak] gentlemen learn. We learn by listening. And the act of listening is a humble moment. You have to actually give yourself over to whoever it is that is telling you something. And your ego needs to be to one side. And that spirit that drives the *manikay*, I think we're in a very fortunate position to be able to take that on board. Maybe that's why this collaboration has worked so well.[29]

The premise of listening "with wide open ears and minds"[30] is an acknowledgement that Yolŋu tradition, while different, possess great depths of meaning and validity—as well as legitimate points of interaction and conversation between cultures. *Manikay* is considered a musical and intellectual sparring partner, which can generate cooperative dialogue and challenge as much as it inspires. The AAO do not consider *manikay* a trove of difference to be plundered but a dynamic and nuanced tradition worthy of engagement.

"To reach and understanding in a dialogue is not merely a matter of putting oneself forward and successfully asserting one's point of view but being transformed in a communion in which we do not remain what we were," Gadamer asserts.[31] This pattern continues in *CRB* as personal and musical relationships between individuals are strengthened. Schäuble agrees: "As with all good musical collaborations, I feel that I have become closer in a personal way to other humans."[32] Carried by the *biḻma* groove, new relationships are forged.

The Spear

As he was searching for a home, Djuwalpada was frightened by the dangerous creatures in the bush. He made ferocious sounds to warn off whatever was lurking, shaking and rattling his spears: "Brrrr!" He holds his spear high, its long shaft quivering; the *biḻma* held by the *manikay* singers rattle, a rapid succession of strikes (fig. 6.2). Djuwalpada looks first south, then north, then east; in none of these directions is his home.

---

28 Gadamer, *Truth and Method*, 355.
29 Paul Grabowsky, "Forum on CRB".
30 Niko Schäuble, interview with the author, Melbourne, 13 October 2011.
31 Gadamer, *Truth and Method*, 371.
32 Niko Schäuble, interview with the author, Melbourne, 13 October 2011.

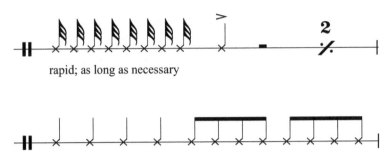

rapid; as long as necessary

Fig. 6.2. Basic *bilma* (clapstick) mode structures for "Gara" (Spear) *throwing* and *dancing* (audio example 6c).

Djuwalpa<u>d</u>a draws back his spear once more, the power in his arm extended by the ga<u>l</u>upu (spear thrower; woomera). "Waahh!" The bi<u>l</u>ma rattle once more, then "crack!" The spear flies towards the west, a single bi<u>l</u>ma strike sending it through the air. Suddenly, the song breaks out of agitated unrest: the spear is sent, cutting through the air toward Ṇilipidji. The bi<u>l</u>ma dance. There is a cathartic release of tension into groove, into pattern, into law. Djuwalpa<u>d</u>a's spear finds home, establishing community, relationship, and ceremony. In celebration, everyone dances together (audio example 6c).

Audio example 6c. "Gara" (Spear), *throwing* mode. Benjamin Wilfred, Daniel Wilfred, Andy Peters, Roy Natilma, and David Wilfred (*yi<u>d</u>aki*), Ngukurr, 7 July 2011.

The *dancing* mode of "Gara" (Spear) grooves because of an inbuilt redundancy of rhythmic repetition; it carries forward with expected regularity. The yi<u>d</u>aki builds complex rhythms onto the underlying bi<u>l</u>ma pattern through a combination of vocables, timbral changes, and overtones. Singers layer together different melodic phrases and syllabic patterns, and dancers cry out syncopated interjections, "Hey-hey, hey-hey." The *dancing* mode connects body and music in kinaesthetic sympathy, paced at a universally typical dance tempo around 112 beats per minute.

This shift is also enacted by the dancers. At the beginning of the song "Gara" (Spear), the dancers hold themselves with poise in imposing stature, brandishing their spears, pointing their elbows, and fixating their eyes. When the rhythmic shift into the *dancing* mode occurs, they immediately spring forward, advancing in a line, involving the whole of their bodies in the realisation of narrative action with regular, synchronised footwork. The drama is heightened by the contrast between unmetered rattling and the metrical regularity of the *dancing* mode.

In many performances and on the first *CRB* album, the AAO musicians realise the powerful aesthetic effect of this rhythmic shift in "Gara" (audio example 6d). The inherent tension and danger in the narrative is intensified by a building dynamic and textural density, through the repetition of the spear-rattling units (table 6.1). On the first *CRB* album, there are four repetitions of this unit before its release into the *dancing* mode. The listening guide below notes key musical elements relating to the building tension.

Audio example 6d. "Gara" (Spear), *throwing* mode. From the first *CRB* album, 2010 (see table 6.1).

Table 6.1. Listening guide: building musical tension in "Gara" (Spear) (audio example 6d).

Biḻma rattle	Time code	Description
i	00:08	Erkki Veltheim (violin) plays a double-stopped tremolo on a tritone (Ab–D), with rapid crescendo and diminuendo—tonally and rhythmically unstable. Paul Grabowsky (piano) and Niko Schäuble (drums) reinforce the final *biḻma* strike with a short, accented diminished octave (G#–G), with cymbal and bass drum strike.
ii	00:15	The violin continues, now at greater intensity of tremolo and dynamic, with a triple stopped, dissonant chord. The piano and drums again reinforce the final *biḻma* strike, accompanied by one of the singers yelling a sharp, accented vocable.
iii	00:21	The bass drum, tom-toms and cymbals add unmetered rhythms to the *biḻma* rattle, increasing the textural and rhythmic complexity.
iv	00:28	The piano joins in this final build up with dissonant arpeggiations. The snare drum builds to the greatest dynamic so far, with a roll leading to the final *biḻma* strike. Tony Hicks (tenor saxophone) joins at the last moment with a rapid trill.

Increasing rhythmic, harmonic, and textural complexity creates growing anticipation, an intensification that seems to be leading somewhere. The *dancing* mode shifts from relatively ambiguous larger-scale units (i, ii, iii, and iv, identified above), to smaller units which are more regular, shorter, and repeated—the singular beats of the *biḻma*. This groove releases energy, and its momentum is ongoing rather than withheld. The narrative of Djuwalpada is felt as rhythmic momentum carries into individual bodies engaged in performance.

The language used to describe the intensification and movement of musical forms above might seem typical of Western music analysis and not *manikay*. Yet terms like *anticipation* and *release*—even the act of analytical description itself—are integral to understanding one culture from another. This is a

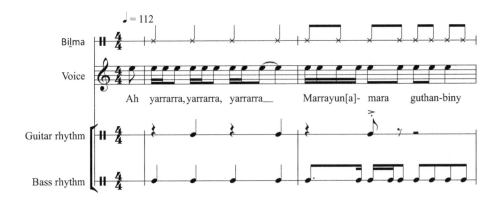

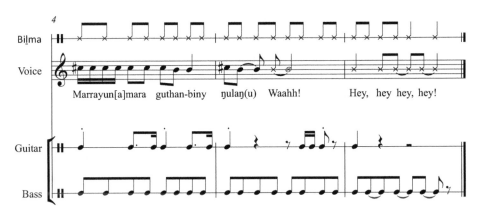

Fig. 6.3. Transcription of "Gara" (Spear) vocal line, with rhythmic transcription of guitar and bass (audio example 6d, from 00:31).

natural process of interpretation, which extends from participation—listening, performing, and dancing. What is most interesting here is the congruence that is suggested in the music, between Wägilak narrative and the shift from Djuwalpaḏa's disorientation to directedness, and the narrative shape of the AAO's contributions. Further, the sensation of groove in the *dancing biḻma* is intensified by the *dancing* drums—*groove* is something that is universal when it comes to dance. This does not mean the music is the same, or that this interpretation is final. Rather, this interaction in "Gara" offers a point of meaningful communication and co-creation.

Jazz musicians are adept at playing in synchronicity with a groove. Frequently in *CRB*, musicians add proportioned, rhythmic layers to the *biḻma* in a way similar to the skipping rhythms of the *yiḏaki*, although without the same degree of nuance and repeatability. In the above audio example (6d), Stephen Magnusson (guitar) plays heavily distorted chords with sparse, articulate rhythms—based on semiquaver subdivisions of the primary beat (see table 6.2).

Both Philip Rex (bass) and Niko Schäuble (drums) reinforce the basic rhythm of the *bilma* with accented crotchets and quavers. The singers also lock into the *dancing* mode with a more regular, proportioned rhythmic setting of the text, transcribed below (fig. 6.3; table 6.2).[33] *Bilma* patterns, fundamental to the narrative of *manikay* remain integral to the music of *CRB*.

Table 6.2. Text for "Gara" (Spear) (audio example 6d).

Time code	Text	*Bilma* mode
00:08	Marrayunmara gara guthanbiny ŋulaŋura, yarrarra Marrayunmara gara guthanbiny ŋulaŋura, yarrarra Yarrarra, yarrarra, yarrarra, waahh! Dancing with the spear, the spear has almost left his hand Dancing with the spear, the spear has almost left his hand Aiming the spear, aiming, aiming, waahh!	
00:30	Ah yarrarra, yarrarra, yarrarra Marrayunmara guthanbiny Marrayunmara guthanbiny, ŋulaŋu Waahh! Hey, hey-hey, hey! Aiming the spear, aiming, aiming Dancing with the spear, the spear has almost left his hand Waahh! Hey, hey-hey, hey!	

"Gara" is a relatively short, energetic song. When the voices and *yidaki* signal its completion with a cadence, the AAO continues to improvise by following the established *dancing* groove—as if they were remaining in the same groove of a record, extending the length of the song (audio example 6e; table 6.3). Benjamin and Daniel Wilfred also groove along to these improvisations, playing their *bilma* in time or dancing across the stage, elbows pointed.

This is an approach frequently taken in concert, and the AAO conclude "Gara" with the correct *manikay* cadence following their improvisations. In the audio example (6e), this is signalled by the piano's continual vamp on the syncopated cadence—a rhythm usually sung by the dancers, "Hey, hey-hey,

---

33 The unmetered beginning of this song still employs the tonal pattern of the Wägilak *ḏämbu* and the rhythms characteristic of the text, even as these are more free and improvisatory, especially in the first half of the song.

hey!" (see table 6.2), after a short period of free improvisation. An extended *liya-waŋa* (coda) improvised by Tony Hicks (tenor saxophone) and Erkki Veltheim (violin) follows.

 Audio example 6e. "Gara" (Spear), *throwing* mode. From the first *CRB* album, 2010. This is a continuation of audio example 6d (see table 6.3).

Table 6.3. Listening guide: analysis of "Gara" (Spear) (audio example 6e).

Point of Interest	Time code	Description
i	00:08	The hi-hat continues to play the same rhythm as the *biḻma* but elaborates this pattern, initially by accenting (dynamically, combined with a slight opening of the hi-hat) the rhythms of the vocal interjections, "hey-hey".
ii		The double bass improvisation suggests a 4/4 metre. The piano layers more complex rhythms onto this groove.
Example fades out and in		
iii	00:24	The piano again vamps on the rhythm of the vocal interjection, anticipating and elaborating the final cadence.
iv	00:37	Correct *manikay* cadence, supported rhythmically by all musicians.
v	00:38	Harmonically, the tenor saxophone and violin improvisation is based on the *ḏämbu* (arrangement of pitch in *manikay*). This will be discussed in the coming sections.

The rhythmic bones of *manikay* are given life in performance, shifting from abstract pattern to an experienced groove that connects individuals in song. Form is only a beginning that is necessarily realised in its performance. Likewsie, Grabowsky muses: "Any work of art, really, its trajectory isn't complete until it is received by somebody."[34] The AAO's sensitivity as they engage with the rhythmic forms of *manikay* permits coincidence of expression. New energy and creativity are brought to the integral forms of Wägilak narrative, basic grooves filled with improvised complexity.

The *CRB* collaboration always extends out from the rhythmic foundations of *manikay*. But it always returns to these rhythmic underpinnings: convergence

---

34 "Australia's Hidden Hit Parade: Paul Kelly with Paul Grabowsky", presentation at *The Monthly Talks* series, hosted by *The Monthly* and Readings Books, Melbourne, 1 October 2012, http://www.themonthly.com.au/australias-hidden-hit-parade-paul-kelly-paul-grabowsky-6543.

is the final theme of *CRB*, pulling discursive, improvised conversation into a celebration of togetherness.

Emerging

During the recording of the first *CRB* album in 2009 and subsequent workshops leading up to a second recording in March 2011 (including the above audio examples of "Gara", 6d and 6e), *CRB* started to come into its own as something more cohesive than a sequence of *manikay* songs interspersed with responsive improvisations.[35] No longer characterised by a musical back-and-forth between distinct groups, the AAO musicians had performed half a dozen times with the YWG and become more aware of the nuances of *manikay*. They sought to develop a fluid, musical narrative that worked not only alongside but through the *manikay*, using new colours and textures appropriate to the *manikay* narratives and musical structures.

There are a huge variety of approaches to improvisation in *CRB* as individuals bring their own voices to the music. The examples selected here demonstrate each musician's consistent sensitivity to the forms of *manikay*. This section examines some of these forms, especially rhythmic cadences, *yidaki* (didjeridu) patterns and the structure of *dämbu* (harmonic/melodic "head").

Concluding the *yutuŋgurr* (thigh; main body) of each *manikay* item is a characteristic cadence, a point of convergence for *bilma*, *yidaki*, singers, and dancers (see table 4.1). In *CRB*, these cadences also form points of convergence for improvisers, a sort of interchange that switches the musical action between partners in a conversation, the AAO and the YWG. In the space between *manikay* songs, improvisations either continue the momentum of the previous song item or build toward the next one. In a sense, *anything goes* in between *manikay* items, just as in local contexts where people break into chatter, cigarette smoking, and talking on mobile phones. After giving the AAO space to improvise, the lead *manikay* singer listens for a suitable point of entrance to begin the next song. Sometimes the AAO lead the *bilma* in by anticipating the correct rhythmic mode and pace. The *bilma* cadence patterns remain an important organising feature (audio example 6f).

Audio example 6f. "Birrkpirrk" (Plover), *brother and sister* mode. From the first *CRB* album, 2010 (see table 6.4).

---

35   The first *CRB* album was released in 2010, the second in 2014.

Fig. 6.4. Transcription of "Birrkpirrk" (Plover) (audio example 6k). Roy Natilma's text is too unclear enough for transcription.

Table 6.4. Listening guide: "Birrkpirrk" (Plover) cadence patterns and *bilma* modes (audio example 6f).

Time code	Description
00:05	♩ ♩ ♩ ♩
	Bilma tapped on ground, second time
00:40	Faster ♪♪ ♪♪ ♩ ♩ ♩

Fig. 6.5. Transcription of Tony Hicks' solo in "Gara" (Spear) (audio example 6k).

Within a *manikay* item, cadences are signalled with a variety of cues both visual and aural. These come predominantly from the lead singer, who conducts the rhythm by striking the *bilma* with larger gestures: "Listen to the *bilma*; follow him."[36] The *yidaki* player anticipates the cadence with a series of syncopated overtones, matched by the dancer's own vocal interjections. The complex rhythms of the *yidaki* are also bound by the cadence, after which it ceases to play during the *liya-waŋa* (coda).

The *yidaki* player has room for virtuosic elaboration within the basic patterns of the *bilma*. Any standard transcription of these patterns would not do justice to the complexities of rhythmic timbral changes, accents, and dynamic shading created by subtle physical alterations inside the player's mouth. David Wilfred introduced the AAO to some new *yidaki* patterns for "Djuwalpada" *brother and sister* mode during a rehearsal in 2011 (audio example 6g; see table 6.5).

---

36 Benjamin Wilfred, interview with the author, Ngukurr, August 2010.

Fig. 6.6. Pitch transcription of improvised *l̠iya-waŋa* (coda) in "Gara" (Spear) (audio example 6k).

Audio example 6g. David Wilfred demonstrates some *yid̠aki* patterns. Melbourne, March 21, 2011 (see table 6.5).

Table 6.5. Listening guide: different *yid̠aki* (didjeridu) patterns (audio example 6g).

Time code	Bil̠ma mode
00:00	"Djuwalpad̠a" *brother and sister*
00:22	"Djuwalpad̠a" *dancing* (double)
00:40	"Gal̠pu" *brother and sister*
00:55	"Gal̠pan̠" *dancing* (double)

In the early rehearsals of *CRB*, the *yid̠aki* was understood as a type of drone, imitated by the trombone and bass clarinet as a sort of tonal grounding (refer to audio example 6a). However, as the collaboration developed, it became apparent to the AAO musicians that the *yid̠aki* was, first and foremost, a rhythmic instrument "like the drums", its complexity located in rhythmic elaboration, invention, and momentum.[37] Sympathetically, Grabowsky often takes a

---

37 David Wilfred, discussion with the author, Ngukurr, June 2011. Unlike *manikay*, West Arnhem Land song styles like *kun-borrk* do use the pitch of the didjeridu as a tonal reference point for

rhythmic approach to the use of keyboard instruments in *CRB*—like a *yidaki*—not limiting himself to the history and design of the piano as an invention with predominantly harmonic potential: "It's not the box, but the brain that controls it that matters."[38]

The below audio example (6h) demonstrates Grabowsky's approach to rhythmic improvisation. Like the *yidaki*, Grabowsky builds rhythmic complexity over the established rhythmic mode, carrying this groove towards its ultimate termination at the final cadence point of each song. Two songs are contained in the below track: the first demonstrates a complex rhythmic scatter effect, the second a tonally ambiguous descent through chromatic scale.

Audio example 6h. "Gara" (Spear), *dancing* mode; "Malka" (String bag), *dancing* mode. Paul Grabowsky (piano) playing on the first *CRB* album, 2010.

Improvisations in *CRB* also weave around the integral Wägilak *dämbu* (intervallic construction; 'head') (see fig. 5.2). Here, the *dämbu* is used to orient melodic or harmonic departure and realignment. This intervallic sequence carries identities of *bäpurru* (lineage) and *wäŋa* (country), and the AAO are brought into this world through performance whether their improvisations emerge in synchronicity or contrast. To perform the Wägilak *dämbu* is to be brought into the world as an image of the underpinning ancestral text.

In *manikay*, the *dämbu* is elaborated through improvisation. Schematically, *dämbu* is a "fairly static intervallic structure",[39] yet in performance it becomes a rich tapestry of vocal relationships. Individual lines weave around one other, the linear patterns of *dämbu* realised through harmonic juxtaposition between melodic lines. The texture of *manikay* shimmers with brilliance and *märr* (essence; vitality), and strong voices emerge over the top, reaching for pitches transposed into the octave above the starting pitch (audio example 6i) (see Chapter Seven). In *yuta manikay* choruses, the effect of coming together in loose unison provides striking contrast to the usual, heterophonic realisation of *dämbu*.

Audio example 6i. "Djuwalpada," *dancing* mode. Benjamin Wilfred and Roy Natilma during recording sessions for the first *CRB* album, 2009.

Märr (ancestral essence; vitality) is also created by extending the *liya-waŋa* (coda) and reiterating the *dämbu* at the end of a song item: "Keeping the song strong, singing with strong voice."[40] Natilma's flamboyant vocal improvisations often begin the *dämbu* at a higher pitch, while retaining its characteristic

---

singers.

38 Grabowsky, "The Complete Musician", paper presented at the Australian National University's public lecture series, as part of the H.C. Coombs Creative Artist Fellowship. Australian National University, Canberra, 14 October 2010. See Chapter Eight for an exploration of the keyboard's potential for musical creation through changes in timbre.

39 Corn, "Ancestral, Corporeal, Corporate", 8.

40 Benjamin Wilfred, interview with the author, Ngukurr, August 2010.

intervallic structure. This is considered highly virtuosic and gives a song greater energy (audio example 6j; table 6.6; fig. 6.4).[41] In this example, Natilma sings around a perfect fifth higher than Benjamin Wilfred, which is an interval that is emphasised in the Wägilak *dämbu*.

Audio Example 6j. "Birrkpirrk" (Plover), *brother and sister* mode. Benjamin Wilfred and Roy Natilma on the first *CRB* album, 2009 (see table 6.6; fig. 6.4).

Table 6.6. Translation of the text for "Birrkpirrk" (Plover) (audio example 6j)

Yawilila yawilila	Plover, plover crying
Moyŋu moyŋu	Djuwalpada dancing, Djuwalpada dancing
Wipa nhaŋu Manungududayi	Flying over the water [at Luṯunba] to land at Manungududayi
Birrkpirrk-nha, moyŋu	Plover, Djuwalpada dancing
Nhabilayi, nhabilayi	Plover, plover [alternate name]
Wipa nhaŋu Manungududayi	Flying over the water [at Luṯunba] to land at Manungududayi
Birrkpirrk-nha, moyŋu	Plover, Djuwalpada dancing
Mmm, mmm, ga-Birrk!	Mmm, mmm, ga-Birrk!
Birrkpirrk, Birrkpirrk, ga-Birrk!	Plover, plover, plover!

Reiteration is contingent on variation and the possibility for variation is contingent on reiteration. This is a fundamental principal of *manikay* and can be seen at work in the improvisations around the Wägilak *dämbu* in *CRB*. Following Natilma's lead, the below examples highlight the freedom and nuance of inflection the improvising musicians take to weaving additional *vocal* lines on their respective instruments, into the overall musical texture. These improvisations do not adhere to the Wägilak *dämbu* as strictly as *manikay* singers, although like *manikay*, the conceptual process that these musicians bring to improvisation also begins with intervals and the variation of sequences of pitch.

Hicks' (tenor saxophone) improvisation (audio example 6k below; fig. 6.5) fits within two descents of the *dämbu*—effectively a double *biḻma* mode with two *gumurr* (chests)—and melodic elaborations occur within this frame. Tonal modifications, such as growls and bends, give vocal-like inflection to the improvisation, and rhythmic momentum is given to sustained pitches of the *dämbu* through breath-accents. In the below transcription of Hick's improvisation, one can see the difficulties of performing the Wägilak *dämbu* without slipping into a pentatonic scale—which the Wägilak singers also start to do. Because saxophone fingerings are relatively fixed, the intervals of the

---

41 Roy Natilma's text is too indistinguishable for clear transcription.

Wägilak *dämbu* are necessarily rendered as alterations to a pentatonic scale. This excerpt again demonstrates that key climactic points in the song series are characterised by greater tonal and rhythmic convergence by all musicians, effecting a sense of cohesion.

In the *liya-waŋa* (coda) following the cadence rhythm, Erkki Veltheim's (viola) improvisation (audio example 6k; fig. 6.6) seeps out of the dense texture. It is characterised by an exploration of intervals around the basic framework of the *dämbu,* much like the improvisation of a *manikay* singer. Rather than a complex rhythmic transcription, the notated example shows the pitch relationships Veltheim and Hick's improvisation, where Veltheim has more flexibility on a stringed instrument than a keyed wind instrument.

It is interesting to listen to discrepancies between these musicians' approach to the fourth pitch (descending) in the Wägilak *dämbu* series (see fig. 5.2). Imitating the *manikay* singers, they try to position this non-diatonic interval with quarter tone shadings and pitch bends. This section is almost bi-tonal, as Veltheim explores the intervals of the *dämbu* around the pitch of G, Hicks around the pitch of F#. The resulting thickness of texture and ambiguity is befitting the tonal complexity of *manikay.*

Audio example 6k. "Gara" (Spear), *dancing* mode. Tony Hicks' (tenor saxophone) improvisation leads into a *liya-waŋa* (coda) with Erkki Veltheim (viola). From the first *CRB* album, 2010 (see figs. 6.5, 6.6).

The end of the song "Gara" in this example (6k) is a very beautiful moment. The rhythmic pace slows and the music comes to rest on the final pitch of the *dämbu.* Veltheim and Hicks intentionally create and sustain an atmosphere of repose, finishing one *manikay* subject and providing space for a new one to emerge in its place.

During moments like these, there is an intense sense of creativity, where process and experience are entwined *in the moment.* As the AAO's improvisations unfold, the sounds invoke—almost palpably—images in the mind of the YWG. Daniel and Benjamin Wilfred vocalise bird sounds, call ceremonial *yäku* (names) of country and ancestors or move purposefully around the stage with stylised poses. In the sounds of the AAO, an ancestral voice is heard. Sometimes, the *manikay* singers just stand and listen carefully, heads slightly cocked to one side, their attention to the music a visible part of its creation. Grabowsky's view of music as an event, experienced anew in the moment of hearing, resonates with *manikay* as an encounter with ancestral creativity:

> All art is latent until the moment it is received by the viewer, listener or
> reader, at which point it ignites, catching fire in the atmosphere of the

141

mind … A work is never the same twice: no matter how many times we encounter it, our experience is dependent on circumstance.[42]

CRB is characterised by improvised responses to Wägilak rhythmic and intervallic forms, demonstrating a sensitivity in hearing and performing that is at once coincidental and creative. The AAO's improvisations are structured by the forms of Wägilak manikay, carried by the grooving biḻma; they also go beyond imitation of these forms, extending the integral structures of manikay with creativity and complexity. But it is in the moments of deliberate interaction—sometimes flamboyant, other times intensely quiet—when the audience is drawn into the experience of hearing, that the act of listening might be recognised as an integral part of song.

For most audiences, without the technical knowledge of manikay forms and narratives, what stands out in CRB is the process of engagement, the conversation between musicians from different cultures, and between performers and listeners. This is not just observed, it is experienced. In this sense, CRB is a ceremonial gathering, holding together tradition and creativity, process and sensation, individuals and collectives, within an animate constellation of sound.

Situated horizons

Musical form is important. To understand an unknown musical world, we must become aware of the processes that give shape to that music, and the structures that underwrite transmission and integrity. Understanding form is necessary to collaboration. Yet paradoxically, as we develop our own voices in response to another tradition, those forms invariably shift and expand. Musical conversation continually shifts our understanding of a musical tradition, and therefore our performed expressions in response to that tradition.

A few years into the CRB collaboration, musicians from the AAO began to enunciate their views on the limitations of imitation as a key approach to manikay. This was partially a desire to develop a deeper awareness of manikay, beyond rhythmic imitation and elaboration of the biḻma grooves. The following observations made by musicians of the AAO were recorded during a rehearsal period in Melbourne, prior to the recording of the second CRB album in 2011.

> I don't think a strong sense of groove is necessarily important to this collaboration … [our grooves] can often seem like mannered versions of the organic sense of groove that the YWG employs.[43]

---

42 Paul Grabowsky, "Art is a River", Comment, The Monthly, October 2012.
43 Violinist Erkki Veltheim, discussion with the author, 2011.

And you know the first bit, the character of the *mokuy* [ghost], it is not a simple sort of being, or a simple *idea* of a being … He's looking for the law—that's such serious stuff—and the sort of rock-and-rolly stuff that I play, it's too unsubtle.[44]

We used to play in a very reactive way, applying very much what we know about playing grooves and these kinds of things, in order to give us internal structure that coincides with what these guys are doing. But actually, the meanings of the songs are so complex … that we have started to think that going into a very heavy groove immediately is probably not necessarily the way to go. And we've been trying to play much more of the story and allowing things to build very, very slowly over time, and also to have areas in the music where there is very little happening … a great deal of space. And, I think everybody felt it was a kind of huge leap that we'd made.[45]

Music emerges out of living relationships. Especially for AAO musicians, the directions of *CRB* are continually negotiated and adjusted. As ease of communication and a nuanced understanding of a musical style grow, so too does the desire to continue to expand our engagement with the forms of tradition—to be creative in the way we carry the tradition forward in new ways, and not just perform reactively by imitating those forms of tradition.

There is an informative coincidence here with Gadamer's hermeneutics. For Gadamer, traditions are not engaged as discrete, objective entities but eventfully, through the ongoing interactions of conversation.[46] Because traditions are inextricably interwoven in our lives, effectively "working on us and in our understanding",[47] engagement with a tradition like *manikay* is necessarily a continual process of translation, transposition, and expansion. Through performance or active conversation with a tradition, "A new horizon is disclosed that opens onto what was unknown to us. In every genuine conversation this happens."[48]

Through their continual negotiations and interpretations, the AAO come to a better understanding of *manikay*. While they bring preconceived ideas to this conversation—such as "groove" "space", "structure"—this language allows interpretation to take place. Undeniably, we come to any conversation with anticipations and preconceptions: "Prejudices, in the literal sense of the word,

---

44 Drummer Niko Schäuble, discussion during *CRB* rehearsal, 21 March 2011.
45 Paul Grabowsky, discussion during *CRB* rehearsal, 21 March 2011.
46 Gadamer's hermeneutics shift from "the theoretical plane of seeing from a perspective to the practical plane of involvement and participation in the ongoing action of dialogue." Gerald Bruns, *Hermeneutics Ancient and Modern* (New Haven, Connecticut: Yale University Press, 1992), 9.
47 Hans-Georg Gadamer, *Gadamer in Conversation: Reflections and Commentary*, ed. and trans. Richard E. Palmer (New Haven, Connecticut: Yale University Press, 2001), 45. See also Gadamer, *Truth and Method*, 272–91.
48 Gadamer, Gadamer in Conversation, 49.

constitute the initial directedness of our whole ability to experience … They are simply conditions whereby we experience something, whereby we encounter what something says to us."[49] While preconceptions become unjustified if we do not allow them to be questioned, they are inescapably the framework of our thought. Yet in conversation, preconceptions are revealed and transformed, as we open ourselves to different voices, situations, and traditions. It is in hearing another possibility that we become critically conscious of our own situated horizons.

In a climate of postcolonialism, many academics in Australia are full of angst, feeling ever "compromised by the forms of knowledge that are traditionally used in the West".[50] Any interpretation of Indigenous Australian cultural, social, or political life made by a non-indigenous academic or musician occur in "a treacherous political space", where the interpreter will potentially "betray people with every move".[51] "Western research" is often framed in opposition to indigenous cultures, considered a particular "cultural orientation, a set of values, a different conceptualization of such things as time, space, and subjectivity" that is brought to bear "on any study of indigenous people".[52] This polarisation between a Western and Indigenous gaze renders Aboriginal cultures as *otherwise*, and therefore inaccessible.[53] The inherent complexity of human perception and understanding is simplified by this posture. In this critical distancing from self, "a fantasy of perfect translation takes over … It reaches a peak in the fear that, being translation, the translation will only be a bad translation";[54] we are left in aporia, unable to speak of difference.

Interpretations of culture are given significance within the frame of encounter and the angle of approach, inherent to any situation. Yet if they are treated provisionally, iterations of understanding generate momentum and ongoing engagement. Although we "grow up into the world through an experience pre-formed by language", Gadamer argues that this is not an ultimate limitation: "The possibility of going beyond our conventions and beyond all those experiences … opens up before us once we find ourselves, in

---

49 Gadamer, *Philosophical Hermeneutics*, 9. Gadamer's somewhat controversial use of the term *prejudice* stems from his dedication to etymology, translated from the the German *vorurteil.*

50 Morgan Brigg, "Political Theory between Two Traditions: Ethical Challenges and One Possibility," in *The Power of Knowledge, the Resonance of Tradition*, ed. Graeme Ward and Adrian Muckle (Canberra: Australian Institute of Aboriginal and Torres Strait Islander Studies, 2005), 118.

51 Brigg, "Political Theory," 118.

52 Linda Tuhiwai Smith, *Decolonizining Methodologies* (London: Zed Books, 2012), 92.

53 Marcia Langton asserts, "There is a naïve belief that Aboriginal people will make 'better' representations of us simply because, it is argued, being Aboriginal gives us 'greater' understanding. This belief is based on an ancient and universal feature of racism: the assumption of the undifferentiated 'Other.'" Marcia Langton, "Aboriginal Art and Film: the Politics of Representation", in *Blacklines: Contemporary Critical Writing by Indigenous Australians*, ed. Michele Grossman (Melbourne: Melbourne University Press, 2003), 115.

54 Ricoeur, *On Translation*, 5.

our conversation with others, faced with opposed thinkers, with new critical tests, with new experiences".[55]

An (imagined) conversational interlude with an imagined Wägilak interlocutor

Another perspective must be recognised before it can be brought into conversation with our own ideas, assumptions, and practices.

But when we recognise another perspective, we come to it with our own lens, with bias. We fall short of that perspective.

Of course, we have bias—hermeneutics isn't maths. Understanding beings in subjectivity.

So how can another voice hold challenge implicit assumptions or even power?

Through conversation that is open-ended, recognising that we only know who we are in relation to others.

Our perspectives are never constituted on their own—life is relational. Nevertheless, the dominance of one culture often mutes the voices of others.

Just as "the unabashed reproduction of primitivism"[56] prevents us seeing the subtle complexities of another culture.

A romantic fascination with *otherness*, in which there is no dialogue, only appropriation.

Like *world music*, a label that has "come to disguise a multitude of musical crimes, in which sampling technology has resulted in widespread looting of cultural artefacts, reducing everything to the status of the *found object*".[57]

So how is *CRB* any different?

Because it foregrounds process, not outcome; it is about dialogue, in which creation is a *doing*. And this *doing* is community.

A playful conversation, in which musical utterances are provisional but give momentum to collective performance—to community in sound.

A playful game: "Understanding can no more be *reproductive* than a game can consist of exact duplications or repetitions of the *same* acts and events of play."[58]

But surely there are still winners and losers, those who do not feel that the emerging conversation represents them with integrity and nuance?

Yes—but this is a reality of human volition and creativity. To play the game of relationality is always a risk. Vulnerability is always a part of relationships.

The risk of listening, in opening ourselves to something new.

---

55 Gadamer, *Truth and Method*, 550–51.
56 Feld, "Sweet Lullaby", 124.
57 Grabowsky, "The Complete Musician."
58 Anthony Thiselton, *New Horizons in Hermeneutics* (London: Marshall Pickering, 1992), 328.

"There is in listening an active component and a passive one simultaneously, in the sense that you are receiving information, and immediately feeding it back into the conversation in order to move it forward."[59]

The same is true of tradition. Tradition is like a conversation: we listen, and we also feed back into it.

"Tradition is not simply a permanent precondition; rather, we produce it ourselves inasmuch as we understand, participate in the evolution of tradition, and hence further determine it ourselves."[60]

"A hermeneutics that regarded understanding as reconstructing the original would be no more than handing on a dead meaning."[61]

Tradition is generative, unfolding through multiple iterations, grooving toward something new. On one level, tradition is "what the ancestors used to do." But this is also what we do today, "for a new generation.

A groove that pulls the past and the present together.

A groove that enfolds us in an ongoing, ancestral conversation.

---

59 Paul Grabowsky, "Art Orchestra, ANAM, and Arnhem Land," presentation at the Australian National Academy of Music's *Fridays@3* public lecture series, Melbourne, 15 April 2011.

60 Hans-Georg Gadamer, *Truth and Method*, 293–4.

61 Hans-Georg Gadamer, *Truth and Method*, 159–60.

7

INTERWOVEN VOICES: A BRILLIANT AESTHETIC

The brilliance and aural vitality of *manikay* captures attention. The *ḏämbu* (head; intervallic framework) of *manikay* is performed in rich heterophony, each voice singing a line that is at once "the same but different". Although individual voices realise their own interpretation of the song text and melodic forms, they are caught up in a greater, coherent pattern. Like the surface of stream, smaller ripples and eddies play within the flow of the water as a whole. In *manikay*, different voices stand out, momentarily capturing attention before subsiding into the flowof the *ḏämbu*. The story of Djuwalpada and the sung names of people and places are carried by this interwoven cascade of voices, from the top to the bottom (audio example 7a).

Audio example 7a. "Gaḻpan̲" (Dillybag), *weaving* mode. Daniel Wilfred, Benjamin Wilfred, David Wilfred (*yiḏaki*), Andy Peters, Roy Natilma. Ngukurr, 8 July 2011.

In *manikay*, singers perform their own melodic realisations of a song within established parameters of rhythm and pitch. As each individual line plays out against the different realisations of other singers, the structure of the *gumurr* (chest)—the body of the song—is infilled with diverse colour and movement. The resulting texture is comparable to the aesthetic of *bir'yun* (brilliance) in painting. This aesthetic is amplified in *CRB*, in which collective improvisation results in a textual density comparable to heterophonic brilliance of *manikay*.

Performing Movement

As eyes shift over a landscape taking in infinitely differing perspectives, ears shift through the layers of sound in *manikay*, delineated but complementary as they build together from a common blueprint. Corn has written: "We are lost in

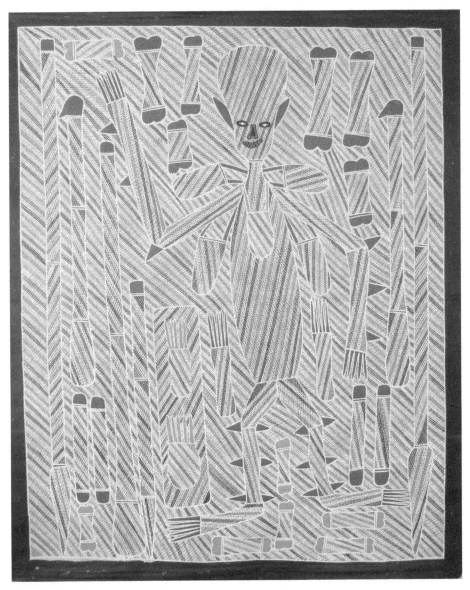

Fig. 7.1. Wally Wilfred, *Devil Devil*, 2012. Showing *rärrk* (cross-hatching). Original, 145 x 117 cm. Reproduced with permission.

these delicately intertwined voices: their melismatic lines gracefully permutating around the ideal of a unified melody."[1] Unique to every performance, every moment, every listener, attention shifts between voices: an individual vocal thread is loosed from the fabric, brought to attention or rising above the others; an individual becomes lost in the texture, subsumed in a living community of sound.

---

1   Aaron Corn and Neparrŋa Gumbula, "Formal Flexibility", 2.

Fig. 7.2. A canopy of palm leaves in Arnhem Land.

In Yolŋu music, dance, and design, *märr* (ancestral essence; vitality) is inseparable from aesthetic affect. While the use of term *märr* varies within different Yolŋu languages, "it always refers to the inalienable relationships of the *bäpurru*, to its sites, language and ancestral essences".[2] *Märr* concerns the ongoing efficacy of ancestral patterns and law, as these enliven present life and give it vitality; where ceremonial expressions bring ancestral precedence to life, they are full of *märr*.

Bir'yun (brilliance; shimmering) might be considered the aesthetic realisation of *märr*. Howard Morphy has explored the attribute of *bir'yunaramirri* (having brilliance) in *miny'tji* (design), created through the technique of *rärrk* (cross-hatching) (fig. 7.1).[3] Creating dynamism and movement, *rärrk* is made up of dense, finely drawn parallel lines that infill figurative forms and surfaces, especially in bark paintings. "The underlying pattern is clearly defined yet the surface of the painting appears to move; it is difficult to fix the eye on a single segment without interference from others."[4]

The aesthetic of *bir'yun* might also be seen replicated in nature (fig. 7.2), as in a dense canopy of palm leaves criss-crossed and moving gently in the

---

2   James, "The Language of 'Spiritual Power'", 251–2.
3   Morphy, "From Dull to Brilliant"; *Ancestral Connections*, 193; *Becoming Art*, 92–6.
4   Morphy, *Becoming Art*, 92.

breeze. *Bir'yun* is conveyed through movement and energy: for example, the shimmering *rärrk* in a painting of a *mäna* (shark) conveys "the flash of pain and fury in the eye of the shark as it tries to escape from the hunter and lashes out in anger. Its fury is also reflected in the energetic steps of the dancers in ritual as they re-enact the stages of its journey."[5]

Like the *dämbu* (pitch sequence) in *manikay*, each *bäpurru* uses their own signature pattern of *rärrk* to generate a continual play of movement, filling and animating the figurative forms of a painting. This aesthetic is not limited to sensual apprehension and stimulation, which the original nineteenth-century definition of the term *aesthetics* as the "perception of beauty by the senses" might suggest.[6] *Bir'yun* is not just a sensual play but could be considered the power of *manikay* to effectively engage someone in life as the expression of ancestral law and patterns for living—following in the "foot tracks" of ancestors. Consequently, the aesthetic of *bir'yun* is inherently political and ethical, in sustaining a view of the world in which family, law, ceremony, and country extend from the original power of ancestral action.

The pervasive groove of *manikay* might also be considered a way of generating *bir'yun*, where melodic realisations of the *dämbu* are energised by rhythm. *Manikay* is inseparable from *buŋgul* (dance) and performances inspire bodies to move. When the *yutuŋgurr* (thigh) section of a *manikay* item begins, dancers leap into action, advancing toward the singers who sit facing them. Their feet move rapidly up and down, pointed elbows quivering with energy. The flick of dust from the ground, the movement of a hand swishing a bunch of leaves, the back-and-forth advance and retreat of the dance formation, the glint of eyes brandishing a spear; all these elements combine with vitality. Bodies are caught up in the rhythmic play of the song, the complexity of movement shimmering as it is carried by the persistent *bilma* groove.

In performance, singers make use of different combinations of text, rhythm, and pitch, with great variety. Singers improvise from a known vocabulary of words that poetically explicate a song subject. Daniel Wilfred explains: "When Djuwalpada walks, he gives those names for the songs, those totems [central narrative tenets]. We call those same words—reverse and forwards—when we sing. Change them around."[7] Words oscillate on the sustained, repeated pitches of the *dämbu* (head); pitches oscillate on the sets of appropriate words for each song subject.

---

5 Morphy, *Ancestral Connections*, 190.
6 Aesthetics as the "perception of beauty by the senses" was a concept first used by German philosopher Alexander Baumgarten (1714–1762). Alan Goldman, "The Aesthetic", in *The Routledge Companion to Aesthetics*, ed. Berys Gaut and Dominic Lopes (Oxon, England: Routledge, 2005), 255.
7 Benjamin Wilfred, interview with the author, Melbourne, 19 March 2011.

INTERWOVEN VOICES: A BRILLIANT AESTHETIC

Märr (ancestral essence; vitality) is also sustained by a singer's strong, independent voice. With conviction, the *liya-waŋa* (coda) extends the expressive and dynamic intensity of the *gumurr* (chest), concluding a song by reiterating key words on a sustained final pitch (audio example 7b). Vocal intensity is only released by the terminal inflection, a pitch fall-off. The longer and stronger the *liya-waŋa*, the more receptive the audience is with cries of "*Yo!*" (Yes!), and "*Manymak*" (Good). With strong voices, the vitality of performance is sustained, before abruptly breaking off into informal chatter and sips of tea in between *manikay* items.

Audio example 7b. "Malka" (String bag), *dancing* mode. *Liya-waŋa* (coda) sung by Daniel Wilfred with Benjamin Wilfred, Roy Natilma, Andy Peters, and David Wilfred (*yidaki*). Ngukurr, 8 July 2012.

The complexity of the *liya-waŋa* (coda) intensifies and grows longer over the course of an evening's performance; the informal rests between songs gradually become shorter. Cries of "one more, one more", spur singers on. After a few hours of outdoor performance, the singers' fatigued voices start to crack with new, rich timbres. This is the time when a singer needs to keep working hard: "Go for it! Die or life", exclaims David Wilfred.[8] More singers are encouraged to join in, getting to their feet and huddling together in a tight circle. In dynamic community, *märr* (ancestral vitality) depends upon individual effort, engaged bodies sweating as they push through one more song. *Manikay* is alive.

SAMUEL CURKPATRICK: How do you make *manikay* powerful?

BENJAMIN WILFRED: You have to keep going. Strong voice; a lot of heart. A lot of going up high [over others] … keep going; keep remembering. The didj has to keep going too. Until you die, then you give up [*laughs*].

SC: When there are more voices, is that more powerful?

BW: Yeah. You just gotta keep doing it. Keep going, until you die.

DAVID WILFRED: I might die while playing *yidaki* [*laughs*].[9]

The way that the individual voices of singers rise momentarily above the thick *manikay* texture is also characteristic of sacred singing performed without the *yidaki* (didjeridu)—in contrast to the public repertoire of *manikay*. Obscured from the view of outsiders, women, and children, a body is moved into its coffin. The

---

8   David Wilfred, interview with the author, Ngukurr, 18 August 2010.
9   Benjamin Wilfred and David Wilfred, interview with the author, Melbourne, 19 March 2011.

voice of a knowledgeable elder is heard rising over song and rapidly striking *biḻma*, intoning the deep names of ancestral figures and places. These sacred *yäku* (names) connect everyone present to a common history and orientation, identifying the strings of connection that form the deceased's *bäpurru*. Sacred *yäku* not only name past ancestors, but merge with the deep names of those present.

In the public context of *CRB*, a similar intoning of *yäku* (names) can be heard when singers "call up" the wind (audio example 7c). The wind also carries like a voice with rich timbre, rising over the top of *manikay*. Just like the structuring forms of *manikay*, the wind is only known as a sensation—experienced through its movement. The wind blows across different individuals, communities, language groups, and homelands (see Chapter Four). This is a narrative the AAO can easily generate.

 Audio example 7c. "Wata" (Wind), *picking up* mode. Benjamin Wilfred calls up the wind with the AAO; Daniel Wilfred is singing. Quai Branly Museum, Paris, 10 November 2012.

As successive generations renew the movements and energies of ceremonial performance, life is animated as *ŋaḻabuluŋu rom* (following law). Strong voices resonate in chests and heads, and bodies are caught up in the momentums of song. Singers are pulled into a lively play of sound, rhythm, and words, their voices combining in a dense heterophonic weave. The *gumurr* (chest) of song is infilled with sound like *rärrk* (cross-hatching), enlivening the structural forms of *manikay* with brilliance.

Shifting Colours

The generation of vitality and movement integral to *manikay* is not impeded in *CRB*. The AAO contribute to *bir'yun* (brilliance) of *manikay* in a variety of ways. Like *manikay* singers, the AAO create complex, shifting timbres with their instruments, and through energetic rhythmic elaboration, the vitality of *bir'yun* is sustained.

In contributing to the brilliance of performance, AAO musicians participate in *manikay* as a living tradition. The content of their improvisations is not a primary concern for Wägilak: whatever sounds they perform are understood as additional voices woven into the already dense texture of *manikay*. What is important is that these voices contribute to the momentum of the *biḻma* and the shimmering play of sound. The aesthetic of *bir'yun* is enhanced through the layering of multiple voices, improvisations and the novel combination of sound. As in Yolŋu painting, such creativity in performance demonstrates "that things are as they have always been: the authority of their forbears is confirmed by the painting as a record of the performance of that authority."[10] The orthodox *ŋaraka* (bones) of *manikay* are filled with new vitality (see Chapter Five).

---

10 Caruana and Lendon, *Painters of the Wagilag Sisters*, 26.

In *CRB,* interwoven instrumental lines form a dynamic, shimmering canvas of sound: *bir'yunaramirri* (having brilliance) is effected through the energy of collective improvisation spurring the *manikay* singers on. In hearing and seeing performances of *CRB*, attention shifts between layers within the overall texture. This is accentuated by the largely unplanned, free-improvisational approach of the AAO in which the event of song is brought to the fore. That is, the generation of rhythm and sound, movement and energy.

As musicians address their attention to a musical idea or theme within *manikay*, new sounds and colours are introduced into the musical collective. Musicians give shape to the direction of the music sensitively, realising their immediate creative intentions within the shape and direction of collective performance. As Grabowsky suggests, "The object of the improvisation is the sublimation of the individual into the process of the group."[11] This is intensely relational. He continues, "Trust is everything in improvising, because your contribution during the improvisation will always be heard in relation to the input of the other players … Know when to lead and when to withdraw, and always engage with an open mind."[12] Flexibility and receptive listening are imperative to sustaining an improvised performance that would otherwise fall into an incoherent heap. Concepts of relationship, responsibility and community emerge through the unfolding event of performance.

Free improvisation draws attention to the dynamic play of musical elements within a work and the individuals involved, to their synthesis, contradiction, and abrupt or fluid variation. That the interplay of sound is brought to the fore itself resembles something of the aesthetic of *bir'yun*. A listener's aural attention alternates between performing individuals, aware of the dynamic relationship between the parts and the whole. Musicians respond to one another—"in the sense that you are receiving information, and immediately feeding it back into the conversation in order to move it forward."[13] It is a continuing dialogue out of which a community of district voices emerges. Grabowsky reflects: "This dynamic play of give and take is an ongoing process, a living thing."[14]

Within the collective, a musician conceives of an idea and brings something of it into play—a timbre, a rhythm, or a combination of sounds. In improvisation, the performance of movement never settles into an fixed representation but is sustained by tensions of anticipation and response, imitation and change. In real time, perspectives shift as the music unfolds. Ultimately, the goal of performance becomes the continuation of this conversation, which is more important than the intermittent results of performance. For Wägilak, this might be expressed as

---

11 Grabowsky, "Art Orchestra, ANAM, and Arnhem Land".
12 Ibid.
13 Ibid.
14 Grabowsky, "Art Orchestra, ANAM, and Arnhem Land".

the continual engagement with *manikay* as a conversation of identity, purpose, and place; ceremony sustains this interplay between ancestral constitution and present context.

Similar to the *ḻiya-waŋa* (coda) which sustains the *märr* (ancestral essence) of a song, improvisations in *CRB* extend a song beyond the final cadence point that concludes each *gumurr* (chest). This is demonstrated in the following audio example (7d), in which the AAO musicians can be sensed *feeling* for a way to continue the song. Benjamin Wilfred hears this as an extension of the *biḻma* mode, adding vocal interjections to carry this *groove* forward; David Wilfred, playing the *yiḏaki* (didjeridu) is also compelled to join. By analogy, the music of the AAO presents a compelling opportunity to sustain the *manikay* tradition.

Audio example 7d. "Djuwalpaḏa," *dancing* mode. Improvisation beginning with the piano (Paul Grabowsky) and clarinet (Tony Hicks); others progressively commit themselves into the mix. Paris, 10 November 2011.

Collective improvisation tends towards the creation of new textures and timbres, rather than integrated structures of melody and harmony as cohesive on a large scale. Consequently, what the AAO brings to *CRB* can be typified by: responsive melodic improvisations, drawing on the Wägilak *ḏämbu*; the generation of rhythmic momentum and groove, in line with the *biḻma* modes; the creation of new colours and sounds that fill out *manikay*, providing a sonic canvas or background of shifting colours, over which the *manikay* remain foregrounded. In these ways, *manikay* is a persistent feature of performances.

The Grain of the Voice

The following selections (audio example 7e) are taken from a live performance in Paris, 2012, and demonstrate different approaches to textural layering in *CRB* (see also Chapter Eight). If *rärrk* (cross-hatching) is used by Yolŋu to fill-out and bring movement to the orthodox, figurative forms of painting—often with bright, fluorescent colours—then a parallel might be drawn with *CRB*. Here, improvisations render the forms of *manikay* by adding colour and movement, also filling out the spaces around these *ŋaraka* structures. The complex density of the collective is befitting the heterophonic brilliance of *manikay*.

Audio example 7e. Three examples of improvised textures in *CRB*: a) "Gara" (spear), a textually dense section of independent voices; b) "Malka" (string bag), note the imitation of *ḏämbu* in the piano (Paul Grabowsky); c) Raki (string), with the synthesiser (Paul Grabowsky) and flute (Tony Hicks) used to create layers of colour alongside the continuing groove. Paris, 10 November 2012.

In the above examples, shifting textures and tone-colours provides the AAO with a means for animating sound; timbral construction and the various combination of different sounds are as important as structures of melody, harmony, and rhythm. Changing the colour of sound allows it to unfold, to shift, to move through time, or develop. Improvisations in CRB create interest through the different timbral grains produced by instrumental voices within the collective.

In manikay, the "grain of the voice"—a term borrowed from Roland Barthes—is an integral element enlivening performance.[15] As Daniel Wilfred explains, "I have the voices for Sambo [Barabara], Roy [Ashley] and mine. I choose which one to use; changing all the time."[16] When performing in CRB, Daniel introduces variety into a performance by imitating different voices of singers and family close to him including Roy Ashley, Sambo Barabara, and his son, Isaiah Wilfred. When he uses Barabara's voice, this makes him sad. During one performance at Museum and Art Gallery of the Northern Territory, he chose to imitate his older brother Barabara, because Barabara's *galay* (wife) was present in the audience.[17] This was something sad but also deeply significant: the use of Barabara's voice connected present listeners and performers with those past, caught up in the greater body of *gurruṯu* (kin) through the generations.

Jazz musicians have historically embraced timbral alteration as an integral element of musical creation: think of John Coltrane's frequent alteration of fingerings on the same pitch or Miles Davis' use of different mutes. Today, guitarists and keyboard players are endowed with a multitude of pedals and effects, which can be used to create new timbres by distorting or altering overtone constructions, and altering note envelopes and the relative amplitudes within a tone. To highly skilled musicians, these are not superficial effects but integral possibilities for sound manipulation and musical creation.

Likewise, wind instrumentalists often play half a dozen instruments—flute, piccolo, clarinet, bass clarinet, alto, tenor, and soprano saxophones—to achieve different sounds (audio example 7f). With all these possibilities on hand, new colours and alterations of timbre are created in collective ensembles primarily through the juxtapositions of sonic layers, an approach evident in CRB. To Grabowsky's suggestion, "So when Benjamin starts singing, Tony, I think we need a timbral change too. We need to mark that somehow," Hicks replies, "With a different instrument? Righto."[18] Hicks emphasises shifts within the *manikay* narrative with these instrument changes, and the use of different colours and timbres within his improvisations (audio example 7f).

---

15 Roland Barthes has identified the aesthetic significance of vocal timbre in contemporary music, naming this difficult-to-define attribute as "the grain of the voice". Roland Barthes. "The Grain of the Voice", in *Image, Music, Text*, trans. Steven Heath (New York: Hill and Wang, 1977), 179–90.

16 Daniel Wilfred, interview with the author, Ngukurr, 18 August 2010.

17 *CRB* was performed in 2012 at the opening of the exhibition *Colour Country: Art from Roper River*. See Bowdler, *Colour Country*.

18 Discussion during *CRB* rehearsal, Darwin, 22 May 2010.

Audio example 7f. Three examples of Tony Hicks' instrument selection (piccolo, flute, soprano saxophone) within the one concert. Monash University students—forming a small brass ensemble—can be heard in the middle of this example. Melbourne, 14 September 2012.

During rehearsal for a performance at the Darwin Entertainment Centre on 22 May 2010, musicians discussed the perceived necessity to create a basic, overarching structure to improvisations, to foster a sense of the unfolding narrative inherent to *manikay*. The intention was to open the concert with a sense of "new beginnings": the very start of Djuwalpa̱da's travels. This approach showed a concern to approach *manikay* as narrative, as well as to imitate *manikay* as a musical form. It was decided that providing a sense of shifting timbres or a changing "sonic canvas" was the way to go about this.

Since that rehearsal, most performances of *CRB* have begun with a slow unfolding of sound, starting from a barely audible dynamic and gradually shifting through different timbres and colours. Over the first few minutes of that concert in Darwin, musicians slowly entered the music one-by-one, adding new pitches and colours to the mix. This created a sense of growth and the disclosure of narrative. The rate of change in the music was slow but not inert, seeming to breathe or pulsate (audio example 7g). Daniel Wilfred also heard this as a narrative beginning.

Audio example 7g. The shimmering opening of *CRB*. Daniel Wilfred: "First song called Wild Blackfella. He went with his spears. This is the song." Paris, 10 November 2012.

Aesthetically, this opening suggests the an extended *ŋurru-waŋa* (nose-speech); in more recent performances, Daniel Wilfred has taken a similar approach, beginning a concerts by slowly humming, searching for his voice. A compounding amalgam of voices introduced progressively into the mix, moving from stillness to shimmering brilliance.

Grabowsky imagines this style of playing evocatively: "This is night. Now, the first rays of sun."[19] The image of a shimmering, rising sun illuminating everything that existed but was not seen, describes a performance of *manikay* that discloses the Wägilak narrative of old into the awareness of the present. With the opening *bilma* strike, the songs of Ŋilipidji are set in motion: Djuwalpa̱da begins to walk.

Textures of Situation

Our lives in a sense are not limited to the dates that define them, but are joined to those who came before us and to those yet to come. This

---

19 Paul Grabowsky, discussion during *CRB* rehearsal, Darwin, NT, 22 May 2010.

is the nub of the human experience, and Australia is home to some of the oldest expressions of this understanding in existence.[20]

Manikay is a heterophonic layering of musical components and voices; it is also a layering of people and situations through time, interweaving different generations and their stories. In every performance, different generations—past and present—come together. A performance of *manikay* is like the single fibre of a string, connected back into the past and also directed into the future, held together by the innumerable fibres twisting around it. When Yolŋu perform *manikay*, they are following in the tracks of those who have gone before, held in the present by the efficacious precedent of ancestral performance.

To the intuitive audience member, the display of Barabara's paintings during performances of *CRB* indicates the complex relations between design, song, and narrative involved in the Wägilak ceremony. Projected on screen, these paintings and other images of people and country from Ngukurr contribute to the heterophonic texture of performance. Barabara's award winning artworks extend the aesthetic of *bir'yun* (shimmering) beyond *rärrk* (cross-hatching) and into the striking use of colour. In his painting, Barabara embraced new materials, such as fluorescent paints, to extend the traditional aesthetic: "His work is firmly embedded in terms of subject matter and style, within the relatively fluid traditions of Arnhem Land, whilst exemplifying great personal innovation."[21]

The projections of Barabara's paintings in *CRB* are as central to the performance of *manikay* as is dance or language. Further, their bright, colourful brilliance seems to mirror the improvisations of the AAO. Grabowsky asserts, "Grandfather's [Barabara's] stuff is the bedrock. That's what we're building the thing on. That's the foundation. That's the root."[22]

The *CRB* collaborators search for ways to reflect this complex interweaving of media, inherent in *manikay,* in their performances. Lighting design, projection of images of country or film, surtitles, body paint, explanatory notes—all these media indicate to the multiple ways that Wägilak narrative might be expressed. An important step in this direction was the inclusion of a video of women dancing, in a concert held at the Australian National University, Canberra, on 22 September 2010. This footage had been recorded during the AAO's trip to Ngukurr in July that year and showed women in brightly coloured clothes dancing to a performance by the YWG. A short segment of a few minutes' length was looped throughout the entire performance that evening.

---

20 Grabowsky, "Art Is a River".

21 Bowdler, *Colour Country*, 69. Barabara's art most commonly depicts ceremonial subjects, including the cypress pine, sandridge goanna, saltwater crocodile, and Djuwalpada (sometimes referred to as *Devil Devil*).

22 Paul Grabowsky, discussion during *CRB* rehearsal, Melbourne, 21 March 2011.

Interestingly, the motion of the dancing on the video—slowed down from real-time and not synchronised with the music on stage—created another layer of rhythmic play within the overall performance. There is a propensity for visual rhythms to link in synchronicity or work against the heard rhythms of music. The different speed of the visual footage—which remained unsynchronised with the live performance—created a certain bi-rhythmic contrast to the rhythms heard in the performance. While the multiple grooves of slow-motion video and real-time performance were experienced simultaneously, the women were really dancing to the same *manikay* groove.

This video was warmly welcomed by all as important addition to the collaboration, especially as it overcame numerous logistical and financial barriers to having these women perform on tour. The video also offered an important point of engagement for an urban Australian audience entrenched in cultures of film. The desire to bring women performers on tour remains one of the main developments that the YWG would like to see happen in *CRB*. Women are an important part of the heterophonic mix of *manikay* performance and *gurruṯu* (kinship).

The layering of media within *CRB* contributes to the intensification of heterophonic experience for the audience, and points toward the complexity of layered narrative. As Wally Caruana and Nigel Lendon have explored in relation to Aboriginal visual art, new media of presentation help to "articulate the artist's authority in the expanded frame of reference of the new social arenas now addressed by the work".[23] Yolŋu readily embrace the possibility of new technologies (Chapter Two).

During the 2010 *CRB* tour to Ngukurr and Darwin, filmmaker Zbigniew (Peter) Friedrich accompanied the AAO, capturing a large amount of footage of people from Ngukurr, the surrounding countryside, the collaboration in rehearsal, performance, and social settings. Guitarist Ren Walters later produced a film to accompany performances of *CRB* that drew heavily on Friedrich's footage, which was first shown in a performance at Monash University on 14 September 2012. This film was subsequently used in performances at the London Jazz Festival and the Quai Branly Museum, Paris, in 2012.

Walters' film is a fragmented collation of images and video clips related to Wägilak *manikay* and *CRB*, depicting: basic figurative designs related to the Wägilak narrative; key song texts and place names; images of family and children in Ngukurr; images of the country around Ngukurr; images of Barabara's paintings. Occasional use of sound in the film also incorporates fragments of people's voices, and children's laughter and games.

Walters' video drew attention to the history of the collaboration, and the wider relationships and events that have shaped *CRB* over time, and which had

---

23 Caruana and Lendon, *Painters of the Wagilag Sisters*, 32.

led to the present iteration of *CRB* on stage. This layering of events and situations resonates with Yolŋu thought as Caruana and Lendon have described: "For the Yolngu, the Western convention of seeing—that is, to see a painting [or film] from the past as if it effects some historical closure—has little meaning insofar as all art exists simultaneously in the present and in the past."[24] Howard Morphy and Philippa Deveson describe the place of film in Yolŋu ceremonial expression in a similar way:

> Films of ceremonies themselves are both whole objects and components to be added to the other manifestations of ancestral action … Yolngu do not see them as an authoritative version that has to be replicated any more that they see sacred objects from the past as more authentic than objects made in the present. They are part of a composite that can be taken apart and put together again."[25]

Opening themselves to conversations outside of local ceremonial contexts, the YWG continue to assert the legitimate, orthodox *ŋaraka* (bones) of *manikay* within *CRB*. Like film, through which the Yolŋu have discovered "an instrument of education and, through this, political and legal persuasion",[26] the YWG "keep culture strong" by embracing new contexts to extend the core identities of land, society, and law carried in *manikay*.

Through film and image, different individuals and situations coalesce into present performance. Gadamer's understanding of history resonates strongly with this notion: "Time is no longer primarily a gulf to be bridged because it separates; it is actually the supportive ground of the course of events in which the present is rooted."[27] In *manikay* and *CRB*, cultural tradition is that which supports and animates present performance. The varied contexts of performances, presentations, and educational workshops are layered together in a collaboration that encompasses a range of events. Each of these contexts allows the Wägilak narrative to be presented in a new forum, opening the conversation to new individuals—"widening possibilities of significance and resonance, extended by the different people receiving it".[28]

CRB shows *manikay* as a complex layering of multiple media and situations, past generations, distant homelands, designs, dances, and narratives, which coalesce together giving shape to a unique present. This is the *bambula*

---

24 Caruana and Lendon, *Painters of the Wagilag Sisters*, 22.

25 Howard Morphy and Philippa Deveson, "Material Expressions of Ancestral Agency: Yolngu Acting in a Virtual Space", paper presented in the *Adrian Gerbrands Lecture* series, Leiden University, Netherlands, 7 June 2011. http://www.fel-leiden.nl/wp-content/uploads/Gerbrandslecture-Howard-Morphy3.pdf: 22.

26 Philippa Deveson, "The Agency of the Subject: Yolngu Involvement in the Yirrkala Film Project", *Journal of Australian Studies* 35, no. 2 (2011): 155.

27 Gadamer, *Truth and Method*, 297.

28 Ibid., 458.

(ceremonial ground), where different families are brought together, and where present performance shapes our understandings of one another and our place in society, culture, and history. Through performance, the present is formed as a brilliant, lively articulation of the past, and as an expression of ongoing ancestral creativity.

8

COLLABORATION AND CREATIVITY

Jazz musicians generally think deeply about the creative drive behind their music. As artists rather than academics, this thinking is directed toward new possibilities, to sounds and processes that extend and innovate. Jazz performances reach toward a future which is energised in the creativity of the moment, imagining something new in response to the sonic environment and traditions around them. The various cultural forms, ideas and expressions a musician is exposed to inspire this creative moment and are skilfully draw into a musician's expression of voice.

Casting his ears back through history, Grabowsky understands jazz as a "music of process ... a child of many parents born out of wedlock."[1] Jazz, which "spins on the pin-head of real time, the result of untold billions of spontaneous decisions", lives in the present but carries with it the voices and fragrances of the past. If *manikay* expresses the immanence of ancestral creativity, jazz expresses the pervasive creativity of human experience that continually expands on what has gone before. Grabowsky continues:

> We have forgotten the original purpose of music, which has something to do with expressing the continual act of creation, which is the meaning of life. The sense that the creation is ever present, that the infinite past is implicit in the present, and that the present is already both past and future, thus music is a way of changing the mode of one's relationship to one's surroundings.[2]

---

1   Grabowsky, "The Complete Musician."
2   Ibid.

As a tradition, jazz contains many contradictions. It is a nebulous concept and musicians performing under this rubric explore widely diverse frameworks and musical languages—yet they nevertheless perform jazz. Commonly understood through the historical progression of styles like blues, swing, bebop, cool, soul, funk, and free, jazz encompass music from America, Europe and Asia; spans the 1920s to the 2020s; intersects with histories of African-American slavery, World War Two, modernism, and postmodernism; and embraces technologies from the LP to the internet. Jazz is this story of historical movement and change. Jazz is what persists through this history as an attitude, the impetus to *find a voice* and the freedom of vocative musical utterance and expression.[3]

In contrast to the present event of creativity at the heart of jazz, writing about music seems second-hand, somehow removed from the reality of participation in performing, listening, or dancing. Similarly, the identification of essential stylistic traits of a performance or transcription itself removes sounds from the relational address of performer to listener. As a relatively stable depiction of musical form, notation underwrites direct, bounded repetition which, as musician and academic Jeff Pressing suggests, "tends to clash … with the idea of the essential uniqueness of the moment that forms part of the jazz attitude."[4] While this may seem anathema to the Wägilak impetus to sustain ancestral forms and narratives, the YWG also encounter a sort of freedom in *CRB*, in expressing their voices within new relationships, places, and technologies. Tradition is given freedom from the past as a living narrative: "Old and new ways are always combining into something of living value."[5]

During a concert of *CRB* in Darwin on 22 May 2010, Grabowsky displayed a slideshow of photographs of African-American jazz greats such as Miles Davis and Ornette Coleman on his laptop, which sat atop the grand piano facing out into the audience. Sitting alongside a projected image of Barabara's painting of Djuwalpada titled *Medicine Man*, these photographs situate the performance within an effective history of jazz, the present performance articulating into an ongoing conversation with those great musicians. As in the Yolŋu world, the creativity and approaches of these leading *songmen* (Davis, Coleman, etc.) from generations past continues to resonate within *CRB* today, through the constitution of the AAO musicians within ongoing conversations of jazz. As in *manikay*, musical performance here perpetuates an awareness of life within coordinates of substantiating history.

---

3   *Vocative* is used here in the sense of the grammatical mood of personal address. Jazz musicians speak, cry, moan, or scat to those who will hear. This metaphor might be contrasted with classical music as *indicative*.

4   Jeff Pressing, "Free Jazz and the Aavant-Garde", in *The Cambridge Companion to Jazz*, ed. Mervyn Cooke and David Horne (Cambridge: Cambridge University Press, 2003), 204.

5   Gadamer, *Truth and Method*, 305.

In *CRB*, we also understand *manikay* as a meeting of difference, with different families, languages, narratives, and musical repertoires coming together in the present act of performance. This does not mean that what the AAO performs is definitively *manikay*. Approached as a set of definitive stylistic idioms and musical forms, free jazz improvisation is unlike *manikay* and even incompatible with it. Yet so long as the YWG claim that *CRB* is performed as an event within the *manikay* tradition, the widely diverse musical forms that coalesce in this event need not be problematised. Similarly, one might observe that the forms of *free jazz* are also unlike those of the blues, and yet the AAO musicians continue to perform within this tradition of *finding a voice* through improvisation, in response to the contexts they find themselves in.

The desire for new expressions of creativity shape the AAO's desire to hear the unique voices of other cultures, such as *manikay*, that these might enrich present musical conversation and challenge assumptions about music and performance. This openness to hearing another voice allows the discovery of *manikay* as a tradition with something to say to the present, enriching the relationships in which it is performed—here, a collaboration between Yolŋu and Balanda. The project has given those involved an experience of co-creation in ways not previously imagined, a shared discourse that is not only respectful of the past but generative, a process opening new horizons of possibility "for a new generation." This is an orientation on which *manikay* and *jazz* might readily agree. AAO violinist Erkki Veltheim reflects:

> I don't think the AAO could lay claim to the term *manikay* [in what they play]. That would seem to me culturally colonialist. I do think something unique must occur as a result of any such dialogue across a great cultural divide, even if it ends up being but a misunderstanding … Perhaps the important thing is not the end product, but the very process of open engagement.[6]

Open Playground

Rather than conforming to stylistic agendas, the liberalism at the heart of jazz—an energetic expression of freedom—allows the music of *CRB* to emerge with substantial variety in every performance. *CRB* is a dynamic, conversational play of voices, like AAO musician Tony Hicks' description of his project with David Tolley, *The Expose Project*: "A playground for engaging in joyous investigation of our relationship[s] through sounding."[7]

---

6   Interview with the author, Melbourne, 17 October 2011.
7   Tony Hicks, "The Path to Abstraction: A Practice Led Investigation into the Emergence of an Abstract Improvisation Language." Masters diss. (Victorian College of the Arts and Music, University of Melbourne, 2011), 65.

Each performer brings a unique set of sounds and approaches to their improvisations. Indeed, playing a specific instrument opens a perspective on music, an approach that is shaped by technology and technical possibility—an instrument's timbre, note envelope, range, and dexterity—as well as the histories, traditions, and pedagogies of which that instrument is a part. Improvisation, then, lives in a productive tension between new possibility and implicit limitation. History effectively shapes our orientation and view of creativity, summed up by Gunther Schuller in the maxim, "Technique is content and content is technique."[8]

When Australians start to look at our geographic place in the world, they begin to realise that most of our inherited cultural forms are a long way from their origins. While the AAO continue to celebrate the rich possibilities of these inherited traditions, they also seek new engagements with the musical cultures present in our global neighbourhood. Seeking to shift dominant paradigms of musical creation and to hear musical voices they have not yet heard, the AAO have constantly sought ways to engage with diverse musical cultures. Typically, this has been approached with an openness to what might emerge, and sustained through friendships and ongoing learning.

> This notion is at the heart of my concept of music as language, and it is in the spirit of collaboration and communication that the AAO has worked in recent years with musicians from different musical language groups, from Bali, from South India, with classical musicians, with musicians from pop and rock and increasingly with musicians from our Indigenous communities.[9]

As we have seen in *CRB*, new structures need to be developed—even in the loosest sense of the word—to allow cohesive performance. Historically, the free jazz movement sought to improvise form and not only content-in-form: improvised sounds were not contained within a structure but gave rise to that structure. Pressing explores the origins of free jazz: "The first unmistakably relevant evidence of free musical improvisation appears to be the home recordings made in the early 1940s in New York by jazz violinist Stuff Smith (Hezekiah Leroy Gordon Smith) and concert pianist Robert Crum. Later, in 1949, pianist Lennie Tristano's jazz group recorded the first spontaneous studio tracks, "Intuition" and "Digression".[10] Free jazz also liberated approaches to timbre, colour, and the raw sounds of multiphonics from the predominance

---

8   Gunther Schuller. Liner notes to the reissue of *Free Jazz* (recording), by the Ornette Coleman Double Quartet. New York: Atlantic Recording Corporation, 1997.

9   Grabowsky, "The Complete Musician".

10   Pressing, "Free Jazz," 207.

of established melodic and harmonic traditions.[11] Ornette Coleman describes this radical approach: "I play pure emotion ... Blow what you feel—anything. Play the thought, the idea in your mind—break away from the convention and stagnation—escape!"[12]

A decade or so after these beginnings, saxophonist Ornette Coleman came to be widely recognised as the great advocate of free jazz, giving name to the concept on his 1960 album, *Free Jazz*.[13] Coleman went on to coalesce his ideas of improvisation into a concept known as *harmolodics*, which also characterises a common approach to improvisation in *CRB*. In *harmolodics*, a group of musicians improvise collectively, basing their improvisations on a distinct musical fragment or theme. Each musician responds to this content in their own unique way, improvising simultaneously. No one line is more important than any other and "the fine points of each player's phrasing and inflection are deliberately invoked to render each voice distinct."[14]

Improvisation foregrounds decision. The largely unplanned, free-improvisation approach of the AAO highlights the event of creativity, as sounds and musical ideas are seemingly brought out of nothing, conceived *in the moment*. Musicians address their attention to an aspect of the ongoing musical conversation and commit a thought to sound, generating ongoing musical discourse. Grabowsky expands on this tactical "thinking on your feet", which has been described by David Ross as a game of what-to-do and when-to-do-it, "creative problem solving in real time":[15]

> Effective improvisation requires a flexibility of response, based on knowledge of what belongs where, and how best and most creatively to make decisions in the moment ... The spur of the moment, a wonderful word-picture, is exactly where improvisation takes place. A true improvisation lives for, and in, the moment of its creation. So you can imagine that an extended improvisation is the sum of countless millions of improvised decisions, each one existing only in the passing flash of its execution and yet somehow managing to be part of something utterly coherent. Even improvisations that are made up

---

11 Expanding conceptions of sound in improvised music reflected movements in the world of visual art and European/American classical music of the period. See Alyn Shipton, *A New History of Jazz* (New York: Continuum, 2007), 539–626.

12 Ornette Coleman, "Discourse: the Harmolodic Manifesto." http://www.ornettecoleman.com/course.swf.

13 Pianist Cecil Taylor was, independently of Coleman, another key architect of the *free jazz* direction of the 1960s. Other players (especially in the United States) with intersecting interests were Sun Ra, John Coltrane, Evan Parker, Richard Abrams and the Art Ensemble of Chicago, Pharoah Saunders, Miles Davies, and Archie Shepp. Pressing, "Free Jazz".

14 Palmer, Robert. Liner notes to *Ornette Coleman, Beauty is a Rare Thing: The Complete Atlantic Recordings*, by Ornette Coleman. New York: Rhino Records, 1993.

15 David Ross, Activating Bodies of Knowledge: Improvisation, Cognition, and Sports Education, *Critical Studies in Improvisation* 7, no. 2 (2011): http://www.criticalimprov.com/article/view/1314.

of seemingly random and disconnected events can have an inherent logic not immediately evident; it remains the quality of the concept, and the ability of its creator(s) to realise it, that makes the difference between good and bad improvising.[16]

Playing the game of improvisation demands a certain reliance on technical ability and musical aptitude—the improviser must throw themselves into this *game*. As Gadamer has written, "The attraction of the game, which it exercises on the player, lies in this risk. One enjoys a freedom of decision, which at the same time is endangered and irrevocably limited."[17] Limitations that define creativity—or possibilities—are created by the sounds and ideas of other musicians. For example, in *CRB*, the presence of *manikay* becomes a framework both limiting and enabling creative performance; *manikay* is embraced as a means of shaping improvisations through apparent divergence and convergence.

In this sense, *manikay* becomes a basic chart for performance, a musical theme generating response, and the nuances of *manikay* become more apparent as the collaboration matures. This represents a shift from Coleman's notion of *free jazz*: "Coleman saw *Free Jazz* as epitomizing liberation from preconception, and its absence of formal structure and harmony as allowing musicians who were normally restricted by their training to discover more about themselves."[18] Where Coleman wanted to do away with any possible preconception of structure—, *CRB* embraces the patterns and limitations of *manikay* as necessary to productive and ongoing musical creation.

AAO musicians are sympathetic to the ŋaraka (bones) of Wägilak *manikay* necessarily underpinning culturally legitimate performance. This approach displays parallels with Bill Evans' description of the seminal Miles Davis album *Kind of Blue* from 1959—even as the music manifests with dramatically different results:

> This conviction that direct deed is the most meaningful reflection, I believe, has prompted the evolution of the extremely severe and unique disciplines of the jazz or improvising musician. Group improvisation is a further challenge. Aside from the weighty technical problem of the collective, coherent thinking, there is the very human, even social need for sympathy from all members to bend for the common result ... As the painter needs his framework of parchment, the improvising musical group needs its framework in time.[19]

Importantly, the long-term viability of *CRB* as an engagement with Wägilak culture depends on healthy and respectful relationships, more so than musical

---

16 Grabowsky, "Art Orchestra, ANAM, and Arnhem Land".
17 Gadamer, *Truth and Method*, 95.
18 Shipton, *A New History*, 572.
19 Evans, *Kind of Blue*, 2.

inspiration (see Epilogue). Likewise, the continuation of ceremony requires the maintenance of reciprocal *gurrutu* (kinship) obligations. To locate the collaboration in *pure sound* reduces creativity to a technical practice removed from the dynamics of human life. Only in performance as a living expression of relationships will *CRB* avoid devolving into the austere trajectory of free jazz critiqued by Evans, and have something creative to say within real contexts of time, culture, language, and place.

In the Neighbourhood

The AAO is, at heart, a collaborative ensemble. Many of their projects involve engagement with different musical styles from around the world. These projects, each in their own distinctive way, require flexibility in listening and improvising with musicians from Chennai, Bali, Japan, and Korea, just to name a few.

Since its foundation in 1993, "One of the primary aims of the AAO has been to create situations allowing for a free and open exchange of musical and dramatic ideas between different cultures and traditions."[20] Each of the AAO's projects manifests in dramatically different ways, and improvisation is at the core of these experimental engagements. As George Lewis explains, "In performances of improvised music, the possibility of internalising alternative value systems is implicit from the start. The focus of musical discourse suddenly shifts from the individual, autonomous creator to the collective."[21]

In 2000, the AAO began working with Balinese musicians and composers in a project named *Theft of Sita*, directed by Nigel Jamieson (audio example 8a). This project incorporated music, song, storytelling, puppetry, and video in a telling of the Ramayana narrative that relayed the ancient Sanskrit epic in Bahasa Indonesia, a modern language, with focus given to themes of revolution, democracy, corruption, and money. Grabowsky worked closely with new-music composer I Wayan Gde Yudane and Balinese poet Ketut Yuliarsa to create this intriguing work.

Audio example 8a. Excerpt from the *Song of Sita*, from the collaboration *Theft of Sita*. The singer is Shelly Scown.[22]

An insistence on equal partnership with Indonesian artists, the respect of different cultural expertise, the use of musical imitation as an important means of engagement, and a commitment to better understanding the forms of Balinese music shaped this collaboration. Grabowsky reflects on *Theft of Sita*

---

20 Australian Art Orchestra. "Australian Art Orchestra: Projects." http://aao.com.au/projects/program/.

21 George E. Lewis, "Improvised Music After 1950: Afrological and Eurological Perspectives," *Black Music Research Journal* 22, supplement (2002): 234.

22 Australian Art Orchestra, *Theft of Sita*, composed by Paul Grabowsky in association with I Wayan Gde Yudane, CD (North Melbourne: Australian Art Orchestra, 2000).

and its dissimilarities with "world music", a gene that started to take shape in the 1980s:[23]

> Cross cultural collaborations are delicate situations. In an age where the term *world music* has come to disguise a multitude of musical crimes and in which sampling technology has resulted in wide spread looting of cultural artefacts, reducing everything to the status of the *found object*, the onus on our creative team has been to approach the composition process as a partnership.[24]

Other collaborations undertaken by the AAO are shaped by similar approaches but with widely diverse results. *The Chennai Sessions* (*Into the Fire*) brings Indian Carnatic musicians, composers and the virtuoso Mridangam player Guru Karaikudi Mani into the AAO, shaping performances that explore complex rhythmic possibilities (audio example 8b): "The rhythmic intricacies and improvising practices that reside at the core of both the South Indian Carnatic tradition and the Western jazz tradition are revealed in this program in virtuosic splendour."[25]

 Audio example 8b. Opening of *Sacred Cow's Tail*, from *The Chennai Sessions*.[26]

The AAO collaboration The Hollow Air, directed by trumpeter Phillip Slater, looks to possibilities of timbral and tonal variation through improvisation with Japanese shakuhachi player Riley Lee. Kura Tungar: River Songs and Stories (also Ruby's Story) was a project with Aboriginal singer-songwriters Ruby Hunter and Archie Roach that has a more fixed compositional/arrangement base. A more recent intercultural collaboration of the AAO is The Return of Spring, with Bae Il Dong and other Korean musicians. Other eclectic projects such as Ringing the Bell Backwards and Soak—influenced by artists such as Arvo Pärt, Henryk Górecki, Brian Eno, Radiohead, Dust Brothers, and Miles Davis— are collaborative in their juxtaposition of multiple strands of European and American traditions and performers. Here, as in all AAO engagements, unique music emerges through the productive interplay of diverse traditions. Schäuble reflects on the place of *CRB* within this oeuvre:

> I see *CRB* as being part of the inter/cross cultural stylistic block— referring to *Into the Fire*, but also to the Hunter/Roach collaboration

---

23 Feld writes about the emergence of the genre *world music*, which began to attract popular attention due to the high profile, highly financed commercial marketing of record companies. Early examples include the Beatles' adventures with Ravi Shankar in the 1960s and 1970s; 'Paul Simon's *Graceland* (1986) with South African musicians; David Byrne's *Rei Momo* (1989) with Latin musicians. Feld, "A Sweet Lullaby", 149.

24 Grabowsky, "Theft of Sita", program notes, http://aao.com.au/projects/program/theft-of-sita/.

25 Australian Art Orchestra, "Projects".

26 Australian Art Orchestra, *The Chennai Sessions (Into the Fire): Australian Art Orchestra and Guru Karaikudi Mani* (North Melbourne: Australian Art Orchestra, 2008).

[*Kura Tungar*], as well as the early *Theft of Sita* project. I think *CRB* is well on the way to matching the degree of interaction within these projects, which have the *advantage* of their artistic traditions being related more closely. These projects are steeped in a mix of traditions, mainly Western classical and jazz, with a typical Australian approach, i.e. having enjoyment of the process and recognising performance as an integral part.[27]

The AAO conceive music as a means for engaging with other cultures and traditions different to their own. By providing space for personal expression and conversation, these projects open the horizons of individuals through interpersonal engagement in sound. This ethos builds on attitudes of vocative expression born in jazz histories. While the original music created by the AAO might herald a distinctive Australian musical identity—drawing on the unique influences and cultures that are held together within society—sound engineer John O'Donnel indicates to one of the most important outcomes: a sense of beauty in creating something new.

It's extraordinary … this band, it's just an extraordinary group of people that, musically, don't seem to have any kind of fear or notions that they can't do something. They sit down there and they go, "That's a challenging piece of music to improvise to," yet somehow they create beautiful music.[28]

Musical Voices

Every musician in *CRB* brings their own sounds and voices to the project. These are the very possibility for creativity; each musician has something different to say. Every improvisation is also a unique response within time and place. Players speak into the musical conversations going on around them, and address broader concerns of tradition. Within the great liberal tradition of jazz improvisation, individual players perform dynamic and colourful responses to Wägilak *manikay*, illuminating jazz as a history of seeking a voice. This process resonates with Gadamer's approach to understanding as an unfolding, conversational process, which has informed the theoretical underpinnings of this book. In the musical conversation of *CRB*, a shared future is opened that cannot be fully anticipated, yet is born of the traditions and perspectives that feed into present performance:

In speaking, one word brings forth another, and hence our thinking gets promulgated. A word becomes real when it proffers itself in our

---

27 Niko Schäuble, interview with the author, 13 October 2011.
28 John O'Donnel, quoted in Australian Broadcasting Commission, "Orchestra Collaborates".

speaking on its own out of however thoroughly pre-schematized a thesaurus and customary usage. We speak that word and it leads to consequences and ends we had not perhaps conceived of.[29]

The following table (table 8.1) describes characteristics that represent the general improvisational approach of each player from the AAO, the approach each brings to the musical conversation. Examples are given from the first *CRB* album, recorded in 2009 and released in 2010, and typify many live performances of *CRB*. On this recording, Wägilak approaches to improvisation are conservative, showing little divergence from the idiomatic forms of Wägilak *manikay* (see Chapter Five). Developments in Wägilak approaches to improvisation are discussed shortly. The below descriptions should only be considered partially representative and, ultimately, as generalisations (audio examples 8c–j).

Table 8.1. Characteristic approaches to improvisation in *CRB*, based on the 2010 album.

Musician	General approach to improvisation on *CRB* album	Audio example
Tony Hicks, winds	Use of rapid passages to create colours around the *yiḏaki* (didjeridu) or *manikay* voices. Frequent changes between different instruments.	**8e** "Djuwalpaḏa"
	Solo improvisations based on the intervallic material of *manikay*, elaborating key pitches with ornaments, tonal inflections, and phrases.	**8c** "Birrkpirrk" (Plover)
Erkki Veltheim, violin/viola	Melodic and harmonic oriented fragments; extended sections of improvisation often follow the intervallic structure of *manikay*. Harmonic sequences and pitch series suggest a strong connection with European traditions, especially in their intervallic construction.	**8c** "Birrkpirrk" (Plover)
Paul Grabowsky, keyboards	Rhythmically repetitive ideas, based on the *biḻma* (clapstick) cadence rhythms, which are shifted complex harmonic patterns or pitch series. Alternatively, simple rhythmic ideas are displaced or undergo rhythmic contraction/expansion.	**8c** "Raki" (String)
	Creation of complex timbres with synthesised sounds or extended piano techniques.	**8e** "Djuwalpaḏa"

---

29 Gadamer, *Truth and Method*, 552.

Niko Schäuble, drums	Alternations between fluid rhythmic gestures and more regular, repetitive (although complex) grooves. Imitation of *bilma* modes and cadences.	**8e** "Djuwalpa_da_"
Philip Rex, double bass	High degree of rhythmic interaction with the *bilma* groove, providing an underlying pulse and energetic drive.	**8i** "Galpa_n_" (Dillybag)
Stephen Magnusson, guitar	Creation of a sonic background over which action occurs. Subtle shifts in timbre and heavy use of effects create interest. Occasional melodic solo.	**8j** "Galpa_n_" (Dillybag)

Being a melodic player, everything I do is like a lead statement. To form those statements, I had to develop new techniques and approaches for exploring micro-tonality, and as my own practice developed and my ears became more attuned to the music, it stopped sounding out of tune. It was as if a whole new world opened up.

—Tony Hicks[30]

I have tried different approaches, including attempting to create incidental sounds that follow the story of the manikay, as well as attempting to deliberately play against the manikay and create a strong musical argument based on my own interests: for example, trying to exaggerate the differences between our two musical cultures.

—Erkki Veltheim[31]

I am trying to grasp the rhythmic flow, which is different from the music I usually play. Having learned about the deeper meaning of the songs, I am approaching playing with the narration/story in mind, as the music of the songs—mostly in regard to pitch—are all very similar. I do try to interpret the meaning of the song and *translate* it into my own musical language, rather than just imitate the Wägilak style.

—Niko Schäuble[32]

The above audio examples (8c–j) and statements show the collaboration as a discursive conversation between ideas and approaches. An engaging performance relies on the skill of musicians to respond tactfully to the *manikay* also performed on stage. Permitting Wägilak concepts and sounds to work into

---

30 Tony Hicks quoted in Power, "Crossing the Divide: Music Bridges Two Cultures".
31 Interview with the author, 17 October 2011.
32 Interview with the author, 13 October 2011.

their own musical language, the music of this collective grows through new colours, shades, textures, and directions.

To sustain improvised performance through an hour-long *manikay* series, players must forgo fixed ideas of how the music should take shape. Within an improvised collective, every player must lead and every player must follow. In every moment musicians are responding to both the immediate sonic situation and their sense of greater musical development or course of events. Questions that run through a musician's head might be: Where is the music going? What could happen next? How can I show my intentions to others in what I perform? What are the intentions of others? How can I support another musician and give them space within the music? These dynamics also engage perceptive listeners.

AAO musicians have, to varying degrees, moved beyond the approaches to improvisation set out in the above table (table 8.1) in recent years. Continual development and musical exploration have always been an aim of *CRB* in rehearsal and concert; recordings only fix instances of this ongoing process. AAO musicians have also explored how their performance practices are shifting as a result of *CRB*. Tony Hicks' research thesis examined his own development as a musician. Tracing his approach to improvisation through different projects, a pervasive goal of Hicks remains the liberation of performance from old "codes of production", seeking to allow "for more contextually sensitive contributions within a range of unconventional music making contexts".[33] Considering *CRB*, Hicks writes:

> A new language was required that could express the raw power and transcultural potential of this collaboration … improvisation can exist to drive evolving creative processes, leading to profound creative transformations and the development of new languages.[34]

Hick's research extends directly into his approach to improvisation within *CRB*:

> By 2012, my individual approach had evolved and matured significantly due to my intensive investigation into textural and microtonal techniques to liberate me from the prejudices and effective histories of my jazz-based melodic language and traditional instrumental techniques. This evolution of approach can be heard by comparing my contributions to the 2009 and 2011 studio recordings and the Paris concert … The process of change that took place was partly inspired by working in CRB. This process involved the gradual dismantling of idiomatic melodic approaches to my instruments in free improvised contexts.[35]

---

33 Hicks, "The Path to Abstraction", 65.
34 Hicks, "The Path to Abstraction", 2–3.
35 Tony Hicks, discussion with the author, 2013.

Within *CRB*, the YWG have also started to find their own voices within this dynamic mix of traditions. *CRB* has allowed the YWG to engage with new ways of performing and to explore ideas of music as interpersonal dialogue and spontaneous creation. Engaging with the AAO musicians—who never play the same thing twice—has presented the YWG with a challenging performance context. Benjamin and Daniel Wilfred have become adept at finding opportune moments during instrumental improvisations at which to lead-in the *yuṯuŋgurr* (thigh) of the next song item, accommodating to the improvisations around them. If the music is soft and gentle, the *manikay* leader will respond slowly, extending the *ŋurru-waŋa* (nose-speech) so that the full singing voices emerge out of the *ŋurru-waŋa* gradually and not abruptly; if the improvisations are intense, then the *manikay* is brought in with great energy and vigour, the *biḻma* cutting through any volume the AAO can muster.

When Daniel Wilfred joined the *CRB* ensemble in 2010, there was a clear shift towards more improvised interaction from the YWG during performance. This has manifest in several ways. Particularly, where the YWG are engulfed by the sound of the AAO or caught up in the groove of the bass and drums, they feel no urgency to begin the next *manikay* item. Instead, they improvise along with the other musicians. Characteristically, David Wilfred improvises repetitive patterns and syncopated *hoots* (by overblowing the fundamental pitch) on the *yiḏaki*; Daniel and Benjamin Wilfred call out with syncopated vocal interjections, mimicking the cry of the *birrkpirrk* (plover); without the *biḻma*, Daniel Wilfred bends his voice around fluidly, reaching up to new pitches outside of the *ḏämbu* (audio example 8c). YWG improvisations occurring between the *manikay* items are a genuine part of the innovative mix.

Audio example 8c. Improvisations by Daniel, Benjamin and David Wilfred in "Raki" (String) and "Birrkpirrk" (Plover). The guitarist is Ren Walters. Melbourne, 14 September 2012.

Similarly, *CRB* concerts often open with material improvised by either by Benjamin and Daniel Wilfred. The example given below is taken from a concert at Monash University, Melbourne (audio example 8d). It is an opening improvised for its drama, the performers looking directly at the audience, with an intense, searching gaze, holding the audience's attention before the *biḻma* break the tension. Daniel explains: "I sing, 'Ahhh, ohhh.' That sound came from nowhere."[36] The other musicians respond, leaping into action.

> You hear Paul [Grabowsky]? You hear that wind sound he makes? We just listen to the orchestra, hear that song. You listen to Tony [Hicks], playing that saxophone [imitates saxophone]. David [Wilfred] plays

---

36   Daniel Wilfred, interview with the author, 15 September 2012.

the bass, that didj—like the drums. We listen; just play along .... I make that new song tonight.[37]

Audio example 8d. Opening of *CRB* improvised by Daniel and Benjamin Wilfred. This excerpt fades back in as the singers return to the same motif at a later stage. Melbourne, 14 September 2012.

We have considered Yunupingu's expression "connectedness in separation is not contradictory" in relation to the concept of *gularri* (floodwaters) (Chapter Three).[38] Similarly, *CRB* is animated by the connections and separations of the musicians on stage. *CRB* is a confluence of different streams: families, individuals, traditions, ideas, and aspirations. Converging together, the waters overflow, flooding the dry land and creating new, lifegiving billabongs. Around these freshwater pools, new families gather to drink, fish, camp, and tell stories, Yolŋu and Balanda together in their differences. The water that sustains them has been swept along from another time and place, but it sustains life presently, in this time and place.

Negotiating Form

Individual improvisation and decision making engages the attention of the listener. The tension between the shape of an individual's musical approach and the way this shapes the course of the music (and vice versa) is a key dynamic animating aural reception. Instead of any singular, structuring point of view, an individual must be actively engaged in relationship with other players visually, aurally, conceptually, and proximately.

Yet creative musical relationships do not always happen *in the moment*. Basic structures are sometimes brought into the mix of improvisation in *CRB*, albeit often temporarily and experimentally. Just like the framework offered by the *manikay* songs, small composed fragments or structural schemes have been used to provide moments of contrast for the listener and underpin ensemble cohesion. Rhythmic or tonal synchronicity can provide relief from dense group improvisation.

The AAO often discuss structuring performance so that it allows for more sparse sections of music, clearings where solo voices have space to emerge. There is also a desire in the ensemble to develop an overarching framework of growth through distinct sound combinations. Schäuble comments on the need for structuring performances: "The whole thing for me is a story that seems to build, and on the CD it's full on right at the start."[39] Grabowsky, Hicks, and Philip Rex also discussed this during one rehearsal:

---

37 Daniel Wilfred, interview with the author, 15 September 2012.
38 Yunupingu, "Vision for the North".
39 Niko Schäuble, interview with the author, 13 October 2011.

PG: I think there is great drama in that, in that music. And I think we are not always really getting that drama.

TH: Cause that's what I'd really like to see is …

PG: Less playing.

TH: Less of everyone playing.

PG: Yeah, that's right: duos, trios, solos.

PR: Breaking it down, less of the frenetic sort of stuff where we're all in.[40]

To this end, the ensemble experimented by including short, composed fragments into one rehearsal of *CRB*. These allowed cohesion at certain points in the music, offering reprieve from the density of free improvisation. Schäuble brought along some charts he thought might suit this purpose to a rehearsal in Melbourne, during March 2011. After a few rehearsals, the charts never appeared again: these composed fragments created a stilted feel and seemed to be juxtaposed against the *manikay*. Some players felt that the music should be completely free from premeditated structures other than the manikay series, allowing for a more fluid evolution of improvisation. During a recording session in May 2011, Grabowsky also brought some composed charts into the studio. These were played once and then abandoned as they did seem to conflict, pastiche like, with the central focus on Wägilak song (audio example 8e). Here, the integration of improvisation with *manikay* was displaced as a primary focus.

Audio example 8e. "Djuwalpada," *brother and sister* mode. Recording session, using composed fragments. Melbourne, 19 March 2011.

More successful experiments with composition have occurred in *CRB*. During a concert at Monash University in September 2012, several brass and saxophone students formed a small ensemble onstage with the AAO. This group played musical fragments from charts prepared by Grabowsky, who directed them to play these short bursts of intense sounds at different moments during the performance. Effectively, this group formed another *instrument* within the collective, offering a unique, pre-configured timbre to be sampled at Grabowsky's discretion.

Negotiations of form in *CRB* are ongoing, shaping discussions within the AAO. Among the YWG, there seems to be no concern over these issues,

---

40 Discussion during *CRB* rehearsal in Melbourne, 21 March 2011.

Fig. 8.1. Rhythmically approximate transcription of the composed pitch-series opening "Wata" (Wind) (audio example 8f).

especially as they do not impact negatively on relationships, participation, and the continuation of the *manikay* narrative. What is more significant for the YWG is that the AAO's awareness of *manikay* continues to grow, in their knowledge of the layered narratives as well as musical subtleties of form and rhythm. The AAO are mindful of any musical developments continuing to build on or respond to *manikay*. The following conversation occurred between Grabowsky, Veltheim, and Hicks in 2011:

> PG: As we now know the songs quite well—or we are getting the know them—I think that we could actually have, from time to time, a little more structured music which goes with the song … And maybe music that launches out of the song into a composed piece of music, which is then a kind of a platform for improvisation. So I want to try and take it to the next level, and I think that all this talk about the look [lighting, visuals etc.] is really important too. *[To EV]* I'd really like you to write some things, little fragmentary compositions that, in turn, set up various sorts of possibilities for exploitation.

> EV: You think that everyone could write something?

PG: If anybody wants to write something they should. I think the more we can collectivise that process, the more interesting the results will be.

TH: Are you talking about – little audio cues? Musical cues?

PG: Well I know what I would do. I would write a little kind of head. Like a head arrangement for something, which would either be designed to sync with a particular part of one of the songs, or it comes out of the *manikay* cadence, and that leads in turn to something; it sets up another kind of environment. So they're the kinds of things I'm thinking about. Like the line in Wata [Wind], that's a good example.[41]

The "line in Wata" that Grabowsky refers to is a composed sequence of pitches played by the AAO at the beginning of this track on the 2010 album (audio example 8f; fig. 8.1). This is an effective addition to the song and not an incongruous fragment, as Grabowsky conceives the motion and timbre of the instrumental sounds sympathetically with the *manikay* narrative: the picking up of a breeze that carries away the spirit of the deceased. This section is structured like a series of breaths, the gentle contours animating an eerie pitch sequence which bends around like a fluid, gentle breeze. The below audio example (8f) also demonstrates the skill with which the YWG introduce their *manikay* into the mix, the composed section invoking an appropriate atmosphere for "Wata" to be performed.

Audio example 8f. "Wata" (Wind), *gentle breeze* mode. A composed section performed with bass clarinet and violin from the first *CRB* album. See transcription below (fig. 8.1).

The negotiation of structures and the composition of melodic fragments, as in Grabowsky's "Wata" (fig. 8.1), begins with the desire for greater cohesion in performance. Yet no definitive structures or approaches emerge from these discussions and the collaboration continues to morph through many different iterations. Conversations about form and cohesion lead to a greater consideration of the voices of others, and the desire for more responsive, nuanced listening between performers. Consequently, each performance of *CRB* becomes a unique telling and retelling of the collaboration itself—a gathering of individuals, musical forms, traditions and relationships—as a collective working out of connectedness in separation.

---

41 Discussion during CRB rehearsal in Melbourne, 21 March 2011.

Something Emerges

CRB emerges out of the distinct musical languages that individuals bring to improvisation and performance. While our languages—musical or otherwise—carry prejudices through which understanding takes place, a language also opens the very possibility of understanding. In grappling with another cultural form like *manikay*, the horizons that initially situate our understanding are expanded.

If any understanding is inherently subjective, the responsible interpreter would suppose that further engagement is necessary to expand, elaborate, refute, or question those very anticipations that enable understanding to take place. Similarly, understanding a tradition like *manikay* is not an objective science but an ongoing process: *manikay* is always perceived from a new point of view, as our orientation is shifted by the process of interpretation: we perform, imitate, reinterpret, push against, dialogue with, and question *manikay*. As we grapple with the perspectives of others, understanding unfolds through a continual fusion of horizons—*horizon*, because interpretation is always situated, yet also looks beyond what is immediate and is not limited to what is nearby.[42]

As well as renewing and expanding horizons, language can be a tool for pulling something into the scope of our own horizons. This book began with the appropriation of *CRB* into the *manikay* tradition, as a performance "just like my Grandfather used to do".[43] For the AAO, this appropriation by Wägilak is deeply appreciated, offering a radical inversion of historical legacies in Australia. Yet Wägilak also value the AAO for what they bring to performance, as *CRB* enables them to carry integral *ŋaraka* (bones) of identity into new situations.

There is a degree of necessary appropriation going on for AAO musicians as well as for Wägilak, although not to the degree of asserting, "What the Wägilak are doing is nothing new, it is just jazz, as we have always played it." During a public lecture at the Australian National Academy of Music, Grabowsky's use of language in response to a question from the audience demonstrated his own grappling with music as culturally situated. In this exchange, Grabowsky was asked, "What entry points did you find, when you first heard this music, were most present for you? Were you looking predominantly at rhythmic construction, or is there a role for harmonic progression [in *manikay*]?" His response, in descriptive language at home in any music conservatory, enabled Grabowsky to communicate his experiences to a new audience eager to understand more about *manikay*.

Interestingly, "what seems to be the thesis-like beginning of the interpretation is in reality already an answer, and like every answer the sense of an interpretation has been determined through the question that is posed"—a

---

42 Gadamer, *Truth and Method*, 301.
43 Benjamin Wilfred, conversation with the author, 12 August 2013.

foundational observation of Gadamer's hermeneutics.[44] The audience member framed their question with terms such as "entry points", "particular musical element", "rhythmic construction", and "harmonic progression". For Yolŋu, such a question might seem absurd. The "entry point" for *manikay* is relational, beginning with people rather than abstracted musical elements, and education begins with narratives and dance learnt in childhood. *Biḻma* modes are not "constructed" but are as they have always been; one is carried along by an established groove and the sticks *sing*. Harmony does not move forward through "progressions" but connects one back to the ancestors.

Still, the question was as fair as any other. Fully aware of the limitations of his musical terminology, Grabowsky's response to the questioner also used common Western musical terminology, including: melody line; micro-detail; uniformity of shape; variations; heterophony; relationship between lines; synchronisation points; line-against-line; 5/8 metre; cadence. Despite many differences between cultural worlds, the languages we use underwrite the possibility of engagement. The concepts we hold allow us to begin a conversation, to look beyond the idiosyncrasies of our language, and begin to create something new together. The point is to recognise these limitations and so remain open to new possibilities.

The following examples show how our situated horizons of understanding can lead to new ways of conceiving the world. In his famous 1953 essay *The Dreaming*, celebrated Australian anthropologist William Stanner argued that we should "*think black*, not imposing Western categories of understanding".[45] Yet in this essay, Stanner's interpretation of the *dreamtime* hinges on the Greek word "*logos*", which brings with it a world of rich association: "A kind of narrative to things that once happened ... a kind of *logos* or principle of order transcending everything."[46] Stanner's use of this term was a prejudgement that seemed necessary, even after years of engagement with Aboriginal cultures.

Through his situated but shifting understandings, Stanner was at the forefront of reshaping Australian knowledge about Aboriginal peoples in a more positive light. His writings achieve this because they transpose aspects of Aboriginal culture into the understandings of a wider audience. Similarly, anthropologist Nancy Williams' use of the term *corporate* to describe Yolŋu landholding groups was necessary to effectively destroy colonial notions of *terra nullius*, the empty land, "in terms that common law can comprehend".[47] And likewise, some Yolŋu have translated the terms Ŋärra' as "parliament" and

---

44 Gadamer, *Gadamer in Conversation*, 49.

45 Stanner, *The Dreaming*, 58.

46 Ibid. *Logos*, "the Word" (Gospel of John, 1:1), is on one level an event of disclosure, a meaning which is only known as it is heard.

47 Williams, *The Yolngu and their Land*, 104.

riŋgitj as "embassy",[48] asserting the equivalence of these institutions with those dominant in Australia.

Musical terms foreign to Yolŋu have been used throughout this book. In interpreting, speaking or performing, we ourselves are *"right there* in the understood meaning",[49] "transformed into a communion in which we do not remain what we were".[50] For the AAO, *manikay* is not a trove of otherness to be plundered but a forum for developing relationships. Something greater than a unique recording or musical performance emerges:

> Apart from the artistic aspects, this collaboration has revealed many things to me, philosophically and socially. As different as our cultures may be, so similar are we as human beings: we all love our family and friends, we all crave respect, we all laugh at silly jokes.
>
> —Niko Schäuble[51]

> The trust earned, ability to listen and understanding of the process by each participant are the rewards of collaboration, and when this occurs across cultures, the benefits are great indeed.
>
> —Paul Grabowsky[52]

Because of their openness to change and nuanced to listening, the AAO have been able to question the musical languages they bring to interpretation, coming to a richer understanding of their differences. Here, performance is about finding new sounds and ways of articulating their own voices and traditions that are both different from and sympathetic to the forms and concepts of *manikay*. That "old and new ways are always combining into something of living value"[53] seems to be a perspective resonant with Daniel Wilfred:

> I always learn about that *munanga* [whitefella] music. I just listen to that sound, how this fits, how the beat goes. I just follow the beat, how they play, how they make the sound: how this [*manikay*] song can go with that beat. I'm learning. What I do, what I learn, I can do it on tour with *CRB* and I can do it in the funeral, back home. We are making a new song for a new generation.[54]

Like the *yuṯa manikay* (new song) "Wäk Wäk" (Black Crow), which tells of the friendships and travels of musicians in *CRB* (Chapter Five), every performance

---

48 See Gondarra, "Assent Law."
49 Ibid., 47.
50 Gadamer, *Truth and Method*, 371.
51 Interview with the author, 13 October 2011.
52 Grabowsky, "Art Orchestra, ANAM and Arnhem Land".
53 Gadamer, *Truth and Method*, 305.
54 Daniel Wilfred, discussion with the author, 2013.

of *CRB* is finally an expression of relationships in sound. Over years of performance, this enduring desire has emerged and has supplanted the drive to create something definitively new: innovative performance has become a by-product of something much more important. Borne along by tradition, the individual voices that shape performance are always opening beyond tradition, searching for creative ways to relate others with integrity.

CRB is a collaboration born of many parents, an expression grounded in multiple cultures and histories. This dense mixture of influences and imaginations sustains deeply embedded cultural orthodoxies, rendered anew through brilliantly diverse realisations. Coming together across cultural distances in present-day Australia—blown together by the *wata* (wind)—the relationships of *CRB* attest to the wonderful possibilities of a new future that extends from intermingling existence.

• • •

CRB is a song for us and our time. Shimmering with *bir'yun* (brilliance), *manikay* is enlivened by the colourful improvisations and voices of individuals grappling with similarity amid difference, and the past within the present. Diverse individuals and situations are drawn together into the event of performance, mutually enfolded within a narrative web of people and place.

The performance of *CRB* sustains a conversation with ancestral reality which has unfolded through the generations, retelling stories of old that continue to shape the lives of communities today. Impelled by the grooving forms of the past, the present generation finds a voice for our time.

While the creativity of performers is directed by intrinsic histories and forms of cultural practice, creativity always grasps beyond what is idiomatic: creativity transforms horizons as it proceeds from those situated horizons. The orthodox *ŋaraka* (bones) of the past enliven new conversations between the individuals, communities, and cultures brought together in performance. Beyond pervasive cultural separations between non-indigenous and Indigenous Australian cultures and people, the *dudutudu* (night owl) and *birrkpirrk* (plover) come together and sit on nearby branches. In their difference, they sing a new song.

EPILOGUE: NEW FRIENDSHIPS

Back in 2012, David, Daniel, Benjamin Wilfred and I were passing through customs at Heathrow Airport. We were on our way to a performance at the Southbank Centre, as part of the London Jazz Festival. David brandished his newly acquired passport, issued especially for this trip as a temporary document, the recorded name reading only "David", without a surname. This was the first time the Young Wägilak Group had travelled overseas.

We were all standing together at the front of the queue when a brusque official called us to the desk. He glanced over our documents, flight bookings, and accommodation details. When he got to David's passport, he seemed confused.

"We have a copy of David's birth certificate, if you want to look at that," I suggested.

The officer responded officiously, "Don't speak for him."

David, looking slightly amused, piped up, "It's OK, he's my son. He can talk for me."

The officer looked us both up and down, seeing only a black man standing next to a white one. He did not know how to respond.

Family connections are greater than direct, biological descent. For Wägilak, family extends to those who take their relationships seriously and are involved in a shared life. Out of such these relationships emerge stories, and the retelling of stories like this one.

Manikay is about shared experience. The *biḻma* (clapsticks) are always present when Yolŋu gather for funerals, circumcisions, celebrations, family gatherings, welcomes, and departures. *Manikay* creates and sustains a complex web of relationships, between different families and countries, languages, stories and metaphors, and as we have seen with *Crossing Roper Bar*, different musical cultures and forms of learning.

Perhaps the most significant outcome of *CRB* has been the genuine friendships between musicians and others associated with the project—management, supporters, photographers, and ethnomusicologists. Where these relationships are ongoing, *CRB* is being extended in new directions.

While performances of *CRB* are now less frequent, the latest occurring in 2017 at the Garma Festival in Gulkula, NT, the collaboration is by no means over. Daniel and David Wilfred continue to visit Melbourne regularly, running school workshops and engaging with university students. New projects with even greater levels of co-creation and nuance of understanding between musicians have been explored. Notably, Paul Grabowsky composed a work titled *Nyilipidgi* for Daniel and David Wilfred and the Monash Art Ensemble, an improvising ensemble of students and staff, in 2016. This work, which won an Australasian Performing Right Association award in 2016 for Best World Music Album abounds with wild tunes, improvised duets and trios, and an array of full-ensemble items in differing jazz styles. The work encourages a greater interplay between *manikay* singers and the ensemble, as Grabowsky's composed sections dovetail into *manikay* rhythmic patterns and respond to the narrative scenes of Djuwalpada's journey. Grabowsky also continues to work with Daniel and David in an improvised trio performance (piano, *yidaki*, and voice), a project known as *Bambula*, the "ceremonial ground". *Bambula* features a series of *manikay* which were not used in *CRB* and tells of the blossoming of the *gadayka* (stringybark tree).

The concept of *bambula* (ceremonial ground) expresses something of the centrality of relationships to *manikay*. Daniel, David, and I made use of this concept during some teaching at the AAO's Creative Music Intensive (CMI) in 2017. The CMI began in 2015 and was an initiative of composer, trumpeter and sound artist Peter Knight, who had taken over from Paul Grabowsky as artistic director of the AAO. The CMI is a two-week residency held in Tarraleah, in the central highlands of Tasmania, and brings together young performers and recent graduates from the major music conservatories around Australia, from classical, jazz, and popular music streams. Participants spend their days attending workshops led by guest artists and rehearse together in small, improvising ensembles, working with the guest artists to explore different musical traditions and concepts.

In recent years, a focus of the CMI has been the Korean P'ansori tradition and *hohŭp* rhythmic processes, working with singer Bae Il Dong (Seoul), vocal artist Sunny Kim (Seoul/Melbourne), bassist Christopher Hale, and drummers Simon Barker and Chloe Kim. Wägilak *manikay* has also featured, with Daniel and David Wilfred leading workshops and rehearsals. Other guests—who have worked closely with these musicians in a professional capacity—include trumpeter Scott Tinkler, AAO artistic director Peter Knight, and myself.

Before the CMI started in 2018, I asked David Wilfred where we should begin our workshops. "Where should *manikay* begin?"

David's reply, "*Nhini numa dawu lakaram ŋapu numa.*" As he translated it, "You and me, together we sit and listen."

We explored this notion using the *manikay* narrative of *bambula* (ceremonial ground). This is the place where everyone comes together in their differences, to sit and listen, sing and dance, and tell stories. *Bambula* is the ground of gathering as an extended, complex, dynamic family.

The most important aspect of the CMI is this invitation to sit together and listen, to form new friendships, and to explore who we are together through sound, with voices that come into their own as they intermingle with others. "Don't be shame," Daniel encourages the participants. "You are here to learn." Many come with a reticence, unsure of how to approach this strange, indigenous, cultural *otherness*. "You just have to go for it," encourages Daniel. "Make something!"

The better we come to know each other, the more our identities extend from our shared lives. So too our music, which extends out of relationships rather than abstract musical forms. Daniel and David jam with the participants long into the night, telling stories and laughing. It is through these emerging friendships that integrity and trust come to characterise our engagements with one another, shaping how and why we play together.

When we sit and listen, something new starts to emerge. Songs that did not seem appropriate to perform in *CRB* have been introduced by Daniel Wilfred into the CMI. "Something new is coming out. The *gaḏayka* [stringybark tree]." As the seasons turn, the *dhaŋgarra* (stringybark flowers) start to emerge. This is a delicate song. It started when we were talking to participants about silence. Silence is not absence but expectation; silence has a distinct quality to it. Often in free-improvisation, musicians just want to jump in and make noise. But silence also leads somewhere. Culturally, we feel a bit awkward with silence, but leaving space means that something unanticipated might emerge, or a voice yet unheard.

Into our shared silence, Daniel was inspired to sing "Gaḏayka" (Stringybark tree), a song about budding flowers, fragrance, and honey. "The [Australian] Art Orchestra always do this music full-on! I don't do this one with them. Your play soft. I listen to you mob. I just think of that song, 'Gaḏayka.'"

New songs and approaches are also emerging within relationships of trust. The following audio examples capture just two moments from the CMI that demonstrate this beautifully. In the first, David Wilfred hears his good friend Bae Il Dong singing during a coffee break and joins in (audio example 9a). In the second, Daniel Wilfred and Sunny Kim have imagined what it is to sing as two birds meeting, one from Arnhem Land, the other from Korea (audio example 9b).

The idea originally came from Daniel, who, on hearing Sunny's improvisations, imagined the cry of two birds singing together. He invited Sunny to sing with him in Korean. This song has now become the basis of a further collaboration, titled *Hand to Earth*, between Daniel, Sunny, and Peter Knight.

Faculty member at the CMI Christopher Hale has observed that new songs are often created when sounds invoke a narrative or image that can dovetail into established *manikay* series. "They find a way for me to sing with them," Daniel explains.[1] In the sounds being performed around him, Daniel hears birds singing or stars shimmering; a narrative scene is imagined which interprets the situation, like two birds meeting, one from Korea and one from Australia.

Audio example 9a. Yolŋu *manikay* meets Korean P'ansori. David Wilfred (*yidaki*) and Bae Il Dong (voice). Informal performance during the AAO's *Creative Music Intensive*, 21 September 2018.

Audio example 9b. "Two Birds," flying and singing together. From the collaboration *Hand to Earth*, performed by Daniel Wilfred, Sunny Kim, and Peter Knight (trumpet and laptop). Produced by Leo Dale, 2018.[2]

One of the lasting experiences of the CMI is this sense of genuine partnership and coincidence of expression. Il Dong reflects, "Even though we are separated from each other, we sing the same music."[3] Il Dong's teachings make clear that this coincidental expression is as much a corporal sharing of space and sound, as it is a technical or conceptual encounter. Fundamental to the P'ansori tradition is the way the voice emanates from and resounds through the body. "P'ansori traditional singing isn't about complicated theory but expressing emotions in the right way. It is breathing and singing."[4] Similarly, Christopher Hale shares his own reflections on Korean *hohŭp*: "Rhythm is produced from a system of body movement and breathing, literally inhalation and exhalation. Not a grid of conceptual subdivisions. This is how Korean musicians play what sound like very complex slippery subdivisions together … rhythm is the sonic result of a body movement."[5]

---

1   Daniel Wilfred, comment during a performance at the symposium, "Interlingua: Extending Improvisational Language in Music", of the Australian Art Orchestra and Melbourne Conservatorium of Music Jazz and Improvisation, 24 September 2018.

2   For a longer video excerpt of this performance, see Australian Art Orchestra, see "Hand to Earth," https://vimeo.com/306922359.

3   Bae Il Dong, "Interlingua: Extending Improvisational Language in Music" symposium of the Australian Art Orchestra and Melbourne Conservatorium of Music Jazz and Improvisation, translated by Chloe Kim, unpublished paper, 22 September 2017.

4   Il Dong, "Interlingua," 22 September 2017.

5   Christopher Hale, "Interlingua: Extending Improvisational Language in Music" symposium of the Australian Art Orchestra and Melbourne Conservatorium of Music Jazz and Improvisation, unpublished paper, 22 September 2017. See also Hale, Christopher Hale, "Ritual Diamonds."

Sunny Kim also recounts the way new musical encounters are opening through the CMI, as friendships and trust underpin an intimacy of shared space and bodies.

> Although it [*manikay*] was very foreign—almost the farthest thing I had experienced from anything I had been exposed to—I really felt a sense of connection and some area within me that was awakened and connected by the presence of the music. It was the last day of the intensive [in 2016] and Daniel said, "Let's sing together." And we were watching the other participants and he said, 'Stars. Let's sings about stars.' And that's all he said.[6]

Daniel, captured by an image of stars; Sunny, captured by the sound of his voice. A year later, that encounter still resounds in her memory:

> The first time I heard Daniel's voice I was really taken by it. Mesmerised and maybe even shocked … I couldn't really understand how he was producing those sounds … That just captured me. And the sheer beauty of it. There's power and strength in it … His song helped me to get closer to my voice, to finding my voice … Since then we've sung about water, about flowers, tall trees and the clouds, the sunset, making fire, and about the two birds, one from Arnhem land and one from Korea.[7]

Refracted through the concept of *bambula*, *manikay* is more than a set of musical forms and narratives. *Manikay* is an invitation to make new connections, to observe, through performance, our shared relationships and stories. It is always a living, expanding web of similarities and variations.

Old forms come to new expression as they intermingle with the environment around. The crack of a voice straining like an old man reminds us of our grandfather. That saxophone sounds a bit like the *birrkpirrk* (plover), but also introduces a little bit of John Coltrane. The didjeridu player inhales with the P'ansori singer, and their deep sounds reverberate across the valley. Two birds, one from Korea, the other from Arnhem Land, come to sing a new song in Tarraleah. *Manikay* sings new connections into being. On the *bambula* performance ground, a unique, sometimes rambunctious mix of family and characters, narratives, and sounds intermingle, carried together in song.

---

6   Sunny Kim, "Interlingua: Extending Improvisational Language in Music" symposium of the Australian Art Orchestra and Melbourne Conservatorium of Music Jazz and Improvisation, unpublished paper, 22 September 2017.

7   Ibid.

BIBLIOGRAPHY

Abbate, Carolyn. "Music—Drastic or Gnostic?" *Critical Inquiry* 30, no. 3 (2004): 505–36.

Australian Art Orchestra. "Australian Art Orchestra: Projects." http://aao.com. au/projects/program/.

Australian Broadcasting Commission and Murray McLaughlin (reporter). "Orchestra Collaborates with Top End Musicians." *7.30 Report*, August 2, 2005.

Australian Bureau of Statistics. "Basic Community Profile: Ngukurr (SSC70143)." *2011 Census of Population and Housing*. http://www.censusdata.abs. gov.au/census_services/getproduct/census/2011/communityprofile/ SSC70143?opendocument&navpos=100.

Australian Institute of Aboriginal and Torres Strait Islander Studies with the Federation of Aboriginal and Torres Strait Islander Languages. *National Indigenous Languages Survey Report*. Canberra: Department of Communications, Information Technology and the Arts, 2005.

Barthes, Roland. "The Grain of the Voice." In *Image, Music, Text*, translated by Steven Heath, 179–90. New York: Hill and Wang, 1977.

Barton, William, and Matthew Hindson. "Kalkadungu (2007): programme notes." http://hindson.com.au/info/kalkadungu-2007/.

Berndt, Roland. "An Adjustment Movement in Arnhem Land, Northern Territory of Australia." Facsimile edition of *Oceania Monograph* 54, [1962] (2004). Sydney: The University of Sydney.

Berndt, Roland M., and Catherine H. Berndt. *The World of the First Australians: Aboriginal Traditional Life Past and Present*. Canberra: Aboriginal Studies Press, 1988.

Bowdler, Cath. *Colour Country: Art from Roper River.* Wagga Wagga, NSW: Wagga Wagga Art Gallery, 2009.

Bowman, Wayne. *Philosophical Perspectives on Music.* Oxford: Oxford University Press, 1998.

Brigg, Morgan. "Political Theory between Two Traditions: Ethical Challenges and One Possibility." In *The Power of Knowledge, the Resonance of Tradition*, edited by Graeme Ward and Adrian Muckle, 115–123. Canberra: Australian Institute of Aboriginal and Torres Strait Islander Studies, 2005.

Bruns, Gerald. *Hermeneutics Ancient and Modern.* New Haven: Yale University Press, 1992.

Buku-Larrnggay Mulka Centre. *Saltwater: Yirrkala Paintings of the Sea Country.* Yirrkala, NT, Australia: Buku-Larrnggay Mulka Centre, 1999.

Caruana, Wally, and Nigel Lendon, eds. *The Painters of the Wagilag Sisters Story 1937–1997.* Canberra, ACT: National Gallery of Australia, 1997.

Chauvel, Charles (director). *Jedda.* California: Columbia Pictures Industries, 1955.

Coleman, Ornette. "Discourse: the Harmolodic Manifesto." http://www.ornettecoleman.com/course.swf.

Corn, Aaron. "Ngukurr Crying: Male Youth in a Remote Indigenous Community." *South East Arnhem Land Collaborative Research Project* 2. Woollongong, New South Wales: University of Woollongong, 2001.

———. "Dreamtime Wisdom, Modern-time Vision: Tradition and Innovation in the Popular Band Movement of Arnhem Land, Australia." PhD diss., University of Melbourne, 2002.

———. "Ancestral, Corporeal, Corporate: Traditional Yolŋu Understandings of the Body Explored." *Borderlands* 7, no. 2 (2008): 1–17.

———. "Sound Exchanges: An Ethnomusicologists Approach to Interdisciplinary Teaching and Learning in Collaboration with a Remote Indigenous Australian Community." *The World of Music* 51, no. 3 (2009): 21–50.

———. *Reflections & Voices: Exploring the Music of Yothu Yindi with Mandawuy Yunupingu.* Sydney: Sydney University Press, 2009.

———. "Land, Song, Constitution: Exploring Expressions of Ancestral Agency, Intercultural Diplomacy and Family Legacy in the Music of Yothu Yindi with Mandawuy Yunupingu." *Popular Music* 29, no. 1 (2010): 81–102.

———. "Indigenous Australian Music and Media," course handbook. School of Music, Australian National University, Canberra, ACT, 2012.

———. "Nations of Song," *Humanities Research* 19, no. 3 (2013): 145–60.

Corn, Aaron, and Neparrŋa Gumbula. "'Buḏutthun Ratja Wiyinymirri': Formal Flexibility in the Yolŋu Manikay Tradition and the Challenge of Recording a Compete Repertoire." *Australian Aboriginal Studies*, no. 2 (2007): 116–27.

Deveson, Philippa. "The Agency of the Subject: Yolngu Involvement in the Yirrkala Film Project." *Journal of Australian Studies* 35, no. 2 (2011): 153–64.

Dewar, Mickey. *The Black War in Arnhem Land: Missionaries and the Yolŋu 1908–40.* Darwin, NT: North Australia Research Unit, Australian National University, 1982.

Dussart, Françoise. Introduction to Part 3: "Sacred Places." In *Aboriginal Religions in Australia: An Anthology of Recent Writings*, edited by Max Charlesworth, Francoise Dussart, and Howard Morphy, 113. Aldershot, Hampshire: Ashgate, 2005.

Feld, Steven. "A Sweet Lullaby for World Music." *Public Culture* 12, no. 1 (2000): 145–71.

Gadamer, Hans-Georg. *Truth and Method.* Translation revised by Joel Weinsheimer and Donald G. Marshall. London: Continuum, 2006.

———. *Gadamer in Conversation: Reflections and Commentary.* Edited and translated by Richard E. Palmer. New Haven, Connecticut: Yale University Press, 2001.

———. *Philosophical Hermeneutics.* Translated by David Linge. Berkeley: University of California Press, 2008.

Garadji, Wurrtjumun Dinah. *The Unknown Struggles of my People: Stories by Wurrtjumun Dinah Garadji.* Goulbourn Island: Warruwi Literacy Centre, 1996.

Gondarra, Djiniyini. "Assent Law of The First People: Views from a Traditional Owner," *National Indigenous Times*, March 3, 2011.

Grabowsky, Paul. "The Complete Musician." Paper presented at the Australian National University's public lecture series, as part of the H.C. Coombs Creative Artist Fellowship. Australian National University, Canberra, October 14, 2010.

———. "Art Orchestra, ANAM, and Arnhem Land." Presentation at the Australian National Academy of Music's *Fridays@3* public lecture series. Melbourne, April 15, 2011.

———. "Art is a River." Comment, *The Monthly*, October, 2012. http://www.themonthly.com.au/comment-art-river-paul-grabowsky-6474.

———. "Theft of Sita: Program Notes." http://aao.com.au/projects/program/theft-of-sita/.

Grabowsky, Paul, and Paul Kelly. "Australia's Hidden Hit Parade: Paul Kelly with Paul Grabowsky." Presentation at *The Monthly Talks* series, hosted by *The Monthly* and Readings Books. Melbourne, 1 October 2012, http://www.themonthly.com.au/australias-hidden-hit-parade-paul-kelly-paul-grabowsky-6543.

Grabowsky, Paul, Benjamin Wilfred, et al. "Forum on *CRB*," panel discussion, Melbourne University, April 16, 2009.

Hale, Christopher. "Interlingua: Extending Improvisational Language in Music" symposium of the Australian Art Orchestra and Melbourne Conservatorium of Music Jazz and Improvisation. Unpublished paper. 22 Sept., 2017.

———. "Ritual Diamonds and Bass Hohŭp: Strategies for Cross-domain Creative Engagement and Influence with Korean Traditional Rhythm." PhD diss., University of Sydney, 2019.

Hanslick, Eduard. *On the Musically Beautiful*. Translated by Geoffrey Payzant. Indianna: Hackett, 1986.

Harris, John. *We Wish We'd Done More: Ninety Years of CMS and Aboriginal Issues in North Australia*. Adelaide, SA: Openbook Publishers, 1998.

Hayes, Deborah. "Review: Sculthorpe's 'Kakadu'" *Notes* 52, no. 3 (1996): 1029–30.

Heath, Jeffrey. "Texts Recorded in the Numbulwar Area." 33 sound files (ca. 60 min.). HEATH_J04, 1974–76. Australian Institute of Aboriginal and Torres Strait Islander Studies Audio Visual Archives.

———. *Ngandi Grammar, Texts, and Dictionary*. Canberra: Australian Institute of Aboriginal Studies, 1978.

———. *Basic Materials in Ritharngu: Grammar, Texts, and Dictionary*. Canberra: Pacific Linguistics, Australian National University, 1980.

Hicks, Tony. "The Path to Abstraction: A Practice Led Investigation into the Emergence of an Abstract Improvisation Language." Masters diss., Victorian College of the Arts and Music, University of Melbourne, 2011.

Il Dong, Bae. "Interlingua: Extending Improvisational Language in Music" symposium of the Australian Art Orchestra and Melbourne Conservatorium of Music Jazz and Improvisation. Translated by Chole Kim. Unpublished paper. 22 Sept., 2017.

James, Bentley. "The Language of 'Spiritual Power': From Mana to Märr on the Crocodile Islands." In *Strings of Connectedness: Essays in Honour of Ian Keen*, edited by Peter G. Toner, 235–61. Canberra: ANU Press, 2015.

Jones, Rhys, and Neville White. "Point Blank: Stone Tool Manufacture at the Ngilipitji Quarry, Arnhem Land, 1981." In *Archaeology with Ethnography: an Australian Perspective*, edited by Betty Meehan and Rhys Jones, 51–87. Canberra, ACT: Australian National University, 1988.

Keen, Ian. *Knowledge and Secrecy in an Aboriginal Religion: Yolngu of North-East Arnhem Land*. Oxford: Clarendon Press, 1994.

———. "Metaphor and the Metalanguage: Groups in Northeast Arnhem Land." *American Ethnologist* 22, no. 3 (1995): 502–27.

———. "A Bundle of Sticks: The Debate Over Yolŋu Clans." *Journal of the Royal Anthropological Institute* 6, no. 3 (2000), 419–36.

Kiel, Charles, and Steven Feld. *Music Grooves*. Chicago: University of Chicago Press, 1994.

Kim, Sunny. "Interlingua: Extending Improvisational Language in Music" symposium of the Australian Art Orchestra and Melbourne Conservatorium of Music Jazz and Improvisation. Unpublished paper. 22 Sept., 2017

———. "Interlingua: Extending Improvisational Language in Music" symposium of the Australian Art Orchestra and Melbourne Conservatorium of Music Jazz and Improvisation, unpublished paper, 24 Sept., 2018

Kivy, Peter. *Introduction to a Philosophy of Music*. Oxford: Oxford University Press, 2002.

Knopoff, Steven. "'Yuṯa Manikay': Juxtaposition of Ancestral and Contemporary Elements in the Performance of Yolngu Clan Songs." *Yearbook for Traditional Music* 24 (1992): 138–53.

———. "Yolngu Clansong Scalar Structures." In *The Garland Encyclopaedia of World Music, Australia and the Pacific Islands*, vol. 9, edited by Adrienne L. Kaeppler and J. W. Love, 141. New York: Garland Publishing, 1998.

Lacoste, Jean-Yves. "The Phenomenality of Anticipation." In *Phenomenology and Eschatology: Not Yet in the Now*, edited by Neal DeRoo and John Panteleimon Manoussakis, 15–33. Aldershot, Hampshire: Ashgate, 2009.

Lakoff, George, and Mark Johnson. *Metaphors We Live By*. Chicago: University of Chicago Press, 1980.

Langton, Marcia. "Culture Wars." In *Blacklines: Contemporary Critical Writing by Indigenous Australians*, edited by Michele Grossman, 164–83. Melbourne: Melbourne University Press, 2003.

———. "Aboriginal Art and Film: The Politics of Representation." In *Blacklines: Contemporary Critical Writing by Indigenous Australians*, edited by Michele Grossman, 109–24. Melbourne: Melbourne University Press, 2003.

Lawn, Chris. *Gadamer: A Guide for the Perplexed*. London: Continuum, 2006.

Leichhardt, Friedrich. "Journal Entries from 1 October 1844 to 2 December 1855." In *Australian Explorers: A Selection from their Writings with an Introduction*, edited by Kathleen Fitzpatrick, 210–52. London: Oxford University Press, 1958.

Lewis, George E. "Improvised Music After 1950: Afrological and Eurological Perspectives." *Black Music Research Journal* 22, supplement (2002): 215–46.

Magowan, Fiona. "It is God Who Speaks in the Thunder: Mediating Ontologies of Faith and Fear in Aboriginal Christianity." *The Journal of Religions History* 27, no. 3 (2003): 293–310.

———. *Melodies of Mourning: Music and Emotion in Northern Australia*. Oxford: James Currey Press, 2007.

Marika, Banduk. "The Story Behind the Project." National Museum of Australia: http://nma.gov.au/exhibitions/yalangbara/about/.

Marika-Mununggiritj, Raymattja, and Michael Christie. "Yolngu Metaphors for Learning." *International Journal of the Sociology of Language* 113, no. 1 (1995): 59–62.

McKenzie, Kim (director). *The Spear in the Stone*. Film and study guide. Canberra: Australian Institute of Aboriginal Studies, 1983.

Merleau-Ponty, Maurice. *The World of Perception*. London: Routledge, 2008.

Merriam, Alan. *The Anthropology of Music*. Evanston, Illinois: Northwestern University Press, 1964.

Meyer, Leonard. *Emotion and Meaning in Music*. Chicago: University of Chicago Press, 1957.

Morphy, Frances. "(Im)mobility: Regional Population Structures in Aboriginal Australia." *Australian Journal of Social Issues* 45, no. 3 (2010): 363–82.

Morphy, Frances. "Whose Governance for Whose Good? The Laynhapuy Homelands Association and the Neo-Assimilationist Turn in Indigenous Policy." In *Contested Governance: Culture, Power, and Institutions in Indigenous Australia*, Centre for Aboriginal Economic Policy research monograph 29, edited by Janet Hunt and others, 113–152. Canberra: Australian National University E-Press, 2008.

Morphy, Frances, and Howard Morphy. "Anthropological Theory and Government Policy in Australia's Northern Territory: The Hegemony of the 'Mainstream.'" *American Anthropologist* 115, no. 2 (2013): 174–87.

Morphy, Frances, and Howard Morphy. "'We Think Through Our 'Marwat' (Paintbrush)': Conceptualising Mind Cross-Culturally." Paper presented at the *Anthropology Seminar Series*, College of Asia and the Pacific, Australian National University, Canberra, ACT, 29 May 2013.

Morphy, Howard. "Now You Understand: An Analysis of the Way Yolngu Have Used Sacred Knowledge to Maintain Their Autonomy." In *Aborigines, Land and Landrights*, edited by N. Peterson and M. Langton, 110–33. Canberra: Australian Institute of Aboriginal Studies, 1983.

——. "From Dull to Brilliant: The Aesthetics of Spiritual Power among the Yolngu." *Man* 24, no. 1 (1989): 21–40.

——. *Ancestral Connections: Art and an Aboriginal System of Knowledge*. Chicago: University of Chicago Press, 1991.

——. "Art and Politics: The Bark Petition and the Barunga Statement." In *Oxford Companion to Aboriginal Art and Culture*, edited by Sylvia Kleinert and Margo Neale, 100–103. Melbourne: Oxford University Press, 2000.

——. "Yolngu Art and the Creativity of the Inside." In *Aboriginal Religions in Australia: an Anthology of Recent Writings*, edited by Max Charlesworth,

Francoise Dussart, and Howard Morphy, 159–170. Aldershot, Hampshire: Ashgate, 2005.

———. *Becoming Art: Exploring Cross Cultural Categories.* Sydney: University of New South Wales Press, 2008.

———. "'Joyous Maggots:' the Symbolism of Yolngu Mortuary Rituals." In *An Appreciation of Difference: WEH Stanner and Aboriginal Australia*, edited by Melinda Hinkson and Jeremy Beckett, 137–50. Canberra, Aboriginal Studies Press, 2008.

Morphy, Howard, and Philippa Deveson. "Material Expressions of Ancestral Agency: Yolngu Acting in a Virtual Space." Paper presented in the *Adrian Gerbrands Lecture* series, Leiden University, Netherlands, 7 June 2011. http://www.fel-leiden.nl/wp-content/uploads/Gerbrandslecture-Howard-Morphy3.pdf.

Morphy, Howard, and Frances Morphy. "Tasting the Waters: Discriminating Identities in the Waters of Blue Mud Bay." *Journal of Material Culture* 11, no. 1 (2006): 67–85.

———. "Soon We Will Be Spending All Our Time at Funerals: Yolngu Mortuary Rituals in an Epoch of Constant Change." In *Returns to the Field: Multitemporal Research and Contemporary Anthropology*, edited by Signe Howell and Aud Talle, 49–72. Bloomington: Indiana University Press, 2012.

Nakata, Martin. *Disciplining the Savages, Savaging the Disciplines.* Canberra: Aboriginal Studies Press, 2007.

National Recording Project for Indigenous Performance in Australia, The. "Garma Statement on Indigenous Music and Dance," drafted by Marcia Langton, Alan Marett, and Mandawuy Yunupingu, 2002. http://www.aboriginalartists.com.au/NRP_statement.htm.

Ngukurr Language Centre. *Ritharrngu/Wagilak Seasons.* Unpublished chart, Ngukurr, NT, Australia.

Normand, Simon. *Stone Country to Saltwater: Recent Artwork and Stories from Ngukurr, Arnhem Land.* Melbourne: Simon Normand, 2004.

Power, Liza. "Crossing the Divide: Music Bridges Two Cultures." *The Age*, entertainment supplement, July 31, 2010.

Pressing, Jeff. "Free Jazz and the Avant-Garde." In *The Cambridge Companion to Jazz*, edited by Mervyn Cooke and David Horne, 202–16. Cambridge: Cambridge University Press, 2003.

Ricoeur, Paul. *On Translation.* Translated by Eileen Brennan. London: Routledge, 2006.

Ross, David. "Activating Bodies of Knowledge: Improvisation, Cognition, and Sports Education." *Critical Studies in Improvisation* 7, no. 2 (2011): http://www.criticalimprov.com/article/view/1314.

Shipton, Alyn. *A New History of Jazz.* New York: Continuum, 2007.

Stanner, W. E. H. "Religion, Totemism, and Symbolism." In *Aboriginal Man in Australia: Essays in Honour of Emeritus Professor AP Elkin,* edited by R. M. Berndt and C. H. Berndt, 207–37. Sydney: Angus and Robinson, 1965.

———. "Some Aspects of an Aboriginal Religion." *Colloquium* 9, no. 1 (1976): 19–35.

———. *The Dreaming and Other Essays.* Melbourne: Black Inc., 2009.

Thiselton, Anthony. *New Horizons in Hermeneutics.* London: Marshall Pickering, 1992.

Thomson, Donald. *Donald Thomson in Arnhem Land,* compiled by Nicolas Peterson. Melbourne: Miegunyah Press, 2010.

Toner, Peter. "When the Echoes are Gone: A Yolngu Musical Anthropology." PhD diss., Australian National University, 2001.

———. "Melody and the Musical Articulation of Yolngu Identity." *Yearbook for Traditional Music* 35 (2004): 69–95.

———. "Sing a Country of the Mind: The Articulation of Place in Dhaḻwangu Song." In *The Soundscapes of Australia,* edited by Fiona Richards, 165–84. Aldershot, Hampshire: Ashgate, 2007.

———. "Form and Performance: The Relations of Melody, Poetics, and Rhythm in Dhaḻwangu *Manikay.*" In *A Distinctive Voice in the Antipodes: Essays in Honour of Stephen A. Wild,* edited by Kirsty Gillespie, Sally Treloyn, and Done Niles. Canberra: Australian National University Press, 2017.

Treloyn, Sally. "Songs that Pull: Jadmi Junba from the Kimberly region of Northwest Australia." PhD diss., University of Sydney, 2006.

Trudgen, Richard. *Why Warriors Lie Down and Die: Djambatj Mala.* Darwin, NT: Aboriginal Resource and Development Services Inc., 2000.

Wallaschek, Richard. *Primitive Music: An Inquiry into the Origin and Development of Music, Song, Instruments, Dances, and Pantomimes of Savage Races.* London: Longmans, Green and Co., 1893.

Warnke, Georgia. *Gadamer: Hermeneutics, Tradition, and Reason.* Oxford: Polity Press, 1987.

West, Margie, ed. *Yalangbara: Art of the Djang'kawu.* Darwin, NT: Charles Darwin University Press, 2008.

Wilfred, Daniel and Nicola Bell (Directors). *Djuwaḻpada.* Ngukurr Story Project. Ngukurr, NT: Ngukurr Arts Aboriginal Corporation and Ngukurr Language Centre, 2019.

Wilfred, Benjamin, interview by Daniel Browning. "Crossing Boundaries." *Awaye.* Radio National, Australian Broadcasting Commission, Melbourne, 2 November 2013.

Wilfred, Benjamin, Daniel Wilfred and Justin Nunggarrgalug, in discussion with Samuel Curkpatrick. "Digital Audio Technologies and Aural Organicism in the Australian Art Orchestra's 'Crossing Roper Bar.'"

Information Technology and Indigenous Communities conference of the Australian Institute of Aboriginal and Torres Strait Islander Studies, Australian National University, Canberra, ACT, July 13, 2010.

Wilfred, Benjamin, interview by Jane Ulman. "Cultural Crossings." Radio National, Australian Broadcasting Commission, Canberra, ACT, August 1, 2010.

Williams, Nancy. *The Yolngu and their Land: A System of Land Tenure and the Fight for its Recognition*. Stanford: Stanford University Press, 1986.

Yunupingu, Mandawuy. *Voices from the Land*. Sydney: Australian Broadcasting Commission Books, 1993.

Yunupingu, Mandawuy. "Vision for the North: Bringing Our Pasts into Our Futures." Keynote address, program one of the annual Charles Darwin University Symposium Series, Darwin, NT, May 21, 2013.

Zorc, David R. *Yolŋu-Matha Dictionary*. Batchelor, NT: Batchelor College, 1996.

DISCOGRAPHY

Australian Art Orchestra. *Theft of Sita*, composed by Paul Grabowsky in association with I Wayan Gde Yudane. CD. North Melbourne: Australian Art Orchestra Recordings, 2000.

———. *The Chennai Sessions (Into the Fire): Australian Art Orchestra and Guru Karaikudi Mani.* CD. North Melbourne: Australian Art Orchestra Recordings, 2008.

———. *Crossing Roper Bar: Australian Art Orchestra and the Young Wagilak Group.* North Melbourne: Australian Art Orchestra Recordings, 2010.

———. *Crossing Roper Bar Volume 2: The Ghost Dances: Young Wägilak Group and the Australian Art Orchestra.* North Melbourne: Australian Art Orchestra Recordings, 2014.

Barton, William. *Kalkadungu: Music for Didjeridu and Orchestra.* CD. Australian Broadcasting Corporation, ABC Classics, 2012.

Evans, Bill. Liner notes to the reissue of *Kind of Blue*, by Miles Davis. CD. New York: Sony Music Entertainment. 2000.

Grabowsky, Paul, Daniel Ngukurr Boy Wilfred, David Yipininy Wilfred, and the Monash Art Ensemble. *Nylipidgi.* Clayton, Victoria: ABC Jazz, 2016.

Lewis, Tom, and Michael Hohnen. *Muyngarnbi: Songs from Walking With Spirits*, audiovisual content on CD album. Katherine, Northern Territory: Djilpin Arts Corporation, 2007.

Palmer, Robert. Liner notes to *Ornette Coleman, Beauty is a Rare Thing: The Complete Atlantic Recordings*, by Ornette Coleman. CD. New York: Rhino Records, 1993.

Schuller, Gunther. Liner notes to the reissue of *Free Jazz*, by The Ornette Coleman Double Quartet. CD. New York: Atlantic Recording Corporation, 1997.

Sculthorpe, Peter. *The Music of Peter Sculthorpe: Sydney Symphony Orchestra*. CD, with liner notes by Graeme Skinner. Australian Broadcasting Corporation, ABC Classics, 1989.

Yunupingu, Gurrumul. *Djarimirri: Child of the Rainbow*. Darwin, Northern Territory: Skinnyfish Music, 2018.

APPENDIX 1: MANIKAY SONG SEQUENCES

**Sequence one: Sung by Andy Lukaman Peters (passed on by Paul Wulkakin)
Homeland: Wuḻku**

Overall theme: *Wukuṉ* (clouds)

• Wukuṉ	Clouds
• Gapu	Freshwater rain
• Ṉäṉuk (Djuwalpaḏa)	*Mokuy* (Ghost)
• Ḏamala	Eagle hawk
• Ḏuḏutuḏu	Frogmouth owl
• Guruwuḏuk	Small magpie, possibly a butcherbird
• Rimu/Waḻkara	Archer fish
• Yolŋu dancing	People dancing; *riŋgitj* wind ceremony
• Boṉba	Butterfly
• Yolŋu	Man stands for punishment, spearing
• Dhaṉarra	White flower, of the *gaḏayka* (Stringybark tree)
• Dhaḻara	King Brown snake

Sequence two: Sung by Andy Lukaman Peters

Homeland: Ŋilipidji
Overall theme: *Riŋgitj* (meeting; alliance)

• Ṉaku	Canoe
• Walpurruŋgu'	Plains turkey
• Birrkpirrk	Lap-winged plover
• Birrkpirrk/Ḏuḏutuḏu	Meeting of plover and frogmouth owl
• Wata	Wind
• Djuwalpaḏa	*Mokuy* (Ghost)
• Yolŋu dancing	*Riŋgitj* ceremony for *wata* (wind) songs

Sequence three: Sung by Benjamin Miyala Wilfred and Daniel Warrathuma Wilfred (passed on by Sambo Barabara)

Homeland: Ŋilipidji
Overall theme: *Guku* (honey); especially for *dhapi* (male circumcision) ceremonies

• Bambula	Ceremonial ground
• Dhaṉarra	White flower, of the *gaḏayka* (Stringybark tree)
• Mäḏawk	Silver crowned friarbird
• Wärrarra	Red sunset
• Waṯu	Dog
• Gurtha	Fire
• Guku	Honey
• Wäkwak	Black crow*
• Bewiyik	Black-faced cuckoo*
• Wata	Wind
• Birrkpirrk	Lap-winged plover
• Guku	Honey

* Wäkwak and Bewiyik are often replaced in this series by their corresponding Nunydjirrpi versions (see Chapter Two)

APPENDIX 1: MANIKAY SONG SEQUENCES

Sequence four: Sung by Benjamin Miyala Wilfred and Daniel Warrathuma Wilfred (passed on by Sambo Barabara)

Homeland: Ŋilipidji
Overall theme: *Wata* (wind); the set of songs used for smoking ceremonies and in *CRB*.

• Djuwalpada (Ŋirriyiŋirriyi)	*Mokuy* (Ghost)
• Gara	Spear
• Galpu	Spear thrower
• Galpan	Dillybag
• Raki	String
• Malka	String bag
• Wata	Wind
• Birrkpirrk	Lap-winged plover

Sequence Five: Sung by Roy Natilma (Dhuwal language, Djambarrpuyŋu dialect)

Homeland: Gupawupa
Overall theme: *Waltjan* (rain)

The Djambarrpuyŋu *waltjan* (rain) songs follow on sequentially from the *wata* (wind) songs of Ŋilipidji and use the same rhythmic constructions.[1]

---

1   This book limits itself to Wägilak songs and it is outside of my scope to detail Djambarrpuyŋu repertoire in significant detail.

APPENDIX 2: SONG TEXTS

Chapter three		
Wukuṉ – **Clouds** (Andy Peters 2012)	Nyalk, galkanan nyalk Gumurr nhäwurlanapu Gel-gel-gel ḻikanangayi nyalk Balaṉayi nyalk mala	Rain, falling down I see the clouds forming The rain is coming, cooling rain Falling on the country
Chapter four		
Birrkpirrk – **Plover** (Wägilak elder Diltjima in McKenzie 1983, 9)[1]	Dirri pala (Birrk Birrk) luyun bawuda Ngulalang Lutunbuy lapa budapurru Dunubawuy Gapu da jindi gunmawili Mayrikbirrk budapurru Mayrikbirrk budapurru Ngulalangba djinbananawuy	From the island to the shore the Plover [Birrkpirrk] waded Reaching the mainland at the rivermouth Where the bay is wide Plover crossed over Where saltwater met fresh, The water swirled.
Dhaṉarra – **White flower**	Wurrpu dilyunayi, dhaṉarra bädun Buluwulu gupurranayi, milimili bädun dilyunayi	Flowers are starting to come out, white Eucalyptus flowers Seeds falling down, flowers withering and dying

---

1   Orthography as in the original

Djuwalpada – *Mokuy* 'Ghost'	Djuwalpada Ŋirriyiŋirriyi Dhawal-wal duy'yun Likandhu-ŋupan Djuwalpada	Djuwalpada, Ŋirriyiŋirriyi Walking across the country Djuwalpada, with elbows pointing
Gara – Spear	Marrayunmara gara guthanbiny Yarrarra, yarrarra, yarrarra Gulyunmirr galpu, madayin-marrayi	Aiming, shakes his spear, runs towards the country Aiming the spear, ready to throw, aiming Thrown from the spear-thrower making the sacred law
Galpan – Dillybag	Galpan galpan wayidjila Birrinyinbirrinyin maninyala	Dillybag dillybag dillybag Carried by the ghost Birrinyinbirrinyin
Wata – Wind	Djiŋala gurru yalagarayi Mawululayi Gumurr-wuma wäkura dädutj-manayi Gumurr yabalayi gumurr-wuma gumurr-gumirrila balayi	He's going up to Ŋilipidji Pulled to the country by his chest Walking back to his place
Wata – Wind	Wata butthun marayi Läplap mirriŋani Djulgarram buma Mokuy mali nhaŋgu Gangul gangul butthun marayi	The wind is blowing The *mokuy* is walking with the wind He is dancing on the ground He is looking at the shadows The *mokuy* flies now
Guku – Honey	Lirrawaya banburr mayipa Guyu-guyu, guyu-guyu, ahhhh, ohhhh Rawarrararay, bulunyirri dalgumirri	The toothed bee [with stinger] is flying, starting to make a hive Buzzing, buzzing, ahhhh, ohhhh [sound of the wind] Like the wind, it flies a long way to make another home
Malka – String bag	Malka dil'yun marrayi bulunyirri Rrr, rrr, rakirri; Rrr, rrr, gawudju	That string bag – now we are painting up Rolling that string; rolling and making it longer

Birrkpirrk – Plover	Yawilila yawilila	Plover, plover crying
	Moyŋu moyŋu	Djuwalpaḏa dancing, Djuwalpaḏa dancing
	Birrkpirrk ŋäthi Luṯunba	Plover crying for Luṯunba,
	Wäŋa Gawirrinydji[2]	[And] the country Gawirrinydji

Chapter five

Word for word transcription

Djuwalpaḏa – *Mokuy* 'Ghost' (Daniel Wilfred)	Djuwalpaḏa	Name of Wägilak *mokuy*
	Ŋirriyiŋirriyi	Name of Wägilak *mokuy*
	dhawal-wal duy'yun	Arriving at his home place
	ŋopurr-ŋopurr	wrist or forearm
	Burrwanyila	Name called by *mokuy*
	ḻikan-dhu	elbow-with
	garrarr'yun	dance
	Mokuy-u	Mokuy Ghost [ergative]
	ŋupana	follow, pointing
	dhawal-wal duy'yun	arriving at his home place
	Gandjalala	Name of Wägilak *mokuy*
	Mokoy-u	*Mokuy* (ghost) [ergative]
	ŋupana	follow, pointing
	Ŋirriyiŋirriyi	Name of Wägilak *mokuy*
	dhawal-wal duy'yun	arriving at his home place

Word for word transcription

Djuwalpaḏa – *Mokuy* 'Ghost' (Daniel Wilfred)	ḻikan-dhu, ḻikan-dhu	elbow-with [repeated]
	Djuwalpaḏa	Name of Wägilak *mokuy*
	dhawal-wal duy'yun	arriving at his home place
	ḻikan-dhu, ḻikan-dhu, ḻikan-dhu	elbow-with [repeated]
	Djuwalpada	Name of Wägilak *mokuy*
	Garrayaŋa, garrayaŋa	place where Djuwalpaḏa walked
	Wakura	place where Djuwalpaḏa walked
	Gurrumirri	place where Djuwalpaḏa walked
	dulumirri	place where Djuwalpaḏa walked
	Gumurrmirri	chest-having
	Wakura	place where Djuwalpaḏa walked
	gurrumirri	place where Djuwalpaḏa walked
	ḻikan-dhu	elbow-with
	gara'yun	spear

---

2   This translation was begun by Aaron Corn on 26 May 2010.

	Word for word transcription	
Djuwalpada – *Mokuy* 'Ghost' (Benjamin Wilfred)	ḻikan-dhu	elbow-with
	Djuwalpada, Djuwalpada	name of Wägilak *mokuy*
	Ŋirriyiŋirriyi, Ŋirriyiŋirriyi	name of Wägilak *mokuy*
	Djuwalpada, Djuwalpada	name of Wägilak *mokuy*
	Nyagulnyagul	name for Mädawk (Silver-crowned friarbird)
	Butjulubayi	place where Djuwalpada began walking
	ḻikandhu-ŋupan	with elbow-pointing
	Djuwalpada	Name of Wägilak *mokuy*
	ŋäkirri, ŋäkirri,	cover [fresh meat in ground oven]
	dhawal-wal duy'yun	arriving at his home place
	ḻikan-dhu	elbow-with
	Djuwalpada	Name of Wägilak *mokuy*
	Ŋirriyiŋirriyi	Name of Wägilak *mokuy*
Mädawk - Friarbird 'Football'	Nyagulnyagul wärrarra dunbirriyunayi	*Mädawk* flies through the red sunset
	'Ŋarra dhu bulyun, ŋarra dhu bulyun'	'I want to play [football], I want to play'

Chapter seven

Gara – Spear	Marrayunmara gara guthanbiny ŋulaŋura, yarrarra	Dancing with the spear, the spear has almost left his hand
	Marrayunmara gara guthanbiny ŋulaŋura, yarrarra	Dancing with the spear, the spear has almost left his hand
	Yarrarra, yarrarra, yarrarra, waahh!	Aiming the spear, aiming, aiming, waahh!
	Ah yarrarra, yarrarra, yarrarra	Aiming the spear, aiming, aiming
	Marrayunmara guthanbiny	Dancing with the spear
	Marrayunmara guthanbiny, ŋulaŋu	The spear has almost left his hand
	Waahh! Hey, hey-hey, hey!	Waahh! Hey, hey-hey, hey!

	Yawilila yawilila	Plover, plover crying
	Moyŋu moyŋu	Djuwalpada dancing
		Djuwalpada dancing
	Wipa nhaŋu Manungududayi	Flying over the water [at Luṯunba] to land at
Birrkpirrk –	Birrkpirrk-nha, moyŋu	Manungududayi
Plover	Nhabilayi, nhabilayi	Plover, Djuwalpada dancing
		Plover, plover [alternate name]
	Wipa nhaŋu Manungududayi	Flying over the water [at Luṯunba] to land at
	Birrkpirrk-nha, moyŋu	Manungududayi
		Plover, Djuwalpada dancing
	Mmm, mmm, ga-Birrk!	Mmm, mmm, ga-Birrk!
	Birrkpirkk, Birrkpirrk, ga-Birrk!	Plover, plover, plover!

APPENDIX 3: YOUNG WÄGILAK GROUP TOUR AND PERFORMANCE HISTORY

2005
• Workshops and performance, *Crossing Roper Bar*, Ngukurr community, NT • Workshops and recording, Okin Studio, Melbourne
2006
• Workshops and performance, *CRB*, Garma Music Festival, Gulkula, NT
2007
• Performance, *CRB*, World Federation of International Song Writing Competitions, Melbourne • Performance, CRB, FINA World Swimming Championships, Birrarung Marr, Federation Square, Melbourne • Performance, *CRB*, National Gallery of Victoria, Melbourne • Broadcast, Radio National's *The Music Show*, Australian Broadcasting Commission, Melbourne • Performance, *CRB*, Queensland State Library, Queensland Music Festival • Performance, *CRB*, Brisbane Powerhouse, Queensland Music Festival • Workshops, Cherbourg State School, Queensland

2008

- Workshops and performances, *CRB*, Top End tour with Tura New Music: Darwin, Katherine, Timber Creek, Kununurra, Warmun, Fitzroy Crossing, Broome, Lombadina, One Arm Point, Beagle Bay
- Performance, *CRB*, Perth Concert Hall

2009

- Performance, *CRB*, Apollo Bay Music Festival, Apollo Bay, Victoria
- Performance, *CRB*, Ian Potter Centre, National Gallery of Victoria, Melbourne
- Performance, *CRB*, Elisabeth Murdoch Hall, Melbourne Recital Centre
- Recording, *CRB*, Alan Eaton Studios, St Kilda, Melbourne
- Forum and performance, *CRB*, Federation Hall, Victorian College of the Arts, Melbourne
- Forum and performance, *CRB*, Melba Hall, Melbourne University
- Workshops, Northern Metropolitan Institute of TAFE, Melbourne
- Performance, signing of the *United Nations Declaration on the Rights of Indigenous Peoples* by the Hon. Jenny Macklin, Parliament House, Canberra
- Performance, *CRB*, Australian Music Centre Awards, The Playhouse, Sydney Opera House

Awards:
- Classical Music Awards: Outstanding Contribution to Australian Music in a Regional Area

2010

- Performance, *CRB*, Australian Performing Arts Market, Adelaide
- Performance, *CRB*, WOMADelaide, Adelaide (Young Wägilak Group only)
- Performance, Erkki Veltheim's *Tract*, Adelaide Town Hall with the London Sinfonietta
- Performance, opening of *Colour Country: Art from the Roper River* exhibition, Museum and Art Gallery of the Northern Territory, Darwin
- Performance, *CRB*, Darwin Entertainment Centre
- Performance and workshops, Ngukurr community, NT
- Forum and performance, Australian Institute of Aboriginal and Torres Strait Islander Studies conference, Australian National University, Canberra, with Samuel Curkpatrick
- HC Coombs Creative Arts Fellowship residency, workshops and performance, Llewellyn Hall and Australian National University, Canberra

Awards:
- Sidney Myer Performing Arts Award – Group Award
- H.C. Coombs Creative Arts Fellowship – Australia National University: recognition of ground-breaking work

2011

- Workshops, Brunswick, Melbourne, with Samuel Curkpatrick
- Recording, *CRB* album, Alan Eaton Studios, St Kilda, Melbourne
- Workshop, Australian National Academy of Music, Melbourne
- Performance with the Australian National Academy of Music (Erkki Veltheim's *Tract* only), Malthouse Theatre, Melbourne
- Broadcast, Radio National's *The Music Show*, Australian Broadcasting Commission, Melbourne, with Samuel Curkpatrick

Awards:
- Australian Jazz Bell Awards: Best Jazz Ensemble – Australian Art Orchestra/ Young Wägilak Group

2012

- Performance, *CRB*, Signal Point Art Gallery, Goolwa, South Australia
- Performances and workshops, *CRB*, Monash University School of Music, Victoria, with Samuel Curkpatrick
- Performance, *CRB*, Musée du Quai Branly, Paris, with Samuel Curkpatrick
- Broadcast, BBC Radio, London
- Performance, *CRB*, London Jazz Festival, Southbank Centre, London
- Workshop and performance, *CRB*, Museum of Archaeology and Anthropology, Cambridge University, Cambridge, with Samuel Curkpatrick
- Workshop and performance, *CRB*, Homerton College, Cambridge University, Cambridge, with Samuel Curkpatrick

2013

- Performances of *CRB* and workshops during tour from Darwin to Perth, produced by TURA New Music: Darwin, Kununurra, Cape Leveque, Djarindjin, One Arm Point, Broome, Beagle Bay, Moonlight Bay, Karratha, Exmouth, Roebourne, Perth

2014

- Performance at Bennetts Lane Jazz Club, *CRB*, Melbourne
- Song and dance workshop, Brunswick, Melbourne, with Samuel Curkpatrick
- Broadcast, ABC Radio Melbourne
- Recording, *CRB* volume two album with the AAO, Melbourne
- Performance, workshop and CD launch at the National Museum of Australia, Canberra
- Performance and workshop, *CRB*, Hong Kong Academy of Performing Arts
- Performance, *CRB*, Garma Festival, Gulkula, NT

2015

- Performance, *CRB*, Museum of New and Old Art, MONA FOMA, Hobart
- Performance, *CRB*, Jazzahead Showcase, Breman, Germany
- Recording, Monash University, *Nyilipidgi* (ABC Jazz)
- Performance, *Nyilipidgi*, Malthouse Theatre, Melbourne
- Broadcast, SBS National Indigenous Television Radio (NITV Radio)

2016

- Premiere of *Nyilipidgi* with Monash Art Ensemble, Melbourne International Jazz Festival.
- Performance and album release, *Nyilipidgi*, Wangaratta Jazz Festival
- AAO's *Creative Music Intensive*, Tarraleah, Tasmania, with Samuel Curkpatrick

Awards:
- APRA AMCOS award, Best World Music Album, *Nyilipidgi* (ABC Jazz)

2017

- Performance, *Nyilipidgi*, Stonnington Jazz Festival, Malvern Town Hall
- AAO's *Creative Music Intensive*, Tarraleah, Tasmania, with Samuel Curkpatrick
- Performance, "Meeting Points" concert series with the AAO, Arts Centre Melbourne
- Workshop and forum, *Interlingua Symposium*, Australian Art Orchestra, with the Victorian College of the Arts, Melbourne University, with Samuel Curkpatrick
- Performance, *Seoul Meets Arnhem Land* with the AAO, featuring Bae Il Dong, OzAsia Festival, Adelaide Festival Centre
- Performance, *CRB*, Garma Festival, Gulkula, NT

2018

- Performance, *Bambula*, Sydney Festival, City Recital Hall
- AAO's *Creative Music Intensive*, Tarraleah, Tasmania, with Samuel Curkpatrick
- Recording, with Peter Knight and Sunny Kim for new AAO project *Hand to Earth*
- Performance, "Meeting Points" concert series with the AAO, Arts Centre Melbourne
- Workshop and forum, *Interlingua Symposium*, Australian Art Orchestra, with the Victorian College of the Arts, Melbourne University, with Samuel Curkpatrick
- Workshop and performance, Melbourne Indigenous Transition School, with the AAO
- Broadcast, "Bambula," *The Music Show*, ABC Radio National

2019

- Performance, *The Expanding Universe,* with Genevieve Lacey, with Erkki Veltheim, Adelaide Festival
- Performance, "Morning Star" *manikay* with Djilpin Arts Black Crow Dancers, Melbourne International Film Festival, IMAX Melbourne (launch of the film, *Australia: The Wild Top End,* directed by Nick Robinson)
- Tour, *CRB* with the AAO, Barunga Festival, Barunga, NT; Ngukurr Arts Festival, Ngukurr, NT
- AAO's *Creative Music Intensive*, Tarraleah, Tasmania
- Workshop and forum, *Interlingua Symposium*, Australian Art Orchestra, with the Victorian College of the Arts, Melbourne University
- Forum, 'Twisted Fibres,' National Institute of Dramatic Arts, NIDAnights, Melbourne, with Samuel Curkpatrick
- Workshop and performance, Melbourne Indigenous Transition School
- Indigenous Singer-Songwriter Residency, Banff Centre for the Arts (Canada) (Daniel and David Wilfred)

Awards:

- Daniel Wilfred, 2019 Northern Territory Arts Fellowship, NT Government

INDEX

INDEX